Hiking Hot Springs in the
Pacific Northwest

Hiking Hot Springs
in the
Pacific Northwest

A Guide to the Area's Best
Backcountry Hot Springs

Fifth Edition

Evie Litton and Sally Jackson

FALCONGUIDES

GUILFORD, CONNECTICUT
HELENA, MONTANA
AN IMPRINT OF GLOBE PEQUOT PRESS

To buy books in quantity for corporate use
or incentives, call **(800) 962-0973**
or e-mail **premiums@GlobePequot.com**.

FALCONGUIDES®

FalconGuides is an imprint of Globe Pequot Press.
Falcon, FalconGuides, and Outfit Your Mind are registered trademarks of Morris Book Publishing, LLC.

Text design/layout: Sue Murray
Project editor: Ellen Urban

Maps © Morris Book Publishing, LLC

Library of Congress Cataloging-in-Publication Data is available on file.

ISBN 978-0-7627-8370-0

Printed in the United States of America

To all the volunteers who struggle patiently and often ingeniously to create and maintain soaking pools for everyone to enjoy and to those who value hot springs in a natural setting enough to pack out the trash left by others, this book is gratefully dedicated.

Contents

ACKNOWLEDGMENTS

When FalconGuides approached me last year to undertake a fifth edition of this guide, I called upon my longtime friend, fellow hot springer and author Sally Jackson, to come on board. Sally, quite a few years my junior, with her much needed twenty-first century skill set and boundless enthusiasm, agreed to step in and carry on the torch. She undertook a staggering amount of fieldwork all across the Pacific Northwest and took over the huge job of revising and updating the text, the maps, and the photos as well adding GPS coordinates to almost all the springs. She also tracked down and added nineteen hot springs, giving us a new grand total of 162! For this amazing feat I'll be forever in Sally's debt. It was a labor of love.

To Skip Hill, former publisher of the *Hot Springs Gazette*; to Chris Andrews, contributor to the Hot Springs and Hot Pools of the Northwest/Southwest books; to the Idaho Dippers; and to Matt Hemmingsen, Wally Dietrich, and Bob Westerberg, I just want to say thanks to each of you for your expertise and good company on some memorable trips out fishing for hot water. For my author photo, I am indebted to Bob Cardell of the Southern Arizona Hiking Club Tucson, Arizona.

And last but not least, I want to express my gratitude to the friendly folks at Falcon Guide for guiding this stray missile to a safe and happy landing. Without their help, it would still be orbiting somewhere over the Pacific Northwest.

Sally Jackson (coauthor, fifth edition): I would like to thank the Idaho Dippers, Chris Andrews, and Hot Spring Harley for sharing their great photos, expert advice, and good company on our trips to "the back of beyond" in search of hot water. Thank you also to my patient friend John Herchenrider for his assistance during our research trip through BC. I'm also very grateful to Tim Messing for sharing his hot springs photos along with detailed trip reports on several Washington springs that I was unable to visit firsthand. Thanks also go to Wayne Estes, John Howard, Blue Meek, Matt Rosenthal, and Michael Rysavy for sharing some of their terrific hot spring photos. An extra special thank you must go to my amazing mother, Margaret, without whose support and understanding this project would never have been completed. And finally I would like to thank my dear friend Evie for her unwavering trust and faith in me as her handpicked reviser and coauthor!

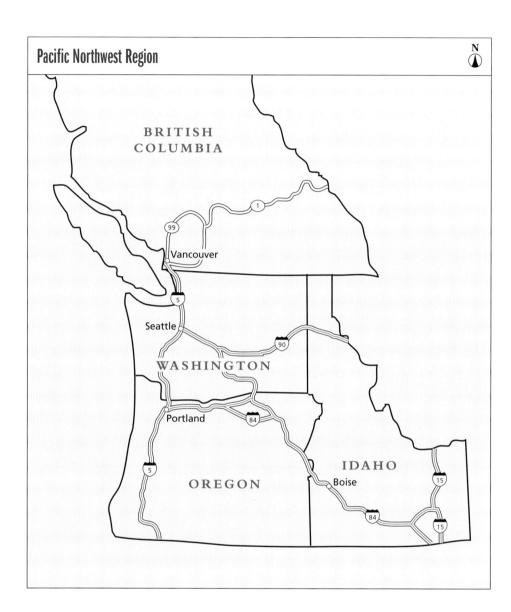

INTRODUCTION

This book was first published in 1990 as *The Hikers Guide to Hot Springs in the Pacific Northwest* and is meant for the active outdoor hedonist who enjoys experiencing the wonders of nature on foot but who also turns on to the contrasting idea of a blissful dip at the end of the trail in one of nature's own steamy creations.

It just so happens that the Pacific Northwest is a mecca not only for superb scenery and hiking but also for first-class primitive hot springs. A chain of these pearls runs through the Cascades of Oregon and Washington, clusters are located across southern British Columbia, and in Idaho you'll discover a total of 109 hot springs—including fifteen buried in the Frank Church Wilderness. Idaho, astonishingly, happens to have more than twice the number of wild hot springs than the total number in Oregon, Washington, and British Columbia combined.

The best of both worlds is presented here in one package: a detailed guide to 162 of the finest natural hot soaks in Oregon, Washington, British Columbia, and Idaho and a trail guide to seventy scenic hikes that either lead to them or begin nearby. Whether you're already a confirmed wilderness buff and hot springs fanatic or you're new to either pursuit, this guide should be a welcome companion to your travels.

How to Use This Guide

Hiking Hot Springs in the Pacific Northwest is a guide to both hot soaks and hikes in Oregon, Washington, British Columbia, and Idaho. The springs marked on the locator maps are listed numerically. Beneath them in the text, you'll find one or more hikes. For example, in Oregon we start with 1 Umpqua Hot Springs, followed by hikes 1a, 1b, and 1c. The hikes fall into three categories: hikes that reach a hot spring, hikes that continue on from the spring, and hikes located in the same area. One or more of these categories may be listed under each hot spring.

Headings for Hot Springs (located less than 1 mile from a road)

General description: Includes what you'll find, the distance from road to spring, and the customary swimwear or lack thereof. Example: A quiet soaking pool cloaked in greenery at the end of a 0.25-mile creekside path. Swimwear is optional.

Elevation: A useful gauge for estimating seasonal access.

General location: Approximate distance and direction of the hot spring from the nearest town. Example: 64 miles east of Roseburg.

GPS: These coordinates will help you zero in on your soaking destination. A vehicle GPS unit, in conjunction with a state map book, makes life a lot easier when embarking on a hot spring road trip.

A handheld GPS unit is an especially worthwhile investment if you plan on spending a lot of time in the backcountry. Most units have screens that show topographic maps, which can save having to buy a bunch of separate paper maps. Sally,

Evie's backcountry researcher, doesn't purchase paper maps for hiking. This guide, along with her trusty Garmin Dakota 20 GPS unit (with the Northwest topo maps downloaded into it), has been more than sufficient for tracking down many a far-flung hot spring—just remember to bring spare batteries! If you purchase the topo map software for your GPS, you should be able to download it into Basecamp (free off the Internet) and then print out your own paper maps.

This guide has listed the GPS coordinates in the degrees format (dd.dddd). Don't panic if your unit is reading in the degrees and minutes format (dd mm.mmm); it's easy to change it to the degrees format by going into the Position Format menu in the Setup/Settings menu. These coordinates should bring you to within about 50 yards of your destination. The accuracy of coordinates varies slightly with the number and strength of overhead satellites being picked up by the GPS unit. Dense foliage and steep terrain can make it more difficult for GPS units to connect with the satellites, but the newer units are getting better at picking up signals in these kinds of situations. Calibrating your GPS's compass after changing the batteries helps with accuracy in most models.

▶ **Punching these coordinates into Google Earth can also give you an interesting and sometimes useful overview of an area.**

There are a few coordinates listed as estimates in this edition. They are based on other people's coordinates, but they should also get you fairly close to your destination. (Please let us know if you end up with some more-accurate ones!)

Map: The best road map for finding your way there. For the US regions this is usually a USDA Forest Service recreation map. (Evie's researchers often bypassed these individual road maps and used a vehicle GPS along with state map books by Benchmark or DeLorme.) For British Columbia, it's the Backroad Mapbook series, as Forest District maps no longer exist. It's noted here whether the hot spring is marked on the map.

Restrictions: You'll see this heading only for sites requiring a special pass; sites with rules, such as day use only; and also for sites with access problems, such as those requiring a major river ford.

Contact: Where to go for more information. Agency addresses and telephone numbers are listed in Appendix A.

Finding the hot springs: The nuts and bolts of getting there.

The hot springs: The quality of the soaking pools, the temperature and any means of controlling it, the general setting and scenery, an idea of how much company you can expect, and a description of how visible the pools are. As a rule of thumb, the swimwear custom equates with the degree of visibility or distance from the road—a useful formula.

Headings for Hikes (usually a mile or longer)

General description: Whether it's a day hike or an overnighter, where it goes, what's there, and the customary swimwear. Example: A day hike to a bubbly soaking box in the Glacier Peak Wilderness. No need to pack a swimsuit.

Difficulty: Determined by overall steepness, with minor adjustments made for length, short steep pitches, or roughness. A hike is rated as easy if the grade is up to 5 percent, moderate between 5 and 10 percent, and strenuous if the grade is more than 10 percent.

Distance: The overall length of the hike.

General location: The approximate distance and direction of the trailhead (not the hot spring) from the nearest town.

Elevation gain: Given in one direction only. A round-trip that gains 1,000 feet and loses 200 feet on the way in would lose 1,000 feet and gain 200 feet on the way out. This would be written: +1,000 feet, -200 feet. Another hike gains 1,600 feet, loses 400 feet, gains another 800 feet, then loses another 200 feet. The total gain and loss would be +2,400 feet, -600 feet. Only one figure is listed if the hike is all uphill or downhill. A loop hike lists just one figure because no matter how many ups and downs, the total gain is always the same as the total loss.

High point: A useful figure when trying to determine the access at different times of year.

GPS: See Headings for Hot Springs.

Hiking quad(s): This heading lists one or more topographic quadrangles. In the United States those most commonly used are the US Geographical Survey (USGS) quads (they can be downloaded for free via www.usgs.gov). In Washington and northern Oregon, a 15-minute series by Green Trails is also listed. The forest service (USDAFS) offers contour maps of most wilderness areas. Although drawn with less detail than the USGS quads, they tend to be more up to date. In British Columbia the standard quads are the National Topographic Series (NTS). These BC maps can be bought online at shop.itmb.ca. It's noted whether the hot spring is marked on the map.

A trail map is also located in the text with each hike. Intended as a general introduction, these maps should not be substituted for the hiking quads or GPS topographical mapping software. (See the map legend for a list of the symbols used.)

Road map: See "Map" under Headings for Hot Springs.

Restrictions: See Headings for Hot Springs.

Contact: See Headings for Hot Springs.

Finding the trailhead: See Headings for Hot Springs.

The hike: Here you'll find a description of the route, the distances between points, any nasty stream crossings or other obstacles to expect, possible extensions or side trips, campsites, and whatever outrageous viewpoints or other rewards lie in wait.

The hot springs: See Headings for Hot Springs.

A note on state geothermal maps: A map that marks hot springs along with other geothermal data is published by each state for the US Department of Energy. These maps are gigantic but very useful for pinpointing possible soaks. They can be found in most university libraries.

Recreational User Fees

The National Recreation Fee Demonstration Program was authorized by Congress in 1996. It allows participating agencies including the Bureau of Land Management (BLM), National Park Service (NPS), and the USDA Forest Service to implement user fees to help finance recreation programs on federal lands. Wherever this fee is required, it's mentioned under the "Restrictions" heading.

In Oregon and Washington the fee is called a Northwest Forest Pass and is required at specified trailheads and parking areas within most if not all national forests. The permit is available at district offices and selected retail outlets as a daily or yearly pass. It covers each vehicle (all passengers) and can be transferred from one car to another. One permit is good in all forests.

Zero Impact

Principles of zero impact camping:

"Some call it low-impact use or the minimum-impact method. Others refer to it as no-trace camping. Whatever you call it, the practice of outdoor ethics is essential in the backcountry. It relies on clear judgment rather than inflexible rules. And not only does common sense protect the backcountry, it can also enhance your outdoor adventures." (Source: *Fieldbook,* Boy Scouts of America)

Three principles of zero-impact camping:

- Leave with everything you brought in.
- Leave no sign of your visit.
- Leave the landscape as you found it.

Concentrate use when in popular or high-use places. Concentrate your use on those places that have already been damaged by previous use. Build campfires only within existing fire rings. Stay on established hiking trails. Cutting switchbacks can lead to erosion.

Disperse use when in pristine areas. Minimize the number of times a place is stepped on, and leave nothing that will encourage others to walk or camp where you did so that the site will have time to recover. Choose a previously unused site to camp. Disperse foot traffic between camp and any water source. Minimize the use of campfires and remove all evidence of fire. In some wilderness areas campfires are not permitted, and where they are, fire pans or fire blankets are recommended and sometimes required. Only hike off-trail if prepared to use extra care. Try to select routes on hard ground. Avoid fragile surfaces like wet places and steep slopes.

Other basic rules. Choose your campsite thoughtfully. Pick a spot (at least 300 feet from water or trails) where you won't have to clear any vegetation or level a tent site. Camp on mineral soil, never in meadows.

The use of backpack stoves conserves firewood. Campfires have been prohibited in many heavily used areas. If a fire is allowed and really needed, dig out the native vegetation and topsoil and set it aside. Don't build a fire ring with rocks. When breaking camp, drown the fire thoroughly, bury the cold ashes, and replace the native soil.

Keep all washwater at least 300 feet from water sources, and don't use soap or detergents near water. Even biodegradable soaps are a stress on the environment. If you must use soap, wash in a basin well away from lakes or streams.

Always answer the call of nature at least 300 feet from any campsites or open water. Dig a hole 6 to 8 inches deep, bury everything carefully when finished, then cover it with sod or topsoil.

Carry out all garbage that can't be burned. This includes tiny items like gum wrappers and cigarette butts. The foil packages commonly used by backpackers don't really burn and must be packed out as well. Never bury food scraps—animals will dig them up.

Note: Many of the designated wilderness areas (the majority of which are in Idaho) have extra regulations with regards to fires, camping, stock, dogs, and group sizes. Be sure to make inquiries in advance and read the trailhead signage carefully.

Hot springs are as fragile as any other water source and should be treated with the same respect. Soaking pools are precisely that. They're not bathtubs where you can lather up with soap and shampoo. Whatever drains out flows directly into nearby streams, and what can't drain out is there for the next user to find. Also, the damp ground around the springs is often steep and easily eroded, and delicate plantlife can be swiftly crushed.

Make It a Safe Trip

Backcountry safety is largely a matter of being well prepared and using common sense. This means carrying proper survival and first-aid equipment. Telling someone trusted where you are going is important before heading into the backcountry. If you are planning extended hiking forays, consider investing in a personal locator beacon, as cell phone coverage is often nonexistent in the backcountry.

Gather information from the ranger station nearest your destination. Rangers can tell you about any potential problems in their area, as well as the current condition of roads, trails, and streams.

The basics in every hiker's gear should include sturdy but comfortable footwear, warm clothing that will keep its insulating properties when wet, plenty of water, extra food, and a dependable tent. You may enjoy beautiful dry weather, but storms can hit at any time.

Select a hike within the abilities of all in your group, and stay together on the trail. If it's getting dark or a storm looks likely, make camp as soon as possible. Be aware of the dangers of hypothermia, and take the proper steps to avoid it.

Don't attempt to ford major streams during the spring runoff. In early summer, creeks and rivers can have ten times their average flow. Leave your boots on for better traction. During runoff the water will be at its lowest level during the morning hours.

Be cautious around hot springs. Some emerge from the ground at temperatures that can boil eggs and would-be bathers alike. Avoid bare feet until you're sure where any hidden hot spots are located. If a soaking pool feels too hot, don't use it unless you can find a way to lower the temperature.

To prevent problems in bear country, keep all food well wrapped in a bear-proof canister, or hang it at night (along with garbage, lotions, and soaps) from a strong tree limb at least 12 feet above the ground and at least 5 feet from the trunk and other branches.

Driving in the backcountry often involves negotiating narrow one-lane roads—some heavily traveled by huge logging trucks and others deserted for hours just when you get stuck. Drive cautiously and exercise common sense. Carry plenty of gas, water, and spare supplies.

Red Spider Mites (Sally's Notes)

Don't forget to bring your reading glasses to check for these annoying little critters (also commonly but erroneously known as chiggers), which frequent a number of Idaho and Oregon hot springs. Barely visible to the naked eye, these tiny orange/red mites scurry with surprising speed upon the surface of the water and the surrounding rocks. They attach to the body, and the bites usually result in mosquito-like itchy welts that can take more than a week to heal. As with many bug bites, different people seem to have varying susceptibilities and reactions to red spider mites. I have seen many at Bog Hot Springs but know of several people who have spent numerous days there and received only the very occasional bite. Sometimes the mites appear then disappear again at certain springs.

My first encounter with these red devils was by far my worst—when I first visited Greylock Hot Springs for a nighttime soak many moons ago. On a recent return visit, the pools were full of algae but not a mite in site; yet the cleaner and obviously more frequented Chattanooga and Atlanta Springs just up the road had a bunch of mites.

I've never seen red spider mites at a sulfur spring; they may prefer less-acidic water. The springs known to almost always have red mites include Bog, Little Borax, Atlanta, Chattanooga, Vulcan, Molly's, Secesh, Magic, Worswick, and Bear Valley. The following website has a page devoted to red spider mites where visitors report the springs with mites: www.idahohotsprings.com/education/hot-springs-red-spider-mites.htm.

Minimizing the Chances of Getting Bitten by Red Spider Mites

- Before taking off your clothes, have a good close-up look around the edge of the pool. If you don't see any tiny orange/red critters, you can relax!
- Check out all your soaking options. Sometimes the mites are at one part of a large spring complex and not another (e.g., Trail Creek, Lynx Creek, and Kwiskwis, where we brought along a tarp and built a pool at the springs where there were no mites).
- If you spy mites, be sure to put your clothes and towel in a plastic bag or hang them in a tree, as the mites can crawl into clothing left on the ground.
- Soak in the center of the pool; the mites tend to frequent the edges.

- Soaking near the outflow sometimes works; the mites seem to know that this is a hazardous location for them.
- Keeping your soak short when there are mites around will greatly reduce your chances of being bitten.
- Dry yourself off thoroughly, immediately after getting out of the pool.
- If you do get bitten, don't scratch; try lotions as you would for other bug bites.

If you can deal with the occasional mosquito and deerfly bite, you're probably going to survive an encounter with red spider mites.

Map Legend

Municipal

≡⬤(5)≡ Interstate Highway

≡(26)≡ US Highway

≡(140)≡ State Road

≡[263]≡ Local/County Road

≡[FR 356]≡ Forest Road

==== Unpaved Road

—-—-— State Boundary

Trails

------ Featured Trail

------ Trail

·········· Cross-country Route

Water Features

(20) Hot Spring

∿ Unfeatured Spring

◯ Body of Water

Marsh

∿ River/Creek

≋ Waterfall

Land Management

National Park Boundary

National Forest/Wilderness Area/
Wild and Scenic River Boundary

Symbols

≍ Bridge

Boat Launch

■ Building/Structure

▲ Campground

Gate

◯ Glacier

Lava

🅿 Parking

⊃⊂ Pass

▲ Peak/Elevation

⊞ Picnic Area

× Point Elevation

Ranger Station/Park Office

Sand

Scenic View

○ Town

□ Trailhead

Turnaround

Oregon

The state of Oregon is richly endowed with primitive hot springs. The ones described in this guide are located in two distinct areas. One group can be found in the Cascade Mountains to the west and another in the desert country to the east, which includes several in the Owyhee River Canyon. The reader will find a total of twenty-seven wild dips marked on the Oregon Map—eight lined up in the Cascades and nineteen spread across the eastern desert.

A tranquil fall morning at Cougar Hot Springs WAYNE ESTES

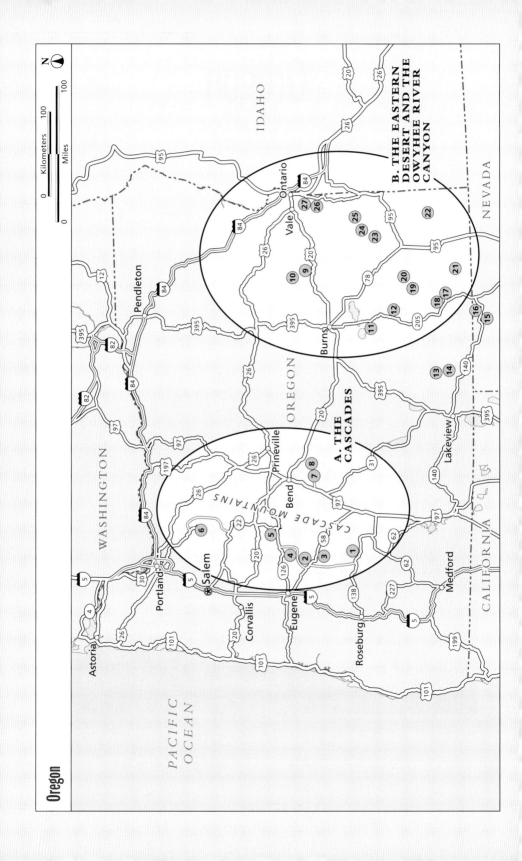

A. The Cascades

Hot spring enthusiasts visiting the southern Cascades can enter primeval forests and discover a chain of inviting soaking pools framed by evergreen boughs. The eight springs listed here are all located in national forests, with easy access via paved roads and short paths.

In addition, superb hikes on nearby trails ramble through lush woods to lakes and waterfalls, ancient lava flows, and overlooks of numerous volcanic cones.

Directions in this section follow from major towns and cities along I-5 and US 97. In general, the forest roads and hiking trails are well maintained and easy to follow, the campgrounds are full in the summer months, and the bubbly soaking pools often brim over with other equally eager beavers.

Hot Springs and Hikes

Umpqua Hot Springs (1) and nearby strolls are located east of Roseburg. Southeast of Eugene near Oakridge, soaks at quiet Wall Creek (2) and popular McCredie (3) mix well with hikes in the Waldo Lake and Diamond Peak wildlands. East of Eugene are the ever-popular Cougar (4) and nearby Bigelow (5), hidden between hikes along the McKenzie River. Southeast of Portland, there's an easy walk to the unique Bagby (6). And south of Bend, on the volcanic east side of the range, comes the hike-in soaks on the shores of Paulina Lake (7) and East Lake (8), as well as an assortment of hikes in and around Newberry Caldera.

Season

All the hot springs can be reached and enjoyed throughout the year except for Paulina and East Lakes, snowbound through the winter months at 6,300 feet, and Bigelow, submerged during spring runoff. Cougar and Bagby see a steady stream of winter visitors that's interrupted only if there's a really heavy storm. The hiking season ranges from almost year-round for the low-elevation hikes near Umpqua and Bigelow to summer-only for the higher routes in the vicinity of McCredie, Cougar, Bagby, and Paulina. Summer weather west of the crest can vary from bright sunshine to damp rain clouds (sometimes in a matter of minutes), while the east side around Paulina stays high and dry.

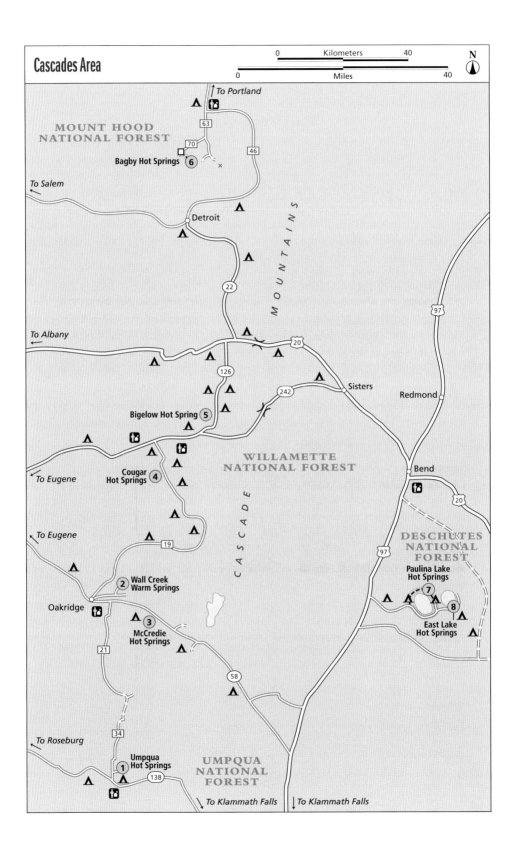

Cascades Area

Kilometers
0   40

Miles
0   40

N

MOUNT HOOD
NATIONAL FOREST

To Portland

63

To Salem

70

Bagby Hot Springs 6

46

Detroit

22

M O U N T A I N S

To Albany

20

126

242

97

Sisters

Redmond

Bigelow Hot Spring 5

WILLAMETTE
NATIONAL FOREST

To Eugene

Cougar
Hot Springs 4

Bend

To Eugene

19

C A S C A D E

97

DESCHUTES
NATIONAL
FOREST

20

Wall Creek
Warm Springs 2

Paulina Lake
Hot Springs 7

Oakridge

McCredie
Hot Springs 3

East Lake
Hot Springs 8

21

58

34

To Roseburg

Umpqua
Hot Springs 1

UMPQUA
NATIONAL
FOREST

138

To Klammath Falls   To Klammath Falls

1 Umpqua Hot Springs

General description: A sheltered travertine pool on a short path, overlooking a canyon. A swimsuit/birthday suit mix.
Elevation: 2,640 feet
General location: 64 miles east of Roseburg
GPS: N43.29674 / W122.36379

Map: BLM/USDAFS Land of Umpqua (springs marked)
Restrictions: Northwest Forest Pass required; self-registration booth at the parking area. The road to these springs is sometimes closed in winter.
Contact: Diamond Lake Ranger District, Umpqua National Forest

Finding the hot springs: From Roseburg drive east on SR 138 about 60 miles to around milepost 59. Turn left onto paved Toketee Rigdon Road (FR 34) and take the first left that crosses a bridge. Continue straight on Toketee Rigdon Road for 2.3 miles, driving past Toketee Lake and Campground before turning right onto Thorn Prairie Road (Road 3401). Drive 2 miles along this gravel road to the parking area, which is on the left. From here the trail goes across the river and to the right for 0.3 mile to the springs. The trail is steep in places, with handrails helping out in some of them. Once you see the restroom you're getting close. You'll emerge from the woods to see a three-sided shelter on the edge of a bluff. You're likely to stay longer than anticipated—don't forget to bring a flashlight!

The Hot Springs

Sculpted from colorful travertine deposits, a pool measuring about 4 × 5 feet perches on a bare cliff 150 feet above the North Umpqua River; the free-flowing curves

The three upper pools at Umpqua Hot Springs SALLY JACKSON

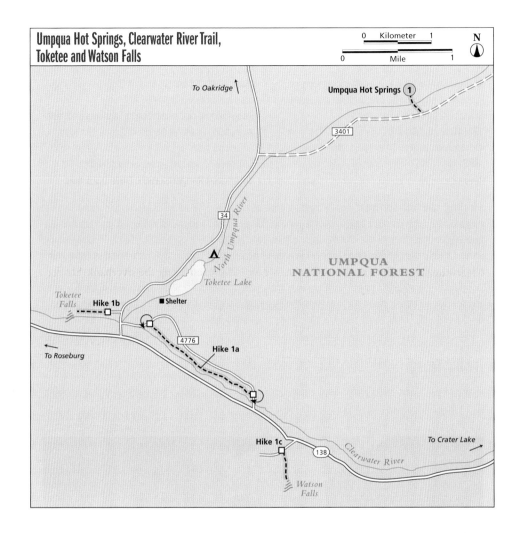

make a uniquely beautiful container for the highly mineralized, 108°F water trickling through it. The hot water feeds in from the source by hose, and the only way to cool the pool is by diverting the hose. Shaded from the elements within a shingle-roofed shelter, a sundeck on the open side provides a pleasing view over the canyon below. Beside the shelter are six other small alfresco soaking pools that tier down the travertine hillside, each one being a little cooler than the one above.

Be warned that these well-known and sometimes abused springs are especially busy on summer weekends. If you can avoid the crowds, these hot springs are a serene place to relax. Left-behind trash can be a problem here—please leave the hot springs cleaner than you found them. Camping is permitted near the trailhead; the nearest official campground is at Toketee Lake.

Hike 1a Clearwater River Trail

General description: A riverside walk through an ancient forest, near Umpqua Hot Springs
Difficulty: Easy
Distance: About 3.4 miles round-trip
General location: 60 miles east of Roseburg

Elevation gain: 200 feet
High point: 2,640 feet
Map: BLM/USDAFS Land of Umpqua
Contact: Diamond Lake Ranger District, Umpqua National Forest

Finding the trailheads: At Toketee Junction on SR 138, take FR 34 to the bottom of the hill. Bear right at the Y onto FR 4776, the west entrance to Toketee Ranger Station. Drive 0.25 mile to a pullout on the right and the west marker. The east trail sign is located 2 miles farther up the road, just before it rejoins the highway.

The Hike

Clearwater River Trail meanders through a twilight forest along the riverbank. Shaded by a dense canopy of cedar and Douglas fir mixed with rhododendrons, alder, and dogwood, it passes lively rapids interspersed with deep pools. The gentle path parallels Toketee Ranger Station Road and can be walked from either end.

The Cascades certainly live up to their name in this neck of the woods, with several famous waterfalls nearby, including Toketee and Watson Falls (see next hikes). Across from the Umpqua Hot Springs is Surprise Falls, which can be reached by a trail on the other side of the river. A free forest service color brochure on the waterfalls in the Umpqua National Forest is available at the Toketee Ranger Station or can be downloaded at blm.gov/or/districts/roseburg/recreation/Thundering_Waters/.

Hikes 1b and 1c Toketee and Watson Falls

General description: Two short strolls through lush woods near Umpqua Hot Springs
Difficulty: Easy
Distance: Toketee Falls, 0.8 mile round-trip; Watson Falls, 1.2 miles round-trip
General location: 60 and 62 miles east of Roseburg

Elevation gain: Toketee Falls, 60 feet; Watson Falls, 230 feet
High point: Toketee Falls, 2,380 feet; Watson Falls, 2,950 feet
Map: BLM/USDAFS Land of Umpqua
Contact: Diamond Lake Ranger District, Umpqua National Forest

Finding the trailheads: For Toketee Falls, drive to Toketee Junction on SR 138 and take FR 34 to the bottom of the hill. Bear left at the Y and follow signs to the parking area. For Watson Falls, drive 2.2 miles east of Toketee Junction on SR 138 (or 0.3 mile east of the east entrance to Toketee Ranger Station) and follow signs to the picnic area parking lot (a right turn on FR 37).

The lower pools with the river still far below at Umpqua Hot Springs WAYNE ESTES

The Hikes

Toketee Falls, a double waterfall plunging a total of 120 feet, lies at the end of an easy 0.4-mile path along the North Umpqua River near Toketee Lake. At one spot, the river tumbles through a tight gorge filled with water-sculpted pools. Mottled sunlight filters through a colorful grove of Douglas fir, cedar, maple, and Pacific yew en route to a viewing platform.

Watson Falls, with its 272-foot drop, is the fourth-highest waterfall in Oregon. A steep 0.6-mile trail follows the plunging creek through an ancient forest of Douglas fir and western hemlock. The understory of ferns, Oregon grape, and salal blends tints of green with the velvet coat of moss draped over the creekside boulders. A foot-bridge along the way offers an excellent viewpoint, and a side path comes to a stop in the misty spray at the base of the falls.

2 Wall Creek (Meditation Pool) Warm Springs

General description: A warm soak in a sylvan setting at the end of a short path. Swimwear is optional.
Elevation: 2,200 feet
General location: 50 miles southeast of Eugene

GPS: N43.8066 / W122.3114 (estimate)
Map: BLM/USDAFS Willamette Cascades (springs marked). See map on page 12.
Restrictions: Day use only
Contact: Middle Fork Ranger District, Willamette National Forest

Finding the warm springs: From Eugene take SR 58 about 40 miles southeast to Oakridge. Turn left to city center, then right onto East First Street, which soon becomes Salmon Creek Road (FR 24). Continue northeast and go 4.5 miles past Salmon Creek Campground on pavement, then turn left onto a gravel road (Road 1934), signed to Blair Lake. Watch for a pullout on your left in 0.4 mile. A 0.3-mile path follows Wall Creek to the pool.

The Warm Springs

A clearing in a virgin forest reveals a pool built directly over the source springs. Bubbles rise gently to the surface in long streamers, heating the water to around 96°F. The pool is roughly 10 × 15 feet and oval in shape. It sits on the bank of a small but lively creek surrounded by countless acres of green solitude.

Bubbles perk up through the sandy bottom of a pool bordered by age-old trees at Wall Creek Warm Springs. SALLY JACKSON

3 McCredie Hot Springs

General description: A busy highway pit stop. As for swimwear, it's a mixed bag.
Elevation: 2,100 feet
General location: 50 miles southeast of Eugene
GPS: N43.70592 / W122.28809

Map: BLM/USDAFS Willamette Cascades (springs named). See map on page 12.
Restrictions: Day use only
Contact: Middle Fork Ranger District, Willamette National Forest

Finding the hot springs: From Eugene take SR 58 about 40 miles southeast to Oakridge. Follow the highway 10 miles farther (0.5 mile past Blue Pool Campground) to a large turnout on the right just past milepost 45, which has a pit toilet and picnic tables. A short path heads upstream to the pools.

The Hot Springs

This soaker-saturated site, sandwiched between Salt Creek and a major highway, offers a variety of soaking pools with temperatures ranging from 95°F to 105°F. The party pool measures about 15 × 20 feet and has a knee-deep bottom that varies in composition from sandy muck to sharp rocks and bits of broken glass.

Any time is party time at McCredie. The social activity varies from mild on weekdays to industrial strength over the weekends. Because there's easy access throughout the year, you're likely to find Winnebago City assembled in the large pullout.

A few quieter pools are located directly across the broad creek. To reach these with dry feet, drive another 0.5 mile east and take Shady Gap Road across a bridge. Bear right for 0.1 mile to a pullout; then hunt for an overgrown path that follows the creek 0.3 mile back downstream.

Update: The parking lot has been paved and the entryway reduced so that trucks and other large vehicles are unable to use the area as a pit stop. Don't be surprised if a small day-use fee is introduced along the lines of that currently charged at Cougar and Bagby.

Early-morning steam shrouds the party pool at McCredie Hot Springs. Evie Litton

Hike 3a Fuji Mountain

General description: A brisk climb overlooking a line of volcanic peaks, near McCredie Hot Springs
Difficulty: Moderate
Distance: About 3.0 miles round-trip
General location: 65 miles southeast of Eugene

Elevation gain: 964 feet
High point: 7,144 feet
Hiking quad: USGS Waldo Lake
Road map: BLM/USDAFS Willamette Cascades
Contact: Middle Fork Ranger District, Willamette National Forest

Finding the trailhead: Drive 23 miles southeast of Oakridge (5.5 miles past McCredie) on SR 58. Watch for a train trestle over the highway; turn left just beyond it onto Eagle Creek Road (Road 5883). Follow this gravel road 10.5 miles uphill to a trail sign on the left and a pullout on the right, at 6,180 feet.

The Hike

With a peak named Fuji, how can you miss? The short climb is a piece of cake, and the summit offers an overview of no fewer than three of the wilderness areas that now link the Oregon Cascades in an almost unbroken line. The route described here is a shortcut to the summit that is overlooked by many hikers.

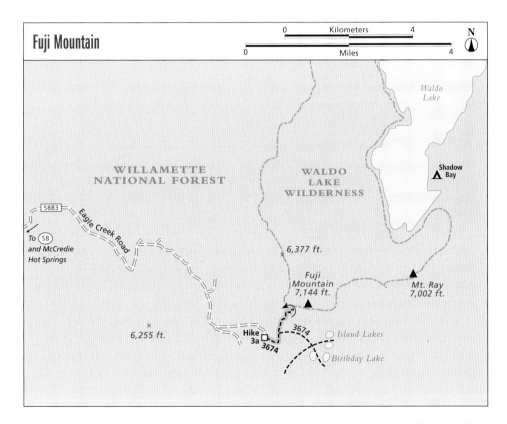

Fuji Mountain

Fuji Mountain Trail (3674) climbs moderately to a signed junction in 0.25 mile and then traverses along the west side of a ridge. The route weaves upward like a needle through a blue blanket of lupine and aster, backed by tall stands of mountain hemlock and true fir coated with tufts of moss. The last 0.5 mile is a steeper grade eased by switchbacks. Snow patches often obscure the route until mid-July.

As you look south from the summit, snowcapped Diamond Peak presides over the Diamond Peak Wilderness (see hike 3b). Waldo Lake, framed by a landscape of wooded knolls and ridges, spreads out directly below. Fuji Mountain itself forms the southern boundary of the 39,200-acre Waldo Lake Wilderness. The massive Three Sisters Wilderness lies just beyond it to the northeast; the glacier-capped peaks of the North and South Sisters, along with several other volcanic cones, can be spotted in a straight line fading into the distance.

Hike 3b Diamond Creek Falls Loop and Vivian Lake

General description: A day hike featuring waterfalls, wildflowers, and a lake in the Diamond Peak Wilderness, near McCredie Hot Springs
Difficulty: Moderate
Distance: About 6.5 miles round-trip, including a 2.5-mile loop
General location: 62 miles southeast of Eugene

Elevation gain: 1,486 feet (loop, 280 feet; 1,206 feet to Vivian Lake)
High point: 5,406 feet
Hiking quad: USGS Diamond Peak
Road map: BLM/USDAFS Willamette Cascades
Restrictions: Northwest Forest Pass required
Contact: Middle Fork Ranger District, Willamette National Forest

Finding the trailhead: From Oakridge take SR 58 about 22 miles southeast (12 miles past McCredie) and through the highway tunnel to Salt Creek Falls Viewpoint and trailhead parking.

The Hike

A pleasant half-day outing through a shaded forest bursting with rhododendrons leads to waterfalls and a wooded lake. The first 1.0 mile is part of a loop trail to Diamond Creek Falls. The route described combines the loop with a 2.0-mile extension south to Vivian Lake.

Diamond Creek Falls Trail (3598) passes the spur to Salt Creek Falls and bridges Salt Creek to a junction. Bear left and begin a gentle climb in a forest of hemlock and Douglas fir. Thickets of bright pink rhododendrons and the solitary white blooms of bear grass highlight the way. The route crosses a dirt road in 0.5 mile and once again just before reaching the far end of the loop.

Take the left fork at the junction to reach Vivian Lake. After crossing the same road once more, followed by the Southern Pacific Railroad tracks and then yet another road, you'll welcome the final crossing—the wilderness boundary line! Next the trail climbs a steep grade beside Fall Creek Falls and then tapers off a bit in the last 0.5 mile along the rushing creek. Thick woods hide the lake until the last minute.

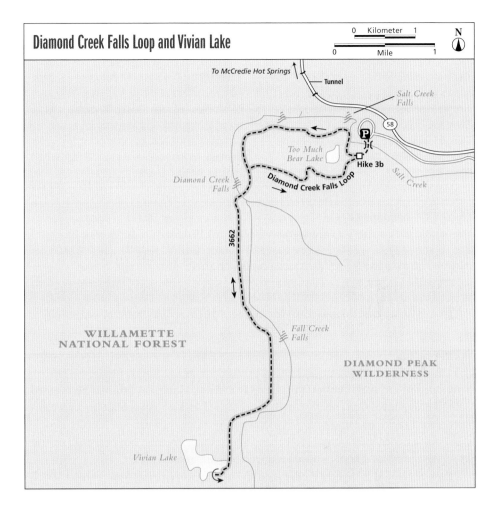

0   Kilometer   1

0   Mile   1

N

To McCredie Hot Springs

Tunnel

Salt Creek Falls

58

Too Much Bear Lake

Hike 3b

Diamond Creek Falls

Diamond Creek Falls Loop

Salt Creek

3662

Fall Creek Falls

WILLAMETTE NATIONAL FOREST

DIAMOND PEAK WILDERNESS

Vivian Lake

The Diamond Peak Wilderness has expanded to cover 52,337 acres centered on the snow-crowned roots of an old volcano (8,744-foot Diamond Peak) and the 7,100-foot and 7,138-foot lava crags of Mount Yoran. The peaks are flanked by forested ridges, tree-rimmed lakes, and a multitude of lakelets gouged out by glaciers.

Vivian Lake, a relatively small lake marked by an irregular shoreline, sits in a shallow basin walled in by trees. A few tiny clearings offer possible campsites or picnic areas. As you look across the green water, Mount Yoran peeks an angular head above the treetops a couple of miles south.

Retrace your steps to the junction, and bear left onto the Diamond Creek Falls Trail to complete the loop. The path soon reaches a close-range overlook of Upper Diamond Creek Falls. The second viewpoint is reached via a spur that drops to bridge the creek and returns to the base of the falls. The homeward route offers a few more vistas across the rugged canyon and a short spur to the rhododendron-rimmed shore of Too Much Bear Lake. Be sure to see 286-foot Salt Creek Falls, Oregon's second-highest plunge, before leaving the area.

4 Cougar (Terwilliger) Hot Springs

General description: An idyllic chain of well-known soaking pools on a short path, near Cougar Reservoir. Officially clothing optional.

Elevation: 2,000 feet

General location: 53 miles east of Eugene

GPS: N44.08339 / W122.23880

Map: BLM/USDAFS Willamette Cascades (springs marked). See map on page 12.

Restrictions: Day use only; purchase day pass from attendants at the parking area. Northwest Forest Pass not valid. Closed Thursdays until noon for cleaning. No glass, alcohol, or pets permitted at the springs.

Contact: McKenzie River Ranger District, Willamette National Forest

Finding the hot springs: From Eugene drive about 41 miles east on SR 126 to Blue River. Continue 4 miles and turn right onto paved Aufderheide Drive (FR 19) toward Cougar Reservoir. Bear right after 0.4 mile and right again at 3.3 miles from SR 126. Continue south along the west side of Cougar Reservoir; 7.5 miles from SR 126 you'll pass a lagoon with a waterfall on your right followed by a parking area on the left. Walk back past the lagoon to the trail sign, where the attendants should be waiting to collect your day-use fee (bring cash). The well-worn 0.3-mile path hugs the shore and then climbs through a darkening forest to the pools. (Please be kind to the soil and stay on established paths.)

The Hot Springs

Enveloped in the dark hues of a primeval woodland, Cougar is brushed by mottled light filtering down from treetops high above. Three soaking pools built up with carefully placed rocks are laid out in steps down a steep ravine. There are usually two or three smaller, user-built pools below these. Springwater emerges out of a small cave at 116°F and tumbles directly into the uppermost, and hottest, pool.

Each rock pool is slightly cooler than the one above, ranging from around 108°F to 95°F. The area receives sustained periods of rain, which can cool the pools down significantly. For updates on this, and other Cougar Hot Spring information, check out friendsofcougar.com.

There's a changing shelter and two compost toilets nearby. The site has been improved throughout the years by the forest service and many volunteers.

The source at Cougar Hot Springs flows out of this small cave directly into the uppermost pool. SALLY JACKSON

5 Bigelow (Deer Creek) Hot Spring

General description: A fern-grotto pool on the McKenzie River, near a paved road. Swimwear is advised.
Elevation: 2,000 feet
General location: 61 miles northeast of Eugene

GPS: N44.23838 / W122.05950 (estimate)
Map: BLM/USDAFS Willamette Cascades (spring not marked)
Restrictions: Day use only
Contact: McKenzie River Ranger District, Willamette National Forest

Finding the hot spring: From Eugene take SR 126 about 57 miles east to Belknap Springs. Continue 4 miles north (midway between mileposts 15 and 14) and turn left onto Deer Creek Road (Road 2654). Cross the river and park just past the bridge. Follow the McKenzie River Trail downstream; then take the first path down the bank to the pool.

The Hot Spring

This little pool is well camouflaged among the many look-alikes along the riverbank. If you were rafting downstream, it would never catch your eye. Walking right above it on the McKenzie River National Recreation Trail (see hike 5a), you wouldn't see the pool through the trees. Even driving across the nearby bridge and looking right at the pool, there are no telltale signs to give it away unless it's occupied.

With the inlet at the bottom of the bubbly pool, hot water seeps in quietly to provide an optimum soaking temperature of 102°F to 104°F. Riverside rocks line the outer edge, while the inner side forms a small grotto carved out of the steep riverbank. Luxuriant ferns overhang the pool, and moisture condenses overhead to drip back down on the steaming surface in cool droplets.

Waking nightmare

I parked by the bridge; mine was the only vehicle on a rainy Friday night. It was my first visit to Bigelow in several years. The next morning I awoke to discover the lot rapidly filling to capacity. People were gathering in small clusters and talking with animation. Huge motorhomes pulled in, and more folks piled out.

I finally squeezed my door open and jokingly asked a lady where the line began. She gave me a blank look and a polite laugh, then hurried off. I finally learned to my great relief that it wasn't Bigelow Hot Spring but a running marathon on the McKenzie River Trail that had drawn the crowd! (Evie)

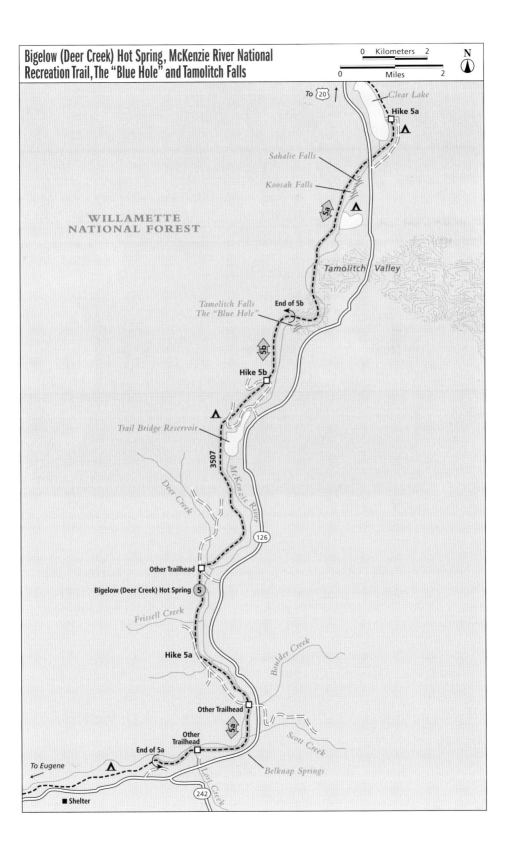

Bigelow (Deer Creek) Hot Spring, McKenzie River National Recreation Trail, The "Blue Hole" and Tamolitch Falls

0 Kilometers 2

0 Miles 2

N

To 20

Clear Lake

Hike 5a

Sahalie Falls

Koosah Falls

5a

WILLAMETTE
NATIONAL FOREST

Tamolitch Valley

Tamolitch Falls
The "Blue Hole"

End of 5b

5b

Hike 5b

Trail Bridge Reservoir

3507

McKenzie River

Deer Creek

126

Other Trailhead

Bigelow (Deer Creek) Hot Spring 5

Frissell Creek

Boulder Creek

Hike 5a

Other Trailhead

Other
Trailhead

Scott Creek

End of 5a

5a

Belknap Springs

To Eugene

Lost Creek

242

■ Shelter

Bigelow Hot Spring bubbles up from below into a fern-grotto pool well hidden along the river-bank. SALLY JACKSON

Nighttime closure: Following in the footsteps of first Cougar and then McCredie, Bigelow has joined the list of hot springs in Willamette National Forest to institute a night closure. The area around the pool is now officially off-limits from sundown to sunrise.

Hike 5a McKenzie River National Recreation Trail

General description: A choice of riverside strolls featuring virgin forests, lava flows, and waterfalls; near Bigelow Hot Spring
Difficulty: Easy
Distance: Variable
General location: Beginning 52 miles east of Eugene

Elevation gain: Up to 1,750 feet
High point: 3,200 feet (Clear Lake)
Map: BLM/USDAFS Willamette Cascades. See map on page 25.
Contact: McKenzie River Ranger District, Willamette National Forest

Finding the trailheads: Drive 52 miles east from Eugene on SR 126 to McKenzie River Ranger Station, where you can pick up a brochure and map listing the many trailheads and exact mileages between points.

The Hike

The riverside path above Bigelow Hot Spring is part of the 27-mile McKenzie River National Recreation Trail. Designated as a National Wild and Scenic River in 1988 and listed as a State Scenic Waterway at the same time, the McKenzie is a whitewater river that originates in the high Cascades. Beginning just west of McKenzie Ranger Station and ending near Clear Lake and the river's headwaters, the route is a gentle climb upvalley parallel to SR 126. There are eleven parking areas along the way that provide a variety of easy access points at signed trailheads.

The lower 8 to 10 miles are usually free of snow year-round. You tread through dim forests of old-growth Douglas fir mixed with hemlock, cedar, and dogwood. Thick mats of Oregon grape, wildflowers, and salal crowd beneath vine maple and other hardwoods. The upper part passes areas where lava flows once spewed from nearby craters, filling the McKenzie Canyon and forcing the once mighty river through underground channels (see hike 5b). Tamolitch, a broad valley of lava, remains a dry watercourse except in times of heavy runoff.

Above Tamolitch Valley the trail passes two impressive waterfalls created by lava. Koosah Falls, a 70-foot drop into a deep pool, is outclassed by magnificent Sahalie Falls, a broad 100-foot plunge over a lava dam followed by a series of cascades that tumble another 40 feet. Clouds of spray billow outward over green banks.

Clear Lake, the next to last stop, was created some 3,000 years ago when a giant lava flow dammed the river and caused the wide valley upstream to fill in. Submerged trees can be seen through the clear surface near the north end, well preserved in the icy, mineral-free water. Springs that average 43°F act as outlets for the buried river and well up from below to feed the lake. Great Springs, one of the largest, can be seen from the trail on the northeast side.

The McKenzie River Trail finally comes to rest near the Old Santiam Wagon Road, just north of Clear Lake. This historic route over the Santiam Pass became an early link between the mid–Willamette Valley and the lands in central and eastern Oregon.

Hike 5b The "Blue Hole" and Tamolitch Falls

General description: A day hike to one of the strangest sights along the McKenzie River Trail, near Bigelow Hot Spring
Difficulty: Easy
Distance: About 4.0 miles round-trip
General location: 66 miles northeast of Eugene

Elevation gain: 240 feet
High point: 2,440 feet
Map: BLM/USDAFS Willamette Cascades. See map on page 25.
Contact: McKenzie River Ranger District, Willamette National Forest

Finding the trailhead: Follow the preceding directions to Bigelow Hot Spring and take SR 126 about 3.5 miles farther north to Trail Bridge Reservoir. Cross the bridge to a junction and bear right (the left fork goes to Trail Bridge Campground). Continue straight where the main road forks right again. As the road makes a left, watch for a small turnout and trail marker.

The Hike

One of the highlights on the McKenzie River Trail (hike 5a) is a spot known locally as the "Blue Hole," a brilliant blue pool of icy water that marks the place where the river rises from its underground channel, near the south end of Tamolitch Valley, to continue its course in a more normal fashion. It's quite a sight to see this strange pool, with no visible inlet, channeling out into a whitewater river.

Follow the McKenzie River Trail north for an easy 2.0 miles through deep woods. At one point you'll cross a fern-laden marsh on a curving bridge hewn from logs. The route gradually emerges into the open at Tamolitch, the Valley of Lava. A drier landscape continues across a riverbed of moss-coated volcanic rock that culminates in a 60-foot drop-off into the Blue Hole. This bone-dry cliff is called Tamolitch Falls on the forest service brochure. It would confound any camera-clicking sightseer out to capture one more waterfall on film or memory card. But so would a river flowing downstream from nowhere.

Note: Tamolitch Falls actually does run water on occasion in the winter months and when warm spring rains cause extensive snowmelt. It's a significant event.

6 Bagby Hot Springs

Hike 6 To Bagby Hot Springs

General description: A day hike through lush woods to the Shangri-la of hot soaks. Swimwear is optional in the private bathhouses.
Difficulty: Easy
Distance: 3.0 miles round-trip
General location: 70 miles southeast of Portland
Elevation gain: 190 feet
High point: 2,270 feet at Bagby
GPS: N44.93580 / W122.17350
Hiking quad: USGS Bagby Hot Springs; Green Trails Battle Ax

Road map: Mount Hood National Forest (springs named on both maps)
Restrictions: A modest soaking fee needs to be paid to the attendants at the parking area— cash only. Northwest Forest Pass not valid. Camping is not permitted at the springs. There is camping 0.25 mile beyond at Shower Creek and also at the trailhead. Alcohol is prohibited.
Contact: Clackamas River Ranger District, Mount Hood National Forest

Finding the trailhead: From Portland take SR 224 to Estacada and on into Mount Hood National Forest. Turn right onto FR 46 at 0.5 mile past Ripplebrook Guard Station, and bear right in 3.5 miles on FR 63. Turn right again in 3.5 miles onto FR 70 and drive 6 miles to the trailhead parking lot. The roads are paved and well marked. Access is sometimes restricted in winter, as roads are not maintained. If you choose to visit Bagby during the winter months, come prepared. The forest service recommends that you drive a four-wheel-drive or equivalent vehicle and have good-traction tires, chains, a shovel, and extra food.

The Hike

The 1.5-mile Bagby Trail (544) is a delight in itself as it undulates through a grand old forest of Douglas fir and cedar with an understory of vine maple. Moss-coated old-growth logs, some 5-foot in diameter, have fallen across the trail, bisecting the path in many locations. The gentle creekside route passes emerald-green pools spaced between rapids. Cross three bridges; then leave the creek behind just beyond the last bridge and climb a short hillside to the springs.

The Hot Springs

A former volunteer group built three rustic bathhouses, fed by two nearby springs, in a sylvan forest setting. The Friends of Bagby added hand-hewn log tubs, decks, out-houses, pathways, and landscaping. What this unique group achieved is a world-class example of the Woodbutcher's Art.

The bathhouse at the upper spring, built in 1983, has a single 6-foot round cedar tub enclosed by minimal walls and maximum trees. The ceiling is pure sky. This is the spot for a family or cozy group to enjoy total privacy. A log flume 150 feet long diverts the 135°F springwater into the tub; a crude faucet admits cold water.

The refurbished communal bathhouse at Bagby Hot Springs MICHAEL RYSAVY

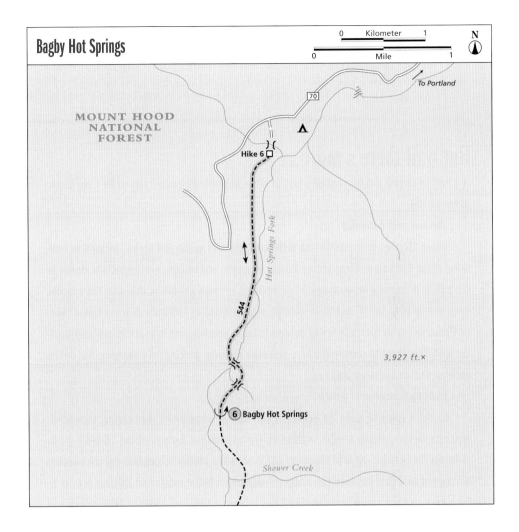

The communal bathhouse, finished in 1984, is another minimal wall–maximum tree and sky affair, but on a larger scale. In recent years the forest service has replaced the three hollowed-out log tubs with four tongue-and-groove cedar tubs. An adjoining bathhouse, completed in 1986, is a fully roofed replica of the original one that burned down in 1979; it offers the remaining five hand-hewn log tubs in private rooms.

A cleverly designed system of log flumes channels 135°F water from the lower spring into each tub, and individual gates may be opened or closed to control the flow. Tub water drains out through another set of gates into long troughs that run beneath each house. One last flume feeds cold water into a centrally located cistern, and buckets are provided to carry it to the tubs.

Note: In 2012 the forest service handed over the operational management of Bagby to Mount Hood Recreation Services. The concessionaire's job is to maintain the unique, charming, and historic atmosphere of the springs and also collect litter, clean toilets and tubs, collect fees, make basic repairs, monitor use, and manage the campground located adjacent to the trailhead. The former problem of parked vehicles being tampered with is now practically a thing of the past, thanks to the presence of the car park attendants.

But wait there's more...

It would be remiss not to mention a trio of other hot springs located not so far from Bagby (down FR 46).

The one with potential . . .

About 15 miles to the northeast is the controversial Austin Hot Spring, located on both sides of the Clackamas River. It's on private property, and despite being officially closed to the public, it receives heavy usage; large amounts of trash get left at this site. The sources are a near-boiling 183°F, and there have been many scalding incidents. A group called "Austin Preservation" is currently trying to raise funds to purchase the hot springs and surrounding land. They want to restore the area and offer soaking, parking, and camping. For online updates visit austinhotsprings.org.

Want to "splash out" a little?

If you're going to make an exception and visit a "commercial" hot spring, then think seriously about spending a night or three at Breitenbush Hot Springs (about 26 miles south of Austin Hot Springs). At first the camping fee sounds a bit exorbitant, but you soon realize it's a great deal that includes three organic vegetarian buffet meals and 24-hour access to the sauna, two hot spring bathing areas, two retreat rooms, and a library. The positive and tranquil ambience of Breitenbush is priceless. It's also possible to book in as a day guest. Breitenbush is located 11 miles northeast of the tiny village of Detroit, and advanced bookings are required. For more information check breitenbush.com.

The rumor . . .

Word has it there's a nice free creekside soak near the turnoff from FR 46 to Breitenbush. I promise to track it down for the next edition! (Sally)

7 Paulina Lake Hot Springs

Hike 7 To Paulina Lake Hot Springs

General description: A day hike to a chain of shallow, primitive hot springs on a lake inside a volcanic caldera. Carry a swimsuit.
Difficulty: Easy
Distance: About 5.0 miles round-trip (or a 7.5-mile loop)
General location: 33 miles south of Bend
Elevation gain: 180 feet
High point: 6,520 feet

GPS: N43.73196 / W121.25154
Hiking quads: USGS Paulina Peak and East Lake
Road map: Deschutes National Forest (springs not marked on either map)
Restrictions: Northwest Forest Pass required to park from May to September. Snow blocks the roads in winter.
Contact: Bend/Fort Rock Ranger District, Deschutes National Forest

Finding the trailhead: Drive 20 miles south of Bend on US 97, then follow signs 13 miles east to Newberry Caldera and Paulina Lake. The springs are on the far shore and can be reached by following the Paulina Lakeshore Loop Trail for 2.75 miles from the Paulina Lake Day Use Area or hiking 2.5 miles from the parking area at the far end of Little Crater Campground.

The Volcano

Newberry National Volcanic Monument is a slice of Deschutes National Forest housing much of the lava lands on the east side of the Cascades plus the largest ice-age volcano in Oregon. Several violent eruptions over the past half-million years formed the 5-mile-wide Newberry Caldera. Within are two scenic lakes. At one time a single body of water, Paulina and East Lakes were eventually split apart by further eruptions. Both lakes are fed by both snowmelt and a multitude of bubbling hot springs, many of which are submerged. Luckily, a few pop up along their shorelines, allowing for bathing when the lake levels aren't too high.

The Hike

Although the round-trip to the hot springs from Little Crater Campground is short and sweet, the full loop hike around the lake is well worth the added mileage. The path hugs the photogenic shoreline, leaving it only briefly to climb a prominent landmark known locally as "red slide." Thick forest shades the way without blocking views of Paulina Peak and the Big Obsidian Flow. The springs can be found between "red slide" and the Inter-Lake Lava Flow, along a meadow-lined beach. There's more lakeside soaking about 0.3 mile to the southeast (GPS: N43.72962 / W121.24671). Look for a short path in the grass leading to the lake—if you're lucky you may find more than one pool.

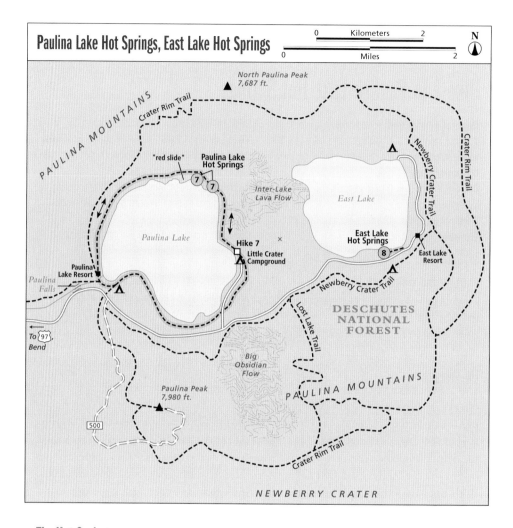

Paulina Lake Hot Springs, East Lake Hot Springs

The Hot Springs

The springs at Paulina are a tad out of the ordinary. Elusive even after you've found them, they lurk not underwater but under red and black volcanic gravel. You can sometimes walk down the beach, turn, and watch your footsteps fill with hot water! The springs range from 96°F to 113°F. Evie consulted a hydrologist and a geologist, both familiar with Newberry Caldera, and was told that the hot springs here bubble up from the depths and simply ride the top layer of the lake's water table. Hot water filters up through the shoreline gravel at the same level as the lake itself.

There's a shallow soaking pool at 113°F over by "red slide" that appears to be a perennial. It sits on bedrock, but it should fill up when the lake level is just right. It has a nice platform spanning one end for a seat and some foot dangling. All you need to do is throw in some cold water.

Just one of many small hot pools along the shoreline of Paulina Lake, with part of "red slide" visible in the background SALLY JACKSON

Other Trips in the Newberry Area

Newberry Caldera

The caldera contains a network of hiking routes to suit every taste. Crater Rim Trail climbs Paulina Peak and then continues around the rim for 20 miles. The caldera can also be entered via the 4.25-mile Lost Lake Trail to create a 10-mile loop or via Newberry Crater Trail, bisecting the caldera's floor from east to west.

Not to be missed are the 0.5-mile Paulina Falls Trail, which offers an exceptional view from the base of the 100-foot plunge, and the 1.0-mile Obsidian Flow Loop, which snakes across frozen cataracts of black volcanic glass. The 1,300-year-old flow is from the most recent volcanic eruption in Oregon. The Paulina Peak and East Lake USGS quads cover Newberry Caldera; the Deschutes National Forest map handles the roads. Visit the Paulina Visitor Center for more information.

8 East Lake Hot Springs

General description: Another set of toasty lakeside soaks. Keep swimwear handy.
Elevation: 6,300 feet
General location: 35 miles south of Bend
GPS: N43.71966 / W121.20449
Map: Deschutes National Forest (springs not marked on map). See map on page 34.

Restrictions: A Northwest Forest Pass is required to park from May to September. Snow blocks the roads in winter.
Contact: Bend/Fort Rock Ranger District, Deschutes National Forest

Finding the hot springs: From Paulina Lake head east a couple of miles and turn left into the Hot Springs boat ramp. Park here and walk west along the south shore of East Lake.

The Hot Springs

If the lake level is not too high, you should soon start to notice hot spots underfoot. Be patient and wait until you've gone around two small points to where the largest spring hides (about 0.4 mile from the boat ramp). It's 140°F and bubbles vigorously at the source. There's often a log-and-rock pool jutting out into the lake.

B. The Eastern Desert and the Owyhee River Canyon

The southeast corner of Oregon is a land of sagebrush hills, cattle ranches, and high lava plains stretching as far as the eye can see. Of the nineteen hot springs listed in this area, thirteen lie scattered to the west and six line the Owyhee River to the east. Most public lands here are administered by the Bureau of Land Management (BLM), with district offices in Burns and Vale.

The desert west of the Owyhee country and south of Burns is a region with a variety of wild hot springs. The springs are bordered by craggy buttes, mountains such as the Steens, lakes, or silvery smooth desert playas. Although vehicle access is long and tedious, all the hot springs do have roadside soaking pools.

To the east the Owyhee carves a rugged canyon through an almost roadless wilderness, draining ultimately into the Snake River. Congress has included nearly 200 miles of the Owyhee and its tributaries in the National Wild and Scenic Rivers System, and many parts are under wilderness study. The state geothermal map lists eight hot springs buried in the canyon. Of these, three are accessible and functional, while another three involve challenging hikes (unless you have a raft).

State highway maps don't begin to tell the story here, and national forest maps don't apply. If you have a GPS unit (highly recommended), then the addition of an *Oregon Road & Recreation Atlas* by Benchmark Maps should cover most of your navigational needs in this area (and for the remainder of Oregon). For those wanting to invest in local maps, the BLM prints both a 30-minute series detailing land features and a series of recreation maps by resource area. The latter maps are more up to date but lack the detail of the 30-minute series. This guide recommends the most user-friendly road map for each hot spring.

Directions are from the few towns scattered along US 95 and SR 205 and SR 140. The access roads tend to be long and dusty, hiking routes strictly cross-country, and campsites primitive and unshaded. The hot springs, with few exceptions, are wild and woolly.

Hot Springs and Hikes

The desert country to the west of the Owyhee River offers a number of remote roadside hot soaks. Shorter routes to Juntura, Beulah, South Harney Lake, Frenchglen, Hart Mountain, Fisher, Virgin Valley, Bog, Borax, and Little Borax (9–18) are followed by somewhat lengthier back roads to Alvord, Mickey, and Whitehorse (19–21). To the east the scenic Owyhee Canyon makes for rugged cross-country hiking as well as long, dusty back roads. Starting upcanyon and south of Jordan Valley at Three Forks (22), we flounder downstream with mad expeditions to Ryegrass, Greeley Bar, and Echo Rock (23–25), the latter accessed along with a companion hike from scenic Leslie Gulch. Farthest north comes a roadside dip at popular Snively (26) and the practically unknown Deer Butte (27).

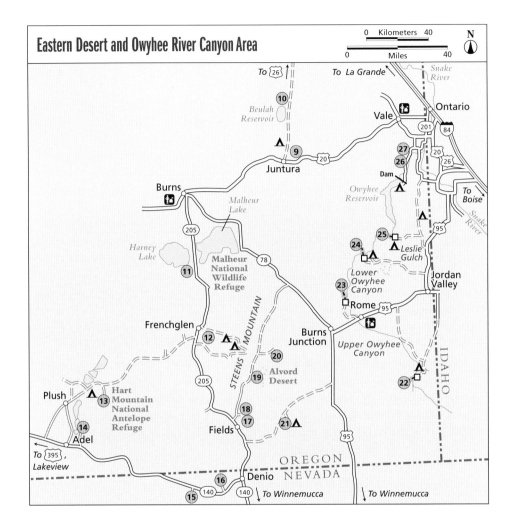

Season

Except for Virgin Valley, Frenchglen, and Borax Lake, which run a bit cool for winter use, the soaks west of the Owyhee Canyon are limited only by road access; the final roads to most are nearly impassable when wet. In the Owyhee Canyon the river level is a second critical factor. Pool temperature restricts Three Forks to warm weather, while summer heat keeps all but "mad dogs and Englishmen" out of the desert. The rafting season, roughly March through mid-June, brings more competition for the hot pools but also more users to keep the algae cleaned out.

Daytime temperatures in the desert often climb to 90°F (and sometimes much higher) through the summer months but drop markedly overnight. The weather tends to be dry and clear, and sunscreen replaces rain gear as the number-one item in the pack.

9 Juntura (Horseshoe Bend) Hot Spring

General description: A desert hot spring on an island in the Malheur River not visible from the nearby highway. Keep swimwear handy.
Elevation: 3,000 feet
General location: 52 miles southwest of Vale; 60 miles northeast of Burns

GPS: N43.77603 / W118.04772 (The spring shows up very clearly when you enter these coordinates into Google Earth.)
Map: BLM Malheur River Country, South Half (spring marked but doesn't show correct access road).
Contact: Vale District, BLM

Enjoying an autumn soak in the large source pool at Juntura Hot Spring SALLY JACKSON

Finding the hot spring: From Vale drive about 52 miles west on US 20 (from Burns go 60 miles east). About 2 miles east of Juntura, the highway crosses the Malheur River at milepost 192. Continue 0.4 mile east before turning toward the river onto an unpaved road. Drive another 0.4 mile and turn right at the closed bridge. Follow the river north around a hill that got in its way—namely, Horseshoe Bend, as it's called on the BLM map. The dirt road curves east, deteriorating to a four-wheel-drive track in the final stretch and ending at the river about 0.5 mile from the closed bridge. It's then a walk, a deep wade, or a swim out to the island, depending on the river level. There is plenty of space for primitive camping along the access road.

The Hot Spring

A 30 × 10-foot source pool hides in the grass on the far side of the little island. It's clear, with a squishy bottom, and more than 3 feet deep in places. The temperature varies considerably with the air temperature and is usually too hot for bathing in summer. During a visit in early October 2012, the ford was knee deep and the pool was registering a perfect 105°F. On the downside, the ferocious goat head thorns are in abundance that time of year—they pierced the thin soles of our sandals, making us thankful for the small plywood deck beside the pool. When the source pool is too hot, users dam up small temporary rock pools at the outflow along the river's edge. The site is used extensively during the fall by hunters, so bright orange swimwear might be in order at this time of the year.

10 Beulah Hot Springs

General description: Alfresco soaking in a domestic bathtub with a charming rural outlook. Wear what you normally take a bath in.
Elevation: 3,400 feet
General location: Northern end of Beulah Reservoir, 17 miles north of Juntura

GPS: N43.94165 / W118.13157
Map: BLM Malheur River Country, North Half (springs not marked). See map on page 38.
Contact: Burns District, BLM

Finding the hot springs: On the west side of the small settlement of Juntura, turn north off US 20 onto Beulah Road. Follow this good unpaved road for 17 miles to the northern end of what is likely to be a dried-up section of the reservoir. Off to the left, about 80 yards from the road, is where you'll see a small shelter.

The Hot Springs

Inside the crude, three-sided plywood shelter is a bathtub that's filled by two pipes connected to the nearby 130°F source pool located in the grass. On a cool October afternoon, these pipes were supplying 107°F water to the tub. Camping is not permitted at the springs.

One of many informal campsites along the edge of Beulah Reservoir SALLY JACKSON

11 | South Harney Lake Hot Springs

General description: Hot pools in a desert meadow near the southeast tip of Harney Lake. Skinnydippable with discretion.
Elevation: 4,100 feet
General location: 34 miles south of Burns

GPS: N43.18021 / W119.05821 (lower pool)
Map: BLM Steens High Desert Country, North Half (springs not marked). See map on page 38.
Contact: Burns District, BLM

Finding the hot springs: From Burns drive 2 miles east on SR 78 to the north end of SR 205. Head south 24 miles to the Malheur National Wildlife Refuge junction. Turn right (west) at an intersection near milepost 24, where a left turn is marked To Refuge Headquarters.

This seasonal road to Harney Lake deteriorates from gravel to rutted clay and deep powder patches. Watching the dust bounce and swirl on your rear window will remind you of an over-soaped washing machine. Stay on the main track for 8.3 miles, then bear right at a fork onto a 0.2-mile spur that goes through a gate to a flat parking area by the pools.

The Hot Springs

Near the gate is a marshy area where numerous sources emerge at temperatures of around 140°F. These join to flow down a channel to where users have dug two soaking pools about 50 yards apart near the parking area. The upper pool is 8 feet square and usually too hot to soak in. The lower one, closer to 10 feet across, tends to hover around a toasty 110°F. The bottoms are knee-deep mud and silt.

The springs are on a small plot of unposted private land within the wildlife refuge. Camping is allowed at the site, but please pack out what you pack in and respect the landowner's rights.

Geothermal note: The Harney Basin is a broad depression in the high lava plains of eastern Oregon that covers a major caldera complex. South Harney Lake Hot Springs is the second hottest, and reportedly the only usable soak, out of twenty-five thermal springs and more than thirty-five thermal wells. The only other possible soaking contender is the Bathtub Springs, a few miles to the west—the name certainly is encouraging! They are visible on Google Earth at N43.19641 /W119.12520.

The spring is located 0.5 mile out from the lake's high-water line. According to the USGS Oregon Geothermal listing, it's supposed to be around 123°F; the National Oceanic and Atmospheric Administration (NOAA) lists 108°F. Neither Evie nor Sally has been to these springs. If you should make it out there, please let us know (nzhotsprings@gmail.com).

The upper pool at South Harney Lake was registering an unsoakable 116°F on this warm October day. Perhaps during the winter months or with some careful water diversion, it could be cool enough to bathe in. SALLY JACKSON

Optional extra: If you're on your way to Frenchglen with time to spare, you might be interested in making a detour to visit the Diamond Craters. This location has been designated an Outstanding Natural Area and has some of the most diverse basaltic features in the United States located within a small, accessible area. From the milepost 24 turnoff on SR 205, head south 18 miles. Turn left at the signed junction to Diamond Craters and continue about 12 miles. There are short hiking trails as well as a self-guided driving tour using a BLM pamphlet (available online).

12 Frenchglen Warm Spring

General description: A warm pool hidden less than 1 mile off the beaten track in the Malheur National Wildlife Refuge. Swimwear is optional.
Elevation: 4,200 feet
General location: 60 miles south of Burns; 52 miles north of Fields

GPS: N42.81499 / W118.90058
Map: BLM Steens High Desert Country, South Half (marked as Barnes Spring)
Contact: Malheur National Wildlife Refuge

Finding the warm spring: Take SR 205 about 60 miles south of Burns (52 miles north of Fields) to Frenchglen, home of a historic hotel and restaurant (closed in winter). Frenchglen has a small store, gas pump, and telephone. There's also an RV resort that's open year-round and a seasonal BLM campground about 3 miles up the Steens Mountain Loop Road. This scenic loop drive, on a seasonal gravel road, climbs to the top of Steens Mountain and overlooks the Alvord Desert.

Take the Steens Mountain Loop Road just south of the Frenchglen Hotel. You'll soon spot a gated spur road to the right with limited parking (the alternative is to park at the hotel and walk the 0.2 mile to the gate). The spur road is closed to motorized vehicles but has a walk-through beside the gate for folks on foot. This old road, on the southern edge of the Blitzen Valley, contours along the base of a hill. In just over 0.8 mile watch for the large rocks and juniper trees on the left from where the pool will be visible. From here scramble down the bank to the pool, watching out for the remnants of a barbed-wire fence. If you reach the grove of cottonwoods in the meadow, you've gone a tad too far.

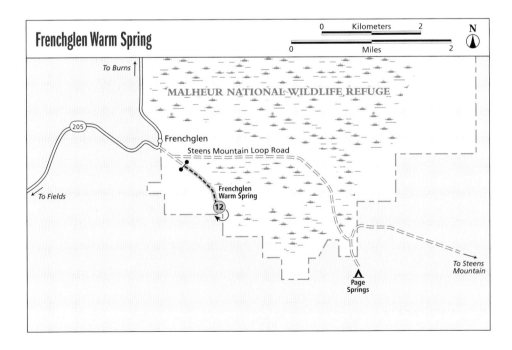

Looking down from the road to the pool at Frenchglen Warm Spring SALLY JACKSON

The Warm Spring

Springwater at 89°F flows out between the boulders just below the road into a shallow pool that's 8 feet across and 20 inches deep in the center. A rocky border is all that separates it from a swamp, so it can be buggy in the warmer months. Many years ago there was a much larger pool and a bathhouse at the site, but even without the frills, Frenchglen Warm Spring can still offer a pleasant dip in a rustic setting. It's a great spot for birding.

13 Hart Mountain (Antelope) Hot Springs

General description: A walled-in concrete tub plus a small primitive pool within Hart Mountain National Antelope Refuge. Skinnydippable with discretion.
Elevation: 6,000 feet
General location: 67 miles northeast of Lakeview

GPS: N42.50168 / W119.68951 (walled pool); N42.50134 / W119.69088 (primitive pool)
Map: Hart Mountain visitors map or BLM Lakeview District, South Half (springs marked)
Contact: Hart Mountain National Antelope Refuge

Finding the hot springs: Most visitors travel to Hart Mountain via SR 140, where two paved roads 12 miles apart head north to Plush. Eastbound travelers exit US 395 at a point 5 miles north of Lakeview and go 15.5 miles to the Plush Cutoff Road (CR 3-13). Westbound travelers coming from Fisher or Bog Hot Springs (see following) turn north at Adel onto Plush Road (CR 3-10). The latter is an 18-mile scenic lakeshore drive; the former, the high route, is 18.7 miles but more direct. Both Adel and Plush offer little more than a small store with a gas pump.

A mile north of Plush a small sign reads Hart Mountain Refuge–23, Frenchglen–73. Turn right onto CR 3-12, which turns to gravel in 13 miles and then climbs Hart Mountain as views unfold of the many lakes below. At the top, 24 miles from Plush, is the refuge headquarters. The all-weather road continues 41 miles northeast to SR 205, so anyone heading to or from the hot springs listed in that area has a third alternative. The headquarters is open year-round and staffed part-time by helpful volunteers and offers a restroom, telephone, and water. A sign points visitors 4 miles south of the complex to the hot springs and camping areas. Bear right at 1.6 miles down this access road; at 4 miles there's a junction with an information board. A left turn leads to the majority of the campsites; a right turn brings you to the springs in 0.2 mile, along with access to the remaining campsites. These primitive campsites have no amenities except for pit toilets.

The Hot Springs

The primary soak at Hart Mountain is a 7 × 10-foot soaking pool bordered by a concrete walkway and 5-foot-high rock walls. The pool is more than 4 feet deep and bisected by a rocky crevice from which springwater perks up in streamers of bubbles at around 100°F. Two changing benches sit beside the pool.

About 100 yards away, across a low white mound to the west, visitors will find a small pool fed by a separate spring. It runs a bit hotter, usually around 106°F, seats three to four

The primitive pool at Hart Mountain Hot Springs affords unrestricted views of mountaintop plateau dotted with groves of aspens. Matt Rosenthal

users, and has a free-form edge in a semi-triangular shape. This pool is fairly shallow with a silty bottom, but it fills the bill for those with an aversion to walls.

Note: Be prepared for cooler nights, as these are the highest elevation springs in the Eastern Desert area. While I was camping here in early October, my water bottle froze solid in the tent!

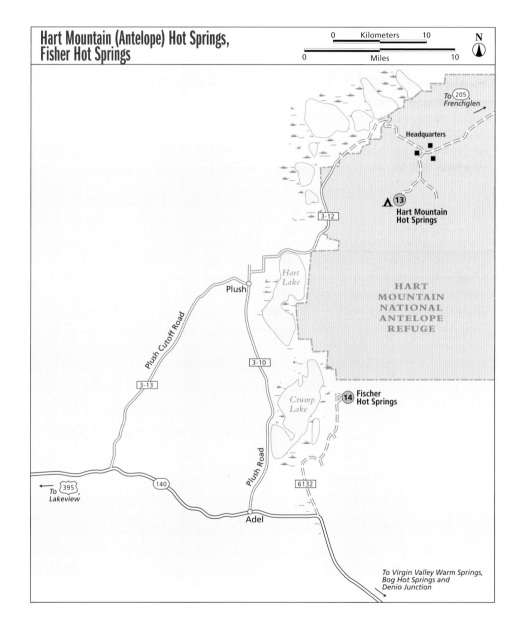

14 Fisher Hot Springs

General description: Potluck tubs on a desert road near Crump Lake and Hart Mountain National Antelope Refuge. Wear what you normally bathe in.
Elevation: 4,600 feet

General location: 48 miles northeast of Lakeview
GPS: N42.29667 / W119.77753
Map: BLM Lakeview District, South Half (springs marked). See map on page 47.
Contact: None available

Finding the hot springs: The back road to Fisher is accessed by SR 140. Eastbound travelers from US 395 proceed 28 miles to Adel, then continue 5 miles east, just past milepost 33, to a dirt road on the left. Those heading west from Denio Junction and SR 205 go about 70 miles to the turnoff. This seasonal BLM road (BLM 6132) shouldn't be used when at all damp. Follow it north through Warner Valley, bearing left at 7.7 miles. Stay on the main track; you'll spot the tubs off to your right in 10.5 miles.

The Hot Springs

Fisher is one of seven thermal springs in the Crump Geyser Geothermal Area and has surface temperatures ranging up to 154°F. The number and types of soaking tubs changes fairly regularly. At last report there were two domestic bathtubs and a square fiberglass tub, surrounded by plywood and planks to help keep feet out of the mud. The super-hot flow is piped into one tub at a time, and users must divert the pipe long enough for the water to cool. If you're lucky, the previous visitors may have been considerate enough to take the hose out of a partially filled tub so that you have some cold water for immediate temperature control. Otherwise you're in for a very long wait. The setting is a broad desert valley with a ridge on either side. The shimmering expanse of Crump Lake is visible to the west.

The springs themselves are on public land, but the soaking tubs and the parking area are on private property. Please respect the landowner's rights, and don't abuse the privilege of visiting.

15 Virgin Valley Warm Springs

General description: A warm pond with a restored historic bathhouse in the Sheldon Wildlife Refuge. Swimwear required in the pond, optional in the bathhouse.
Elevation: 4,800 feet

General location: 25 miles west of Denio Junction; 59 miles east of Adel
GPS: N41.85300 / W119.00189
Map: BLM Vya 1:100,000. See map on page 38.
Contact: Sheldon National Wildlife Refuge

Finding the warm springs: Virgin Valley may be located in an isolated part of Northern Nevada, but it's not off the beaten track if you're traveling between Fisher and Bog Hot Springs. On Nevada SR 140, 10 miles east of Cedarville Junction (CR 8a) and 0.5 mile east of a large rest area, turn south at the signed turnoff to Virgin Valley and Royal Peacock Mine. Traveling west from Denio Junction, it's 25 miles (and 16 miles from the turnoff to Bog Hot Springs). From this turnoff, proceed 2.4 miles past numerous ponds to reach the springs, where the bathhouse will be visible on the left side of the road.

The Warm Springs

The circular pond is 30 feet across and 5 feet deep and ranges from 85°F to 90°F, depending on the air temperature. It's home to a colony of curious small fish that may try to nibble at you. (It feels strange but doesn't hurt!) Inside the basic bathhouse there are two lukewarm showers that run 24/7. The adjacent campground is open year-round, providing drinking water and pit toilets but no garbage or septic dumping facilities. Camping is free, with a fourteen-night limit.

With its warm pond and bathhouse, the campground at Virgin Valley makes a welcome respite from the desert. SALLY JACKSON

16 Bog Hot Springs

General description: Roadside soak in a desert ditch, near the Oregon-Nevada border. Swimwear is first come, first served.
Elevation: 4,300 feet
General location: 38 miles southwest of Fields

GPS: N41.92170 / W118.80083
Map: BLM Denio 1:100,000 (springs marked). See map on page 38.
Contact: None available

Finding the hot springs: The road to Bog can be reached from the east or the west on SR 140, from the north by SR 205, and from Winnemucca via US 95 and SR 140. Traveling east on SR 140, the turnoff to Bog is 16 miles past the turnoff to Virgin Valley Warm Spring. Westbound travelers pause at Denio Junction, where the Fields-Denio Road and SR 140 connect just south of the border in Nevada, then head west on SR 140 for 9 miles. Turn north on a gravel road and go 4.2 miles, then bear left for 0.2 mile to a large parking area by the ditch. The Bog, as it's called by many users, may not quite lie in Oregon, but it sure doesn't miss by much.

The Hot Springs

Hot water gushes into a large soaking pool that's been dug out and dammed within a wide ditch that transports the water to an irrigation pond 0.5 mile away. This enlargement of the ditch creates a pool that usually measures at least 105°F and is big enough to accommodate quite a few soakers. It has a sandy bottom and is well over waist deep in places. There are more soaking options upstream for at least 250 yards (the dirt track leads to another parking area to access this part of the hot stream).

There are often a lot of red mites at the water's edge (see page 6 for information and advice on dealing with spider mites). The water also has a strong, pungent smell (not sulfurous though). This privately owned site is open to the public. It's a classic desert soak with lots of level space for nearby camping.

It's a hop, skip, and a jump from the truck to the pools at Bog Hot Springs. SALLY JACKSON

17 Borax Lake Hot Springs

18 Little Borax Hot Springs

Hike 18 To Both Hot Springs

General description: A short rewarding hike to a salty thermal lake and hot pots in a desert valley. Skinnydippable with discretion.

Difficulty: Easy but with many unfenced geothermal hazards—not a suitable destination for dogs or young children

Distance: About 2.0 miles round-trip from a locked gate

General location: 5 miles north of Fields

Elevation gain: Minimal

High point: 4,080 feet

GPS: Borax Lake Hot Springs, N42.32740 / W118.60440; Little Borax Hot Springs, N42.33610 / W118.60243

Map: BLM Steens High Desert Country, South Half (Little Borax springs marked)

Contact: Burns District, BLM

Finding the trailhead: The only trick here is finding Fields, which hides about 111 miles south of Burns via SR 205 and 97 miles north of Winnemucca via US 95 and SR 140. FIELDS STATION, as the sign reads, does have gas and water (an obligatory pit stop) and a small store/cafe.

Drive 1.6 miles north from Fields and continue straight at the junction onto East Steens/Alvord Ranch Road. Continue 2.4 miles north before taking an unsigned turnoff to the right. Proceed down this dirt road for another 2.4 miles, ignoring all tracks bearing left, and park at the locked gate (there is an unlocked gate at 1.4 miles). Most cars should make it in dry conditions. There is an alternative route from the power substation 1.8 miles north of Fields, which is not recommended. It is longer, and there are a lot more alkali powder patches to contend with.

The Hike

Beyond the locked gate, proceed on foot on a four-wheel-drive track for just over 0.4 mile to reach Middle Borax Lake, which is just beyond the northern tip of the cool Lower Borax Lake. This is the site of an old borax works, where white powder was once extracted from the water by evaporation and then hauled by mule train to Winnemucca.

The Hot Springs

Superheated, 196°F water gushes up through vents in the bottom of Middle Borax Lake, cooling as it disperses to a temperature in the mid to high 80s that varies in different parts of the lake and at different times of year. It's a modest lake, only about 300 feet across, and only a foot or so deep until you're well out from shore. The center is quite deep and makes for very pleasant swimming on a warm day. An air mattress or inner tube would ease the trip out.

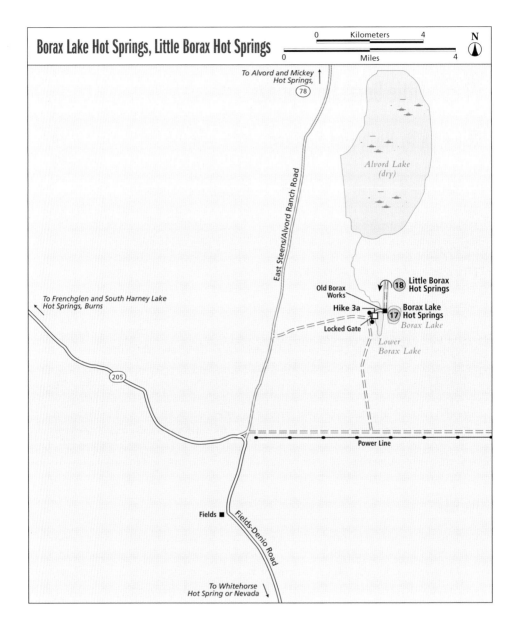

Little Borax, as it's called by some, refers to the last in a string of small "hot pots" that runs north from Middle Borax Lake. Reach it by following a track 0.7 mile due north from the rusting borax works. The pools, called ephermial vents, come in various sizes and flows. They're all deep, sometimes dangerously hot, and subject to occasional sudden surges in temperature.

You'll find two side-by-side pools at the end of the line. The first, roughly circular and 12 feet across, is sometimes lukewarm, although in October 2012 it was measuring

The two potential soaking options at Little Borax. Sudden temperature fluctuations are common, so take care to check the water before jumping in. SALLY JACKSON

100°F. The temperature in the last pool varies from far too hot to just lukewarm. The pool is about 50 × 12 feet wide and 6 feet deep, with a sloping silty bottom and a deep hole at both ends. It's worth checking out, but do use extreme caution.

Middle Borax Lake and Little Borax are on a private plot owned by The Nature Conservancy but open to the public. The small lake, rimmed by grass, sits in a broad valley just south of Alvord Lake, which is nearly dry. In addition to the salty borax, the water also has a high concentration of arsenic. Be sure you don't ingest it.

19 Alvord Hot Springs

General description: A roadside shack and hot tanks set between the Alvord Desert and Steens Mountain. Keep swimwear handy.
Elevation: 4,080 feet
General location: 23 miles northeast of Fields

GPS: N42.54390 / W118.53317
Map: BLM Steens High Desert Country, South Half (springs marked). See map on page 38.
Contact: Burns District, BLM

Finding the hot springs: Follow the preceding directions to Fields and the East Steens Road. Drive 23 miles northeast (only the first 12 miles are paved) to a large parking area on the right. From here a short gravel path leads to the crude bathhouse, which is visible from the road.

The Hot Springs

Two adjoining concrete tanks, 10 feet square and 3 feet deep, are recessed into the ground. One is open to the elements; the other is walled in by a boxy bathhouse minus a roof. The walls form a windbreak as well as a sunshade, and the open top promotes nighttime star gazing, a highly recommended activity out here. A changing room with a bench adjoins the shack, and a plank deck with another bench wraps around two sides.

Several springs emerge into the field at a staggering 172°F but cool to a mere 125°F as the water flows through a ditch. The incoming pipes each have a plug to stop the flow; it's crucial to keep them plugged up except when draining and refilling the pools. Each tank also has several upside-down spin tubs from old washing machines

scattered around for seating and occasional toe-stubbing.

Alvord Hot Springs looks out across the vast satin-finish playa of the Alvord Desert to the east and the silhouette of rugged Steens Mountain to the west. There's a campsite across the road and another with more privacy up Pike Creek, 1.6 miles north. The springs, privately owned but open to the public, are usable year-round.

The stunning mountain vistas help make up for the rustic soaking situation at Alvord Hot Springs. SALLY JACKSON

20 Mickey Hot Springs

General description: One modest soaking pool, plus a geothermal display on a very remote desert road. Clothing is optional.
Elevation: 4,040 feet
General location: 40 miles northeast of Fields

GPS: N42.67854 / W118.34837
Map: BLM Steens High Desert Country, South Half (springs named). See map on page 38.
Contact: Burns District, BLM

Finding the hot springs: Follow the directions in hike 18 to Fields and the East Steen Road. Drive 34 dusty miles northeast (10.5 miles past Alvord) to a point where the road turns north after heading east for the last mile preceding it. For anyone coming south from SR 78, it's 31 miles (the first 11 miles are paved).

Turn south on a seasonal road, then turn left after 1.9 miles and continue 4.8 more miles to a parking area on the right. A large BLM sign on the entrance gate welcomes visitors with a warning of hot springs at near-boiling temperatures and thin breakable crusts—not the best hot spring for dogs and young children.

The only soaking pool at Mickey Hot Springs, with its 125°F source pool just beyond
MATT ROSENTHAL

Mickey is a miniature Yellowstone. It has bubbling mud pots, pressure vents that hiss thin clouds of steam, a tiny boiling geyser, steamy channels snaking through the grass, and hot pools of all sizes and shapes, including a scalding 125°F deep blue-green pool that's 15 feet across. But the really important thing to remember is that Mickey has only one tiny soaking pool. The rest look great, but their temperatures run from 120°F to 180°F. The display varies in intensity from one year to the next. There's no guarantee of a good show or a good soak.

A 4 × 8-foot soaking pool with a knee-deep silty bottom is located about 150 yards from the parking area. It is fed by a tiny channel from the 125°F pool a mere 30 feet away; it may be possible to slowly cool the bathing pool a little by careful placement of rocks near the head of this channel. If you ease your own bottom in gently and manage to keep it suspended, the silt won't stir up. The temperature ranges from 103°F to considerably higher, so check it carefully before climbing in.

The geothermal basin is rimmed by rolling hills and Mickey Butte to the north, while a butte to the west is backed by a panoramic shot of Steens Mountain. Camping is permitted in the parking area but not around the springs. Mickey is on a private plot but open to the public and managed by the BLM.

The beautiful but dangerous source pool at Mickey Hot Springs, which is way too hot for bathing SALLY JACKSON

21 Whitehorse (Willow Creek) Hot Spring

General description: Hot and warm pools back to back on a far-flung desert road. Skinnydippable with discretion.
Elevation: 4,520 feet
General location: 34 miles east of Fields

GPS: N42.27555 / W118.26534
Map: BLM Owyhee Canyon Country, South Half, and Steens High Desert Country, South Half (spring named). See map on page 38.
Contact: Vale District, BLM

Finding the hot spring: Follow the directions in Hike 18 to Fields, and go south on pavement for 8.2 miles. Turn east at the Y, a junction located 13 miles north of the Nevada border, onto an all-weather gravel road signed to Whitehorse Ranch. Drive 23.5 dusty miles and look for a hill on your right. Take the dirt road just beyond it, but only in dry conditions, especially if you don't have four-wheel drive. It's the first right after passing the Willow Creek bridge. Bear right in 1.8 miles and circle the hill for 0.3 mile to the spring.

Westbound travelers will drive 21 miles south of Burns Junction on US 95, then west on White-horse Ranch Road for 23.5 miles. Turn left 0.8 mile past where the power line crosses the main road, 3.3 miles past the ranch, and follow the preceding directions. There is an alternative access road that turns off where the power line crosses the road, but it isn't recommended; it's longer with more stretches of deep alkali powder.

The Hot Spring

Water perks upward at 115°F into the hotter of two pools separated by a concrete dam. Depending on the wind and air temperature, the pool's temperature ranges from 102°F to 110°F. The larger adjoining pool varies from 75°F to 100°F. An anonymous finger has inscribed HOT and COLD, with opposing arrows into the dam, for those with no sense of touch. It's a rare treat, especially in a desert hot spring, to have two temperatures to choose or alternate between.

The hot spring, backed by the rocky double-tipped hill, overlooks a vast expanse of high sagebrush plains. Despite the remote location, Whitehorse is seeing a surprising influx of visitors. Camping is allowed but must be at least 100 feet away from the spring. Quieter campsites are located on the other side of the hill. The BLM has installed a concrete outhouse at the site.

Enjoying the hotter of the two pools on an unusually cloudy day at Whitehorse Hot Spring JOHN R. HOWARD

22 Three Forks Warm Springs

Hike 22 To Three Forks Warm Springs

General description: A day hike to secluded springs and a warm waterfall pool in the upper Owyhee Canyon. Swimwear is optional.

Difficulty: Easy

Distance: A 5.0-mile loop

General location: 35 miles south of Jordan Valley

Elevation gain: 260 feet

High point: 4,000 feet

GPS: N42.53020 / W117.18456

Hiking quad: USGS Three Forks (springs marked)

Road map: BLM Jordan Valley 30-minute or Owyhee Canyon Country, South Half (Warm Springs Canyon marked)

Restrictions: River must be running low enough to ford.

Contact: Vale District, BLM

Finding the trailhead: Two gravel roads 15 miles apart travel south from US 95 to Three Forks. Either way, it's a long haul. Travelers coming from Burns Junction continue 30 miles east (17 miles past Rome) to a road signed THREE FORKS at milepost 36. Bear right at a signed junction 7.4 miles along this road, then bear left at 8.3 miles. This route has the bonus of passing the Owyhee Canyon Overlook (at 16.6 miles).

If you are coming from Jordan Valley, head south at the signed turnoff in the middle of town. Bear right at a fork in 3 miles and right again at the next fork in just over 7 miles, where pavement turns to gravel just past a school. Then turn right again at a fork signed THREE FORKS 14. The western access road is generally in better condition than the one beginning at Jordan Valley.

The two roads join up around 30 miles from the highway and 3 miles from the canyon rim. The final 1.4-mile stretch to the bottom (for high-clearance vehicles) is quite steep; never attempt it when the road is muddy. At the bottom there is a T junction; turn right and you'll see the parking area by the BLM toilets. There are several primitive campsites near the river, accessed by rough tracks.

The Hike

This remote spot, traditionally accessed by anglers and a few hardy river runners, marks the confluence of three tributaries of the Owyhee River, hence the name Three Forks. The Middle and North Forks of the Owyhee come together 0.5 mile to the east and flow into the main fork of the river at the BLM camp and launch site.

A 3-mile four-wheel-drive road takes a roundabout route from Three Forks Camp to the warm springs. This is the principal access, but when the river level is low, usually from June to October, you can make a nice loop by walking up the river canyon to the springs and then following the road back to camp.

The route starts by fording the combined Middle and North Forks just upstream of their confluence with the main fork of the Owyhee. There is no official trailhead, and you may have to bushwhack a little before picking up the path on the other side of the ford. Jagged walls shadow the deep canyon, and a faint, overgrown path reaches

There's an abundance of warm water and spectacular scenery when you visit Three Forks.
SALLY JACKSON

the springs about 2.0 miles upstream. To complete the loop, follow the jeep road up the steep bank on the east side and swing east to breathtaking views of the gorge. The track curves around a hill at the high point on the hike, then dips across a sagebrush valley. After 2.4 miles, a fork to the right drops to ford the Middle Fork.

The North Fork is bridged, and the rocky gorge upstream makes an inviting side trip. The road improves in the short distance back to camp, tempting the unwary driver to try it, but it offers some surprises and almost no place wide enough to turn around when you change your mind. (A map or GPS unit would be useful, as there are several turnoffs along this 3-mile stretch of road that could cause confusion.)

Note: If walking a jeep road doesn't ring your bell, a pleasant alternative is to hike up the river carrying a life jacket and then float back down the canyon wearing it. It's a gentle 2.0 miles, the river feels good on a hot day, and you can just lie back and watch the scenery go by.

The Warm Springs

Clusters of 90°F to 95°F springs are located on both sides of the river, and the rugged Owyhee Canyon forms a magnificent backdrop. On the opposite bank from the track, several thermal waterfalls pour into the river at 3,750 liters per minute, all emanating from Warm Springs Canyon. You may spot a rope descending from a boulder above the largest falls. That's your target. But don't aim for it during the spring runoff

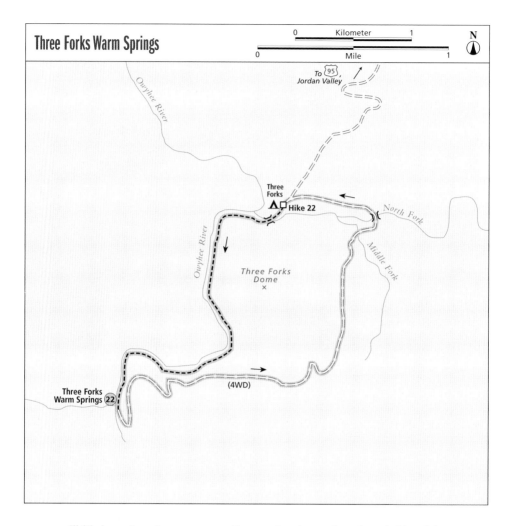

or you'll likely end up downstream at Rome. On the track and road side of the river, there are a couple of small 90°F pools well up the bank, one sporting a pipe to provide a sit-down shower.

If you are able to ford the river safely, you then climb up to a large soaking pool enclosed between boulders. (Sally avoided the weathered-looking rope that was hanging down the slab of rock.) The first pool is a gem that is a good 3 feet deep and has a gravel bottom. The scouring action of three cascades pouring into the pool keeps it clean as a whistle; the resulting warm whirlpool effect is delightful. Another large pool just above this one is reached by more careful clambering, but beyond the source the side canyon is dry. With the cold river and a lukewarm soak, Three Forks should be saved for a hot day.

Note: The springs are located on unposted private land. Please pack out what you pack in, observe fire restrictions, and respect the landowner's rights. As the springs are within the Wild and Scenic River corridor, no development of any kind is allowed.

23 Ryegrass Hot Spring

Hike 23 To Ryegrass Hot Spring

General description: A cross-country day hike or overnighter in the lower Owyhee Canyon to a spring known only to river runners. Swimwear is optional.

Difficulty: Moderate

Distance: About 8.0 miles round-trip

General location: 24 miles north of Rome

Elevation gain: 440 feet

High point: 3,560 feet (at trailhead)

GPS: N43.07160 / W117.69732 (estimate)

Hiking quad: USGS Lambert Rocks

Road maps: BLM Crooked Creek and Skull Spring 30-minute (spring not marked on either map). Springs are marked on page 10 of BLM *Owyhee River Guide* pamphlet.

Contact: Vale District, BLM

Finding the trailhead: Take US 95 to Rome, the launch site for raft trips down the lower canyon. Go 4 miles west (0.2 mile east of milepost 58) and watch for a stop sign on the north side of the highway at the crest of a low hill. Nothing else marks the spot. Do not take this primitive, seasonal road if the ground is at all damp. You'll never make it.

Drive 3.5 miles north to a ranch on Crooked Creek, and take the obscure right fork just past the ranch. Bear left in just over 0.5 mile, then proceed about 1.8 mile and take the right fork onto what becomes Tub Springs Road. The route continues north and roughly parallels the Owyhee Canyon, just visible to the east. It's slow going over rocks, potholes, and sandy washes. You'll eventually cross a plateau strewn with lava rocks and drop into the broad valley of Ryegrass Creek. At 10.5 miles along Tub Springs Road, watch for a Y in the road. Bear right and continue about 1.8 miles; park near a fork in the road.

The sensible approach: As is true for the following two hot springs, the most logical route is by raft—in this case, downstream from the BLM launch site in Rome. What follows is an alternative for the self-motivated adventurer.

The Hike

This off-trail route is a gentle downhill grade; the trick is to keep track of key landmarks on the provided trail map. The banks of Ryegrass Creek are visible across the valley, and the route parallels the canyon. Notice a rounded hill close to a long low one. Make sure you keep those hills on your right or you'll end up in another drainage.

Strike out in a northeast direction between the creek canyon and the rounded hill, and work your way over a grassy desert floor scattered with sagebrush and lava rocks. Soon you'll see a pyramid-shaped hill over by the creek. At a point midway between the two hills, the canyon veers north. Continue straight, aiming for a peninsula across the river. A faint drainage system, named Ryegrass Creek on the BLM map, will lead you eastward to the easiest route down the rocky bank. The spring is located a short distance upstream, at 3,120 feet.

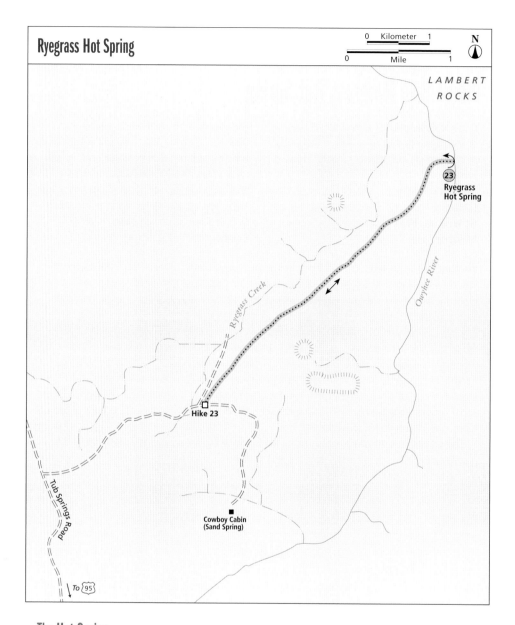

The Hot Spring

Water emerges from the ground at 110°F, and several steamy channels lined with orange algae flow down the bank into one or two small pools hidden in the tall grass at the river's edge. The pools get some TLC and cleaning during the float season, roughly March through June, but at low water you'll have them all to yourself. If you decide on a soak, you'll need a bucket to cool them down with river water. But the river may look a lot more inviting on a hot summer day.

The river runners' camp is a grassy beach near the big bend downstream. A colorfully banded rock formation known as Pruitt's Castle stands out to the north at the true outlet of Ryegrass Creek. Across the river a jeep track winds down the steep peninsula by Lambert Rocks.

The spring lies within the Wild and Scenic River corridor in a wilderness study area, so no development of any kind is allowed. Please treat it with respect and practice low-impact camping techniques. Camping is prohibited within 200 feet of the hot springs.

24 Greeley Bar Hot Spring

Hike 24 To Greeley Bar Hot Spring

General description: A long day hike or overnight bushwhack to a soak you could have rafted to, on the far side of the lower Owyhee Canyon. Swimwear is optional.
Difficulty: Moderate, plus a major river ford
Distance: About 9.0 miles round-trip
General location: 37 miles northwest of Jordan Valley
Elevation gain: Minimal
High point: 2,760 feet (Greeley Bar)
GPS: N43.20780 / W117.54615

Hiking quads: USGS The Hole in the Ground and Jordan Craters North (spring not marked)
Road maps: BLM Skull Spring and Sheaville 30-minute (spring not marked). Springs are marked on page 12 of the BLM *Owhyee River Guide* pamphlet.
Restrictions: Should be done when the river is low. The road is closed from late November to mid-February.
Contact: Vale District, BLM

Finding the trailhead: From Jordan Valley drive 8 miles north on US 95. Turn left between mileposts 13 and 12 on what starts out as an all-weather gravel road marked JORDAN CRATERS 24. In dry conditions, most high-clearance passenger cars can make it all the way to Jordan Craters. To the right, the Birch Creek junction, signed OWYHEE RIVER 6, is about 24 miles from US 95. Take the right fork 1.4 miles to the canyon rim. The final 4-mile stretch is a steep plunge, recently upgraded from a four-wheel-drive track to a high-clearance road, ending at a staffed BLM outpost with a primitive campground, a launch site for rafts, and a historic ranch.

 The sensible approach: As with Ryegrass and Echo Rock, the only sane approach to this extremely remote site is by raft—in this case a 45-mile trip downstream from the BLM launch site in Rome.

The Hike

The hike and rock-hop upstream to the hot spring starts just beyond the ranch house that now serves as a BLM outpost (starting from the river campsites makes for a longer hike). Follow an abandoned jeep track for the first mile then an intermittent path for the remaining 3.5 miles. The route stays on the south bank of the Owyhee Canyon all the way.

 The shoreline route is a boulder-hop over lava rocks choked with cockleburs and poison ivy. In some areas you can shortcut across the slope above, but beware of rattlesnakes in the tall grass in warm weather. Watch for a distinctive cliff above a lava-strewn hillside on the far bank. The jagged wall's outline rises from left to right. This is the landmark you need to locate the hot spring hidden in the marsh below.

 To cross the river—which at this point is broad, smooth, and deep—you might find an inner tube or air mattress (with a life jacket) useful. Launch a bit upstream.

This cliff is the landmark for the river crossing to Greeley Bar Hot Spring. EVIE LITTON

Sally managed to ford the river, but it was waist deep in spots even in mid-September. There isn't a right time to go or an easy way to cross, and by late season there's no guarantee of a soak.

Note: The day cooled as we hiked out, and about a mile from the trailhead we noticed a steaming geothermal area across the river adjacent to where the trail winds around an exposed bluff.

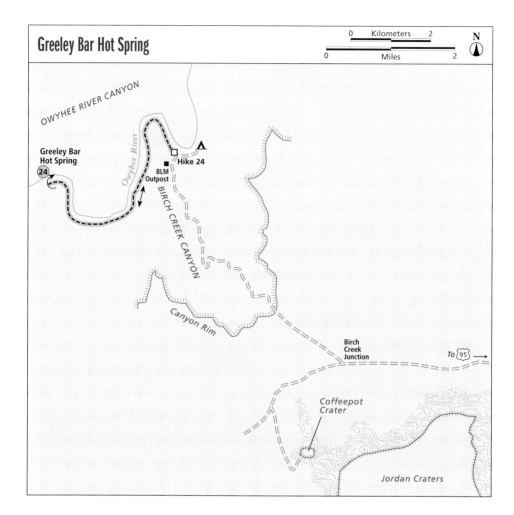

The Hot Spring

Those who make it to the hot spring will find a source pool at 110°F tucked away in the tall reeds. In early summer you can mix the river into the pool by moving a rock or two in the dam. The pool will be stranded on the bank as the river recedes, with no way to cool it off without a bucket. Greeley Bar is a popular stop during the float season, and the boaters who stop to soak keep the algae cleaned out. In the nonfloat season, you can count on having the pool, as well as the cleaning, all to yourself.

Note: The spring lies within the Wild and Scenic River corridor; no development of any kind is allowed. Remember to practice low-impact camping techniques. Camping is prohibited within 200 feet of the springs.

25 Echo Rock Hot Spring

Hike 25a To Echo Rock Hot Spring

General description: A geologically stunning day hike or overnighter to a hot shower and pool on the Owyhee Reservoir. Wear what you normally bathe in.

Difficulty: Moderate if the reservoir is low; strenuous if it is high

Distance: About 8.5 miles round-trip (10 miles via high-water route)

General location: 43 miles northwest of Jordan Valley

Elevation gain: Low route: minimal; high route: +400 feet, -320 feet

High point: 2,700 feet

GPS: N43.30184 / W117.38461 (upper spring); N43.30246 / W117.38505 (lower spring)

Hiking quads: USGS Rooster Comb and Diamond Butte

Road map: BLM Sheaville 30-minute or Malheur River Country, South Half (spring marked on both maps). Springs are marked on page 12 of the BLM *Owyhee River Guide* pamphlet.

Restrictions: Should be done when the reservoir is low

Contact: Vale District, BLM

Finding the trailhead: From Jordan Valley take US 95 about 18 miles north. Turn left onto a gravel road signed to Succor Creek State Park. Follow signs to Succor Creek for 10 miles, then turn left onto a gravel road marked Owhyee Reservoir–15. This road eventually twists down a canyon marked by vertical towers and pinnacles jutting from steep slopes (see following hike). Even without the hot spring, it's worth the drive just to see and experience Leslie Gulch. The road ends at a boat ramp on the reservoir, where rafts running the lower Owyhee Canyon take out. If you have high clearance and the lake level is low, you can probably drive and park a short way along the lake's edge (there's no parking at the boat ramp).

The sensible approach: As is true for the two previous soaks, the easiest route to Echo Rock is by raft. In this case there's even a shortcut. You can put in at the BLM launch site at Leslie Gulch and simply paddle straight up the reservoir. Barring that option, what follows is the least-complicated alternative.

The challenge: Experienced rock-hoppers can reach this remote spring on foot by following the reservoir's shoreline upstream from the boat launch, but only when the water level is low—usually from August to November, although some years this lasts through the winter and into early spring. The shoreline's one major obstacle, located less than a mile upstream from the boat launch, is a rock outcrop attached to a huge hill that can block the low-water route access. When the water level is high, a challenging traverse, best suited to bighorn sheep, would be required that adds almost 0.5 mile each way to the hike.

Note: The road access to the boat launch is not always accessible due to flash flooding and winter conditions.

The Hike

The low-water route simply involves following the shoreline upstream and picking up all-terrain vehicle (ATV) trails after reaching Spring Creek. If the water level is too

Be sure to have your camera fully charged for your hike to Echo Rock Hot Springs, especially if you have an interest in geology! SALLY JACKSON

high to skirt below the initial rocky outcrop, you have two options: Hike Leslie Gulch instead (see next hike) and come back another time when the water has receded; or make like a mountain goat and follow the faint animal trails up and around the rocky outcrops before descending steeply back down to the reservoir at Spring Creek. From here the going should be a piece of cake compared to the initial section. Just follow the long reservoir 2.5 miles upstream from the confluence with Spring Creek, tracking the bends with those on the map.

About 0.3 mile before reaching the springs, bear away from the river slightly and follow ATV tracks over a low hill. When you reach a gated fence, back up 100 feet and head down the rocky hillside to reach the upper pool.

Note: The route is surrounded by towering yellow and orange cliffs composed of rhyolite tuff (consolidated volcanic ash). A high point across from the boat ramp is aptly named the "Rooster Comb." On a calm day, the cliffs reflect magnificently in the water.

Echo Rock Hot Spring, Juniper Gulch

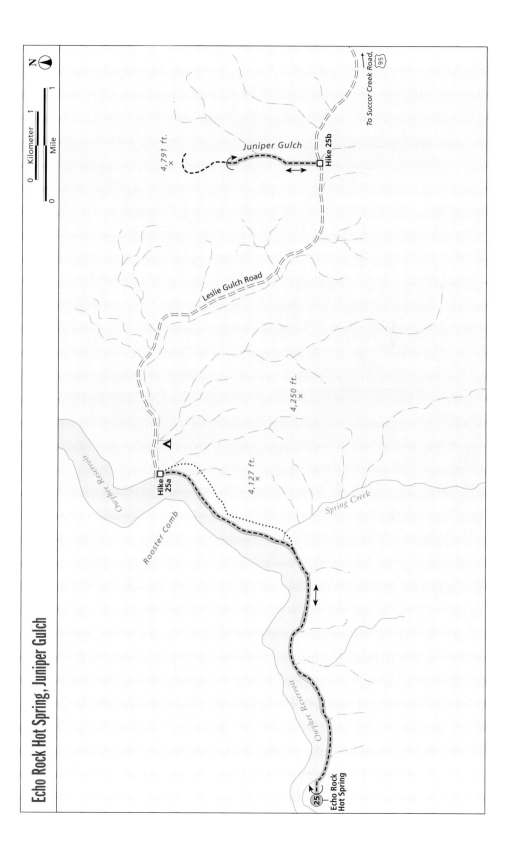

The reverberating sounds of some uninhibited hollering and yodeling from this pool at Echo Rock Hot Springs confirmed that it's been aptly named! SALLY JACKSON

The Hot Spring

Hidden among the volcanic rocks is a toasty soaking pool that in 2006, according to etching in the cement, received a major upgrade by volunteers with the installation of some elaborate plumbing. In 2012 this pool was leaking in places, which meant the inflow of 114°F water couldn't be shut off to let it cool. The result was an exceedingly hot soak—probably too hot for most. This pool is best enjoyed in the colder months, especially considering there is no shade. To prevent algae buildup, drain the pool before you leave. About 180 feet below this pool, toward the river, is an ingeniously rigged shower pipe with an outflow of around 100°F.

Hike 25b Juniper Gulch

General description: A spectacular day hike up a side canyon in Leslie Gulch, not far from Echo Rock Hot Spring
Difficulty: Easy
Distance: About 3.0 miles round-trip

General location: 40 miles northwest of Jordan Valley
Elevation gain: 1,200 feet
High point: 4,600 feet (at the crest)
Map: USGS Rooster Comb
Contact: Vale District, BLM

Finding the trailhead: Follow the preceding directions to Leslie Gulch and drive about midway between the overlook point and the boat ramp at the end. Watch for a prominent pullout on the north side of the road, 0.5 mile west of a cabin. You'll find restrooms, garbage cans, and a wilderness study area sign near the trail.

The Hike

Leslie Gulch is a moonscape of bizarre rock formations capping steep hills. Of igneous origin, the talus slopes are said to be an ash flow tuff from volcanic eruptions fifteen million years ago, with a harder core of more erosion-resistant rhyolite, which forms the spires. Side canyons offer access, but with few exceptions they are too vertical to be feasible routes. Juniper Gulch, however, provides easy access up slot canyons into a land of swiss-cheese rocks and eerie shapes. The hike culminates at an eagle-shaped spire perched on the crest, with an 800-foot gain in the final 0.5 mile.

A well-defined path follows Juniper Gulch north between high walls that gradually converge. Early on you'll pass a huge Cheshire cat grinning down at you. Bear left into a second slot canyon 0.5 mile up; you'll soon see the eagle rock standing tall on a skyline of convoluted shapes up ahead. Using care, it's possible to scramble all the way up to stand beside it. From the crest you can enjoy a face-to-face confrontation with the towering bird as well as a panoramic view of Leslie Gulch.

Note: Leslie Gulch, including all of its side canyons, is an Area of Critical Environmental Concern (ACEC) administered by the BLM. Activities are limited to day use, and camping is permitted only at Slocum Creek Campground, near the boat ramp.

26 Snively Hot Spring

General description: An all-too-popular road-side and riverside attraction at the lower end of the Owyhee Canyon. Swimwear is advised.
Elevation: 2,280 feet
General location: 30 miles south of Ontario; 10.5 miles from Owhyee Junction

GPS: N43.73021 / W117.20304
Map: BLM Malheur River Country, South Half (spring named). See map on page 38.
Restrictions: Day use only; no campfires
Contact: Vale District, BLM

Finding the hot spring: From Ontario head 20 miles south on SR 201 to Owyhee Junction. Follow signs south toward Lake Owyhee State Park. From a prominent pipeline spanning the mouth of the canyon, continue 1.5 miles. If you miss the concrete standpipe on your left, where springwater boils up from the bottom at 135°F, you can't mistake the BLM sign announcing SNIVELY HOT SPRING RECREATION SITE.

The Hot Spring

Scalding water flows from the standpipe through a ditch into one large, shallow pool dammed by rocks. The result is a startling swirl of hot and cold currents as the source and the river mix. The hot floats on top of the cold, so you'll have to keep stirring it up to stay comfortable. The overall temperature is adjustable by shifting the riverside rocks.

Unfortunately, Snively exhibits symptoms of overuse/abuse due to its easy access via paved roads. As a result, evenings, especially in summer, tend to be boisterous parties. Mornings are usually a peaceful scene marred only by the beer cans and other litter from the night before.

The setting is nothing short of spectacular. Red rock cliffs and graceful cottonwoods line the deep canyon on both sides. Snively can be reached and enjoyed any time of year except during the spring runoff.

We arrived on a frosty October morning to find the large soaking pool to be an unbearable 120°F. The river was running so low that it was stagnant and full of algae—we wouldn't have wanted to add this water to the soaking pool even if it had been possible to do so. We were later informed by a reliable source that there is usually a smaller, cooler pool fed by a separate spring a hundred yards or so downstream; it's worth checking out. (Sally)

27 Deer Butte Hot Springs

General description: A lonesome roadside hot spot en route to popular Snively Hot Springs. Swimwear is advised.
Elevation: 2,260 feet
General location: 1.5 miles downstream from Snively Hot Springs

GPS: N43.73861 / W117.17856
Map: BLM Malheur River Country, South Half (spring marked). See map on page 38.
Contact: Vale District, BLM

Finding the hot spring: Nine miles from Owyhee Junction and 1.5 miles before reaching Snively Hot Springs, park in the small pullout on the right side of the road, 120 yards before reaching the giant pipeline that spans the road. Be careful not to run over the innocuous looking puddle, which is actually the small but superheated (184°F) source pool.

The Hot Spring

The outflow runs under the road through a pipe and into a two-person tamarisk-lined pool that's visible when you're standing on the south edge of the road. This small murky pool runs about 107°F and provides a possible backup option if there are issues with the soaking conditions at Snively.

The modest soaking situation at Deer Butte Hot Springs with the landmark pipeline in the background SALLY JACKSON

Washington

The Evergreen State has surprisingly few hot springs on public land. The eight springs on the Washington map are all in magnificent hiking country. Although they don't form a chain like those in Oregon or convenient clusters like those in Idaho, the majority of Washington's scattered springs are still worth a visit.

The hot springs are located in two highly scenic areas—one gem in the Olympic Mountains, the range that forms the jagged core of the Olympic Peninsula, and the rest in the northern Cascades, with their many sharply sculpted glacial peaks. Both areas abound in craggy summits that rival the Swiss Alps, alpine meadows bursting with wildflowers, shrouded rain forests, and seething rivers with waterfalls that thunder into vast canyons. Opportunity here is limited only by your imagination.

This guide gives directions from major towns along SR 14, I-5, and US 101. Generally, the access roads are paved and well signed, the campgrounds heavily used, and the hiking trails maintained and teeming with avid hot springers during the short summer months.

Hot Springs and Hikes

We start at the Columbia Gorge with a soak at Wind River (28) and hikes to waterfalls and views. Next, trails lead to Goldmyer (29) and Scenic (30), both privately owned but open to the public. Forest roads out of Darrington access hikes to very elusive soaks at Kennedy (31), Sulphur (32), and the super-remote Gamma (33). Baker (34), northeast of Mount Vernon, has an easy-access dip and a companion climb to glacier views. On the Olympic Peninsula, soaks at Olympic (35) mix well with alpine rambling in Olympic National Park.

Season

Although summer and fall are the prime times for hot springing, some pools are accessible and usable in the off-season. Winter road closures and deep snow impede access to Baker, Kennedy, and especially Sulphur and Gamma. Spring runoff won't bury the uppermost pools at Olympic, and you can access them through the winter months on cross-country skis. The springs at Wind River are submerged during high water.

Hiking trails in the Columbia Gorge are enjoyable all year, but the high-country hiking season doesn't get comfortably under way until late July, and even then you can't be sure you'll get blue skies. In an average year the mountains west of the Cascade crest are cloud-free one day out of every six. The months of November through April bring torrents of rain to the lowlands and snow to higher elevations. Intermittent storms are common through June and likely to return by early September.

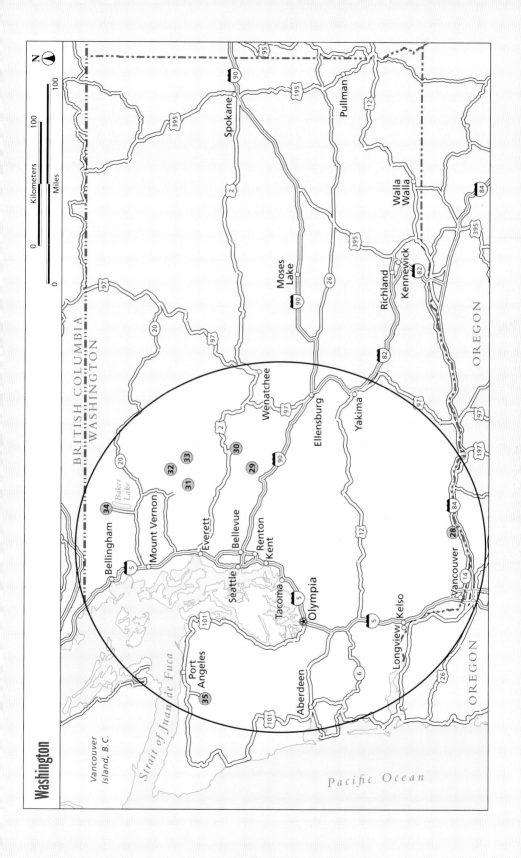

Washington

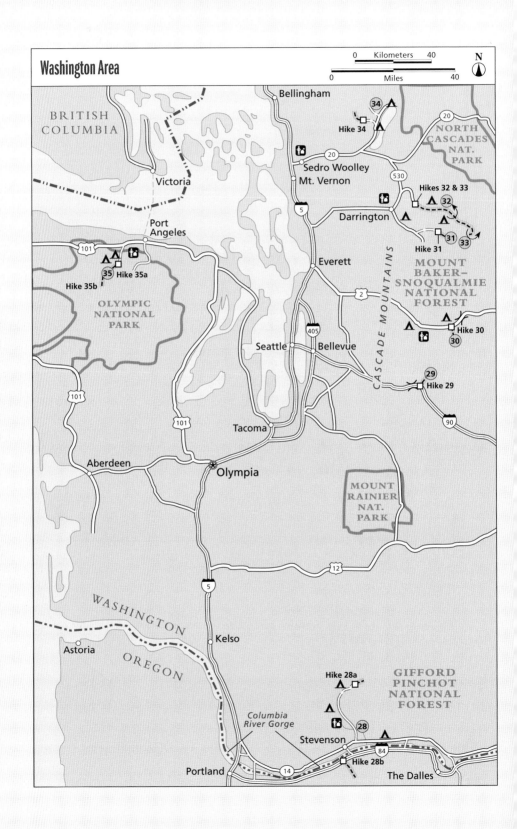

Washington Area

BRITISH
COLUMBIA

Bellingham

Hike 34

NORTH
CASCADES
NAT.
PARK

Victoria

Sedro Woolley
Mt. Vernon

Hikes 32 & 33

Hike 32

Port
Angeles

Darrington

Hike 31

Hike 33

Hike 35a

MOUNT
BAKER–
SNOQUALMIE
NATIONAL
FOREST

Hike 35b

Everett

OLYMPIC
NATIONAL
PARK

Hike 30

Seattle

Bellevue

Hike 29

Tacoma

Aberdeen

Olympia

MOUNT
RAINIER
NAT.
PARK

WASHINGTON

Kelso

Astoria

OREGON

Hike 28a

GIFFORD
PINCHOT
NATIONAL
FOREST

Columbia
River Gorge

Stevenson

Hike 28b

Portland

The Dalles

CASCADE MOUNTAINS

28 Wind River (St. Martins on the Wind) Hot Springs

General description: Late-season, riverside pools with serious access issues, near the Columbia Gorge. A swimsuit/birthday suit mix.

Elevation: 160 feet

General location: 7 miles northeast of Stevenson

GPS: Hot spring, N45.73486 / W121.80263 (estimate)

Map: Gifford Pinchot National Forest (springs not marked). See map on page 76.

Restrictions: Can only be accessed during low water. No camping is permitted near trailheads or springs. (See "The bad news" below.)

Contact: Columbia River Gorge National Scenic Area (Oregon)

The bad news: As of 2005 the St. Martins family, who owns the adjacent property, has denied public access across their land because of garbage and liability issues. There are reports of parked vehicles sometimes being towed from Indian Cabin Road. The St. Martins family is considering reintroducing a system of fee-parking on their land and then allowing access to the river. For an update, try reaching them at (509) 427-8532.

The good news: The pools are technically on public land, as they are below the high-water level of the river. This area is in transition and may be added to the Columbia River Gorge National Scenic Area. This might safeguard the springs from commercial activity (but could also add restrictions). Time will tell as to what the future holds for this special place.

Finding the hot springs: Follow SR 14 along the Columbia River Gorge about 5 miles east of Stevenson, or 15 miles west of Hood River, to Home Valley. Take Berge Road 1 mile north, then go left on Indian Cabin Road; park beyond the power pole tower. The road is narrow and parking spots are limited—don't block the gate at the end of the road or your vehicle is likely be towed. The springs are located less than 1 mile from the road's end. To avoid trespassing, you need to stay in the riverbed. You then have to negotiate thickets of poison oak and scramble over slick boulders en route. The river needs to be running low to attempt this route. When a small waterfall upstream comes into view, you've reached the first pool.

The Hot Springs

Wind River Hot Springs consist of two bedrock soaking pools beside the river. Water bubbles up through the bottom at 107°F, its ample flow keeping the pools clean. You can lower the temperature by adjusting rocks at the river's edge.

The downstream dip is smaller and registers a few degrees cooler. The upper pool sits a tad higher on the bank and enjoys a longer season of use. Users often dig a gravel pool at one end to mix the outflow with river water for a cooler soak. Thick forest borders the river, and the upstream view includes Shipherd Falls.

The springs are sometimes accessed from the west bank of the river. A swing bridge a short distance upstream near the falls is posted NO TRESPASSING and involves a hazardous climb around a cliff to reach the springs. When the river is low, some hardy (foolhardy?) folk have been known to ford the river. The Wind River "Hot Holes" are still regularly visited by locals despite the access issues.

Hike 28a Falls Creek Falls

General description: A day hike to a triple waterfall near the Columbia Gorge and Wind River Hot Springs

Difficulty: Easy

Distance: 3.5 miles round-trip

General location: 20 miles northeast of Stevenson

Elevation gain: 600 feet

High point: 2,000 feet

Hiking quads: USGS Termination Point; Green Trails Wind River

Road map: Gifford Pinchot National Forest

Contact: Mount Adams Ranger Station

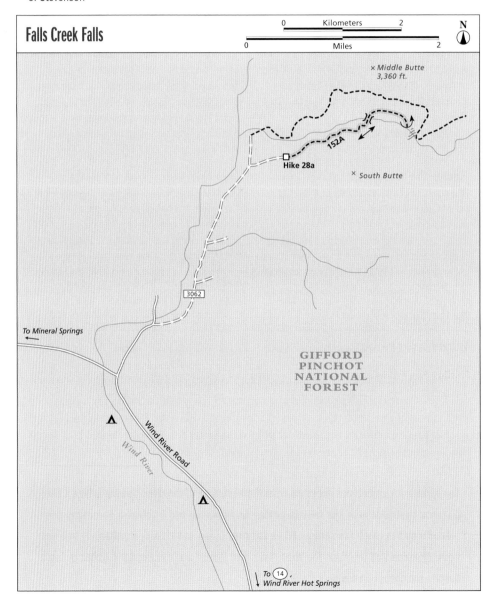

Falls Creek Falls

Finding the trailhead: Follow SR 14 along the Columbia Gorge, 3 miles east of Stevenson (2 miles west of Home Valley if you are coming from Wind River Hot Springs). Turn north onto Wind River Road and go through Carson. Pass the road to the ranger station at 8.5 miles and the turnoff to Mineral Springs at about 14 miles. Take a right in 1 mile onto gravel FR 3062. Bear right in another 2 miles onto a road signed Lower Falls Creek Falls–Trail 152A. You'll soon reach the road-end trailhead, a total of 17 miles from SR 14.

The Hike

For connoisseurs of waterfalls, this one is a must. A broad cascade pours over cliffs high above, churns over a shelf partway down, then another shelf, and reaches the bottom in a total of 250 feet in three graceful tiers. Clouds of spray billow out across the narrow canyon. If you're taking pictures, afternoon is the best time to catch sunlight on the falls.

Trail 152A wanders through a forest of Douglas fir, hemlock, and larch along the south bank of Falls Creek. It bridges the creek at the halfway point, then climbs above the north bank at a moderate grade. Shortly after you cross a boulder-strewn ravine, watch for a view of the upper and middle tiers just before the final viewpoint across from the middle and lower sections of the falls.

Hike 28b Eagle Creek Trail

General description: A popular day hike or overnighter to waterfalls on the Oregon side of the Columbia Gorge near Wind River Hot Springs

Difficulty: Easy

Distance: About 12 miles round-trip

General location: 7 miles south of Stevenson; 41 miles east of Portland

Elevation gain: +1,080 feet, -320 feet

High point: 1,200 feet

Hiking map: Trails of the Columbia Gorge

Road map: Mount Hood National Forest

Restrictions: Northwest Forest Pass required

Contact: Columbia River Gorge National Scenic Area

Finding the trailhead: From the Portland area take I-84 east to Eagle Creek Park (exit 41). Westbound travelers must make a U-turn at Bonneville Dam (exit 40) to reach exit 41. Those coming from the Wind River area cross into Oregon over a toll bridge at Cascade Locks and continue west as outlined above (12 miles total). Follow signs past the campground to parking for the Eagle Creek Trail (440).

The Hike

The Oregon side of the Columbia Gorge is famous for its profusion of waterfall hikes, and the Eagle Creek Trail into the Mark O. Hatfield Wilderness ranks as one of the finest. It gets the heaviest use in summer, but low elevation makes it enjoyable during the off-season as well. Highlights include a verdant forest backed by cliffs, views from high bridges, and a succession of waterfalls along narrowing canyon walls.

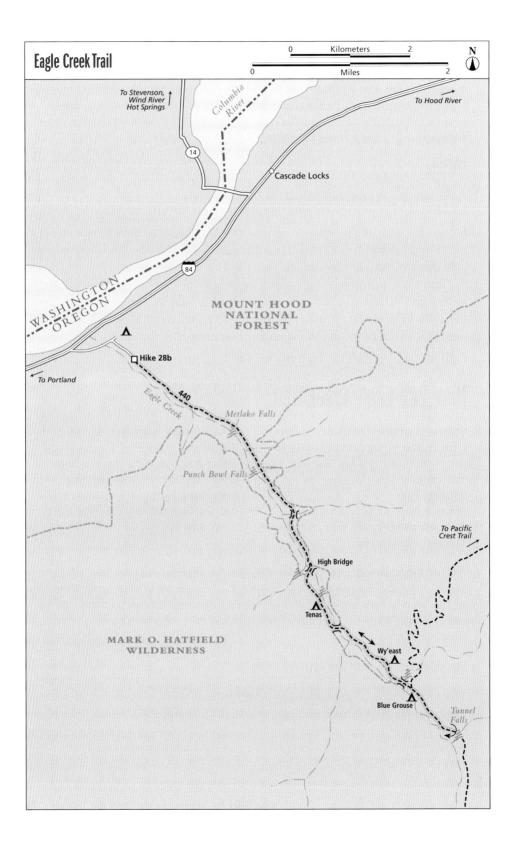

A variety of loops can constitute a longer trip, but the sheer drop of Tunnel Falls at the 6.0-mile mark makes a good destination for a day hike.

Eagle Creek Trail (440) meanders through old-growth woods above the glacially carved canyon of Eagle Creek and soon traverses a railed section carved from rock. A spur at 1.5 miles leads to a distant view of Metlako Falls, and another drops to Lower Punch Bowl Falls. The main trail comes to the upper falls at 2.1 miles. Punch Bowl Falls may be a bit modest as waterfalls go, but it's exquisitely graceful. It forms a perfect punch bowl in its delicate descent, spilling over rimrock into a circular pool below. Nearby benches offer a pleasant overlook.

Next the route spans two lush side canyons on high steel bridges. At 3.3 miles it crosses the now narrow gorge of Eagle Creek itself, a full 80 feet below, on High Bridge. The route soon passes Tenas Camp, then bridges the gorge once again to pass more tent sites at Wy'east Camp.

At 5.0 miles, just beyond the wilderness boundary, reach the junction with the Eagle-Benson Trail, which climbs 2,900 feet in 3.0 miles to the Pacific Crest Trail (PCT) and Benson Plateau. Pass another waterfall nearby, then Blue Grouse Camp at 5.3 miles, the last stop before Tunnel Falls.

The route past Tunnel Falls actually slices a 25-foot tunnel through sheer rock behind the falls. Spray drifts across the side canyon to shower anyone nearby, and the roar reverberates from nearby walls. Seen from across the ravine, hikers approaching the plunge resemble a trail of ants.

Beyond are more waterfalls, views, and remote camps. Side trails offer tempting choices. A backpacker could loop back via Eagle-Tanner and Tanner Butte Trails or continue on to join the PCT at Wahtum Lake, returning across beautiful Benson Plateau or perhaps down quiet Herman Creek to Government Cove.

29 Goldmyer Hot Springs

Hike 29 To Goldmyer Hot Springs

General description: A day or overnight hike to unique, privately owned hot springs nestled in the foothills of the Cascade Mountains. Clothing is usually optional at the springs.

Difficulty: Easy

Distance: 9.0 miles round-trip

General location: 25 miles east of North Bend; about a 3 hour drive from Seattle

Elevation gain: 600 feet

High point: 2,000 feet

GPS: N47.48401 / W121.38994 (caretaker's cabin)

Hiking quads: USGS Snoqualmie Lake and Snoqualmie Pass; Green Trails Mount Si #174 and Skykomish #175

Road map: Mount Baker–Snoqualmie National Forest. See map on page 76.

Restrictions: Reservations for both day and overnight visits are highly recommended. If you arrive without a confirmed reservation, you will be turned away if Goldmyer has reached its twenty-person-per-day limit. Weekends can be full year-round, as well as midweek during summer. Use fee required; check goldmyer .org for rates. No smoking, fires, weapons, glass containers, or pets are allowed on the property. No potable water is available.

Contact: Goldmyer is a minimally developed wilderness area owned by Northwest Wilderness Program, a nonprofit organization established in 1976 to protect the springs and their pristine surroundings. To make a reservation call (206) 789-5631 and leave a message (the office is open Tuesday and Friday 1–7 pm). There is an online reservation calendar to help you plan your visit at goldmyer.org, but reservations can only be made by phone.

Finding the trailhead: See driving directions from Seattle at goldmyer.org. The last 15 miles of road to the Dingford Trailhead is unpaved and is usually passable by regular clearance vehicles from late spring to early fall. The road is not plowed in winter; check the Goldmyer website for updates on road conditions.

The Hike

It's an easy 4.5 miles of hiking on an old forest road to reach the springs. Walk (or mountain bike, snowshoe, etc.) through the large metal gate at the Dingford Trailhead (located down FR 5620). After 4.0 miles the old road widens and forks. Head to the right and go downhill to cross the river on a footbridge. Once on the other side, turn right; a short distance later, turn left at another junction. Proceed 0.25 mile more to reach the caretaker's cabin. Please ring the bell and check in upon arrival.

From here it's a stiff 0.25-mile hike up to the springs through impressive old-growth forest. Down near the cabin, another path leads to the campsites, which are dispersed along the edge of Burnt Boot Creek.

Note: An alternative hiking route on a foot trail also starts at Dingford Trailhead but involves several unbridged stream crossings. It is not recommended if the water

The lower pool and nearby changing area at Goldmyer Hot Springs SALLY JACKSON

is running high and also not recommended in winter. The details for this hike are on the Goldmyer website.

The Hot Springs

The crystal-clear, 125°F source issues out of a 30-foot horizontal mine shaft. The water is lightly mineralized with a pH of 8.5. The "cave" pool is around 111°F, and it's like being in a sauna. Be brave and go right to the back, where you can perch out of the water. The water cascades out into two smaller and cooler pools. There's a cold plunge pool a few steps away, as well as a large wooden changing cabana.

30 Scenic Hot Springs

Hike 30 To Scenic Hot Springs

General description: Rustic soaking on a private parcel of land surrounded by national forest. Clothing is optional at the springs and on the trail.

Difficulty: Moderate

Distance: About 4.0 miles round-trip

General location: 60 miles southeast of Everett near Steven's Pass

Elevation gain: 1,100 feet

High point: 3,500 feet

GPS: N47.70894 / W121.13806 (estimate)

Hiking quads: USGS Scenic; Green Trails Stevens Pass

Road map: Mount Baker–Snoqualmie National Forest. See map on page 76.

Restrictions: Online reservations required (you must carry the written permission to be legally on the property). No children permitted under the age of 6. No camping or night use. No fires or dogs permitted.

Contact: E-mail: scenichotsprings@gmail.com

Finding the trailhead: Directions are given with the reservation. Check website for updated road conditions and pool temperatures: scenichotsprings.blogspot.com.

Background

In the 1890s a hotel was built near the springs then known as Madison Hot Springs. Its name was later changed to Scenic, and it operated as a commercial venture until 1928. Construction of an 8-mile tunnel under the pass spelled the end for the springs' commercial operation. Largely forgotten until the 1970s, the springs then became popular, with volunteers constructing four wooden soaking boxes. In 2001 these springs were closed and the tubs torn out due to liability and environmental issues; they were also removed from the fourth edition of this book. In 2011 they were conditionally reopened to those whom the owner has given permission to visit (via an online booking system). The owners are currently not operating as a commercial, for-profit venture, as they are undergoing a permitting and renovation phase. Check their website for updates.

The Hike

Tucked away high on a hillside overlooking the broad canyon just west of Stevens Pass, Scenic Hot Springs lives up to its name. Two-thirds of the trail is on a dirt access road; the last third is the steepest (and hardest!).

Soaking up some good water as well as the rustic ambience at Scenic Hot Springs CHRIS ANDREWS

The Hot Springs

There are two tarp-lined soaking boxes at Scenic. The "Lobster Pot" pool runs between 106°F and 108°F but is susceptible to temperature fluctuations during spring runoff and also after periods of heavy rain. The "Bear's Den" pool runs a constant 102.5°F. There's room for six soakers in each pool and no need to worry about overcrowding—there's a daily maximum of twelve visitors permitted. (This can be reduced to six in the cooler months when there's often only enough hot water for one pool.)

31 Kennedy Warm Spring

Hike 31a and 31b To Kennedy Warm Spring

General description: What used to be a day hike to a soaking box is now a rugged multiday mission to springs located in a badly eroded area of the Glacier Peak Wilderness. Swimwear is the least of your worries!

Difficulty: Strenuous—verging on impossible thanks to a problematic river crossing just before reaching the springs

Distance: At least 30 miles round-trip, depending on which way you access the springs

General location: 62 miles northeast of Everett

Elevation gain: 3,300 feet (hot spring)

GPS: N48.11820 / W121.19462 (estimate)

Hiking quad: Green Trails Glacier Peak

Road map: Darrington Ranger District Map (spring named). The 2005 edition doesn't show the White Chuck Road closure.

Contact: Darrington Ranger District, Mount Baker-Snoqualmie National Forest

The bad news: A massive storm hit Kennedy Warm Spring and the surrounding area in October 2003. The soaking box, campground, and ranger cabin were all buried by silt, rock, and flood debris. The White Chuck Road and Trail, many miles of the Pacific Crest Trail (PCT), and most of the connecting routes in the vicinity of Glacier Peak were also wiped out. The White Chuck Trail has been decommissioned, and it's estimated that two-thirds of it has been washed away. This is no longer considered a viable way to reach Kennedy Warm Spring. The forest service has also decommissioned the last 5 miles of road that leads to the former White Chuck Trailhead.

The good news: There are recent reports of the spring bubbling back up to the surface behind a log pile. The flow is estimated to be about one-quarter of what it was, and the temperature is around 100°F. There's definitely potential for another pool, but you're going to have to be an intrepid mountain goat to get there.

Hiking Options

Hike 31a: Since 2003, only a handful of strong and experienced hikers armed with good navigational skills have made it to what's left of Kennedy Warm Spring.

There's a great trip report on soakersforum.com (along with photographic evidence) describing a serious 15-mile bushwhack that starts at the end of White Chuck Road (FR 23). This involved 5.0 miles on the old road followed by 1.5 miles on the White Chuck River Trail (643) negotiating multiple slips and tree-falls before crossing Fire Creek Bridge. Half a mile later they took a left fork to follow overgrown Mountain Meadow Trail (657) for about 2.0 miles before hanging a right onto the abandoned Glacier Way (which avoids the worst of the washed-out sections of White Chuck Trail). This almost invisible route is more of a cross-country bushwhack that traverses Pumice Bench before dropping down to cross Glacier Creek to rejoin with White Chuck Trail; from there it's not too far to the river's confluence with Kennedy Creek. Here's the last big problem: There's no bridge across the cold, swift-flowing

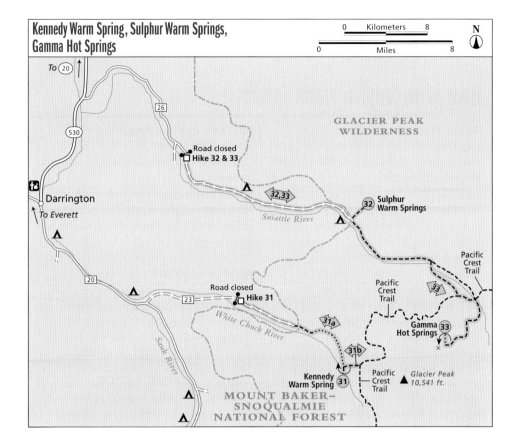

White Chuck River. If there's a suitable tree-fall spanning the flow, you might have a way to cross to visit the spring.

Hike 31b: For those on the PCT, it's also possible to reach this area via the Kennedy Ridge Trail (639); see Hike 31b on the map. To state the obvious, this option is going to be part of a multiday epic from either the north or south that also requires alpine experience as well the as the aforementioned skills. This trail still also brings you to the "wrong" side of White Chuck River. Your best bet for accessing this part of the PCT is probably from the trailhead at Sloan Creek Campground that leads up the North Fork Sauk River.

Be sure to check the forest service trail updates online, and run your plan by the Darrington Ranger District office. The district is undergoing a slow process of recovery, and some bridges, roads, and trails may be repaired in the future, which could improve the access to this area.

The Warm Spring

Highly mineralized warm water trickles out of the riverbank and in one spot has formed a large cascade of orange travertine. The potential soaking options are hidden among the rubble a short way downstream from this obvious location.

32 Sulphur Warm Springs

Hike 32 To Sulphur Warm Springs

General description: A daunting hunt for seeps hiding in a primeval forest in the Glacier Peak Wilderness. Swimwear is superfluous.

Difficulty: Strenuous

Distance: About 25.0 miles round-trip (3.6 miles from Sulphur Creek Campground plus 21 miles from where Suiattle River Road (FR 26) is gated at mile 11.5)

General location: 65 miles northeast of Everett

Elevation gain: +480 feet, -120 feet

High point: 2,040 feet

Hiking quads: USGS Lime Mountain and Downey Mountain

Road map: Darrington Ranger District Map (springs named). The 2005 edition doesn't show the Suiattle River Road closure. See map on page 87.

Restrictions: A Washington State Discovery Pass is required to park off the paved section of Suiattle River Road (not required for trail-head parking).

Contact: Darrington Ranger District, Mount Baker–Snoqualmie National Forest

Note: Save this one for fall, when the water level is down, the creek safer to cross, and any pool more likely to have surfaced. Also check with the forest service on current road and trail conditions.

Finding the trailhead: From I-5 north of Everett, take SR 530 about 40 miles east and north, past Darrington, to the Suiattle River Road (FR 26). Drive about 11.5 dusty miles east to where the road has been gated due to storm damage ahead. Check with the forest service on this road's status; it will be undergoing repairs in 2014 to allow vehicle access up to the original trailhead near Sulphur Creek Campground. During these repairs, there are likely to be long periods when there is no public access up this road.

The Hike

In this neck of the woods, Sulphur Warm Springs ranks second only to Gamma for sheer elusiveness. It's pinpointed on the maps on the edge of Sulphur Creek at the 1,920-foot contour line and listed by the forest service as located across the creek from a point precisely 1.8 miles up Trail 793, but stumbling across it on the ground is another matter.

The first 10.5 miles of hiking is up the remainder of Suiattle River Road to Sulphur Creek Campground (some folks choose to cycle this stretch). Sulphur Creek Trail (793) begins across the road from the campground, climbs the bank, and contours past gullies through a dimly lit forest. This trail is not used much and can be hard to follow; be sure to take the right fork after about a mile. As it finally drops, you'll enter a wildland of fallen logs and rushing water.

The trick is to gauge the 1.8-mile point, beyond which the trail fades into a fishermen's route, and then watch for a faint track angling downhill to a haphazard line of footlogs crossing the torrent (if they haven't been washed away). If you've picked the right track and managed to balance your way over the right logs, the springs should be lurking close by. Keep an eye out for some stone steps leading to them. If you should unearth any hot water in this neck of the woods and would like to share some more clues, then drop us a line at nzhotsprings@gmail.com.

The Warm Springs

One (older) guidebook stated: "Several hot springs seep and flow down a heavily vegetated slope from the south into Sulphur Creek. The main spring issues from a crack in the bedrock immediately adjacent to the creek bank. There is a pool that will accommodate two people comfortably dug into the bank." The flow was listed at 10 gallons per minute (gpm) and the temperature as 98°F.

The forest service printout had this to say: "The springs consist of small colored pools, smelling of hydrogen sulphide gas, and are not large enough to take a dip in." The temperature listed was a mere 80°F. I also met a ranger from Gifford Pinchot National Forest who claimed that he'd not only found a pool at the described location but had actually soaked his bones in it. When he was pressed for a description, a secretive smile crossed his lips as he simply replied "not too bad."

And what did your fearless reporter discover firsthand after zigzagging back and forth across every log in sight at least twice and bushwhacking for hours through primeval ooze armed with machete, magnifying glass, divining rod, and infrared scanner? Nothing. Not even a two-bit seep. Conclusion? If some industrious elf has gotten there ahead of you and dug a cozy little soaker and perhaps heated it up a few notches, then, if you're persistent and lucky enough to find it, you might possibly end up with something to write home about. But, come to think of it, maybe "the one that got away" makes a better story. (Evie)

33 Gamma Hot Springs

Hike 33 To Gamma Hot Springs

General description: A challenging expedition, for hard-core fanatics only, to hot springs buried deep in the Glacier Peak Wilderness. Swimwear? You gotta be kidding!

Difficulty: Extremely strenuous

Distance: About 55 miles round-trip (allow at least five days)

General location: 65 miles northeast of Everett

Elevation gain: +5,800 feet, -1,200 feet

High point: 6,300 feet

GPS: N48.1524 / W121.0634 (estimate)

Hiking quads: USGS Lime Mountain and Gamma Peak

Road map: Darrington Ranger District Map (springs named). The 2005 edition doesn't show the Suiattle River Road closure.

Restrictions: A Washington State Discovery Pass is required to park off the paved section of Suiattle River Road (not required for trailhead). There are several unbridged creek crossings, and heavy snowpack can persist well into the summer.

Contact: Darrington Ranger District, Mount Baker-Snoqualmie National Forest

Warning: The 2003 storms that wiped out the Kennedy Warm Spring area also made getting to Gamma even more of a challenge.

Finding the trailhead: Refer to the preceding note and directions to Sulphur Creek Campground.

The Expedition

First conjure up a pristine hot spring emerging from bedrock at the head of a canyon framed by jagged peaks, light-years from the nearest outpost. Then fit your humble body into the scene, boldly going where few have gone before, seeking out secret soaks.

This vision is known as the call of the wild hot spring, and the only cure is to follow it. But treatment can be risky unless proper precautions are taken. Check with the forest service on current conditions. Get a weather forecast, and travel prepared. Go late in summer or fall, when the streams are low. This expedition to the hottest-known spring in the North Cascades, in addition to hiking 23 miles to reach Gamma Ridge, involves a series of steep switchbacks up the ridgeline trail followed by a nasty scramble down Gamma Creek to reach the goal.

Note: Don't even consider Gamma Creek as an alternate route up. It's an extremely steep canyon, and those who have tried it report deadfalls and impassable waterfalls. Another approach not recommended is attempting to follow the 5,000-foot contour line across to the hot springs from Gamma Ridge Trail.

Authors' note: Evie and Sally have not been to these springs. Although we spoke with several people who have done this hike, the following directions and distances should only be considered an approximate outline of what to expect should you choose to take up the Gamma challenge.

From the Sulphur Creek Campground, continue walking another 1.0 mile southeast to the Suiattle River Trailhead (784), 12.5 miles from the gated road. Hike 6.0 miles to Canyon Creek; about 0.5 mile later there's a junction where it joins with the new section of the Pacific Crest Trail (PCT). Turn right and head south to cross the Suiattle River on the new bridge (the one just upstream of Miners Creek no longer exists). Continue 5.5 miles to the junction where the old PCT (now part of the Upper Suiattle River Trail) crosses Vista Creek. There might be a small trail sign here. Vista Creek must be forded; then, about 1.0 mile later, you reach unbridged Gamma Creek. These creeks can both be challenging, as they run high and discolored year-round from being fed by glacial melt. From here the trails are no longer maintained and it's easy to lose the way.

Head east about 2.0 miles from the Gamma crossing to reach the junction where the old PCT used to turn north to cross the old Skyline Bridge over the Suiattle River (0.25 mile away). Turn right onto Gamma Ridge Trail (791). After about 1.5 miles (it will seem longer) you will come across a small creek coming off Gamma Ridge, where there may be the remains of a campfire ring—this is often the last place to get water on the ridge.

The faint trail then starts to climb steeply up toward Gamma Peak. After 3.0 miles of climbing, at around 6,000 feet, you reach open meadows where there's a more well-defined hunters' camp. Continue another couple of miles or so until you reach a pass overlooking the headwaters of Gamma Creek. You may see another faint campsite near the base of Gamma Peak, 100 feet or so below the ridge. You can scramble from camp directly down the Gamma Creek drainage on a web of goat trails.

About 750 feet down the hill, you'll cross a feeder creek on your right and continue down Gamma Creek on a track maybe 50 feet up the bank. Take great care in this stretch—the ground is very steep and crumbly. There's also likely to be snowpack in sections of the creek. Gamma Creek forms a series of waterfalls about half a mile before reaching the springs. These need to be skirted by climbing about 100 feet away from the creekbed on the right side of the valley. Gamma Hot Springs issue out of a steep rocky bank just above the right side of the creek (facing downstream).

Local note: In late August 2011, a Darrington ranger reported that it took 7 hours to hike 3.0 miles of the Gamma Ridge Trail due to massive amounts of windfall and that the springs were unreachable due to late snowpack.

The Hot Springs

Scalding water seeps up at 149°F through rock fractures and flows through a tiny pool into the glacier-fed stream. The slope is quite steep, which makes any user-built pool or dam difficult to maintain without a tarp. The pool temperature is a bit on the toasty side, but you can channel water in from the creek with the aid of small logs and a little ingenuity.

At last report there was a register tucked into a nearby tree. It's a 6-inch piece of PVC pipe with end caps, and it holds some good stories. Sign it if you can find it. And

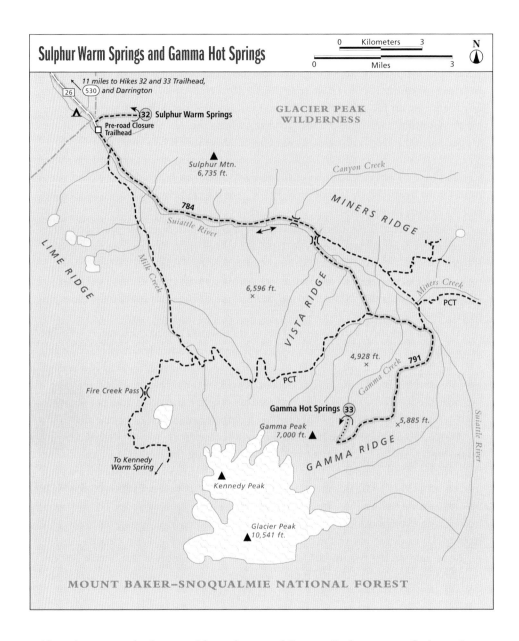

Sulphur Warm Springs and Gamma Hot Springs

0   Kilometers   3

0   Miles   3

N

11 miles to Hikes 32 and 33 Trailhead,
26 (530) and Darrington

(32) Sulphur Warm Springs

Pre-road Closure
Trailhead

GLACIER PEAK
WILDERNESS

Sulphur Mtn.
6,735 ft.

Canyon Creek

784

MINERS RIDGE

Suiattle River

LIME RIDGE

Milk Creek

6,596 ft.
×

VISTA RIDGE

Miners Creek

PCT

4,928 ft.
×

791

Fire Creek Pass

PCT

Gamma Creek

Gamma Hot Springs (33)

Gamma Peak
7,000 ft.

×5,885 ft.

To Kennedy
Warm Spring

GAMMA RIDGE

Suiattle River

Kennedy Peak

Glacier Peak
10,541 ft.

MOUNT BAKER–SNOQUALMIE NATIONAL FOREST

if you happen to do the scramble to the top of Gamma Peak, you may find a register
up there as well—a film canister tucked into a rock cairn at the summit.

The deep canyon is sandwiched between serrated ridges, and the hot springs nes-
tle in the shadow of the 7,000-foot peak. A bit beyond, Gamma Ridge slices a jagged
line between two massive glaciers on the north flanks of 10,541-foot Glacier Peak.

34 Baker Hot Springs

General description: An evergreen-framed pool often brimming with bathers, at the end of a short path. Swimwear is recommended when others are present.

Elevation: 1,500 feet

General location: 56 miles northeast of Mount Vernon

GPS: N48.76382 / W121.67170 (estimate)

Map: Mount Baker–Snoqualmie National Forest (springs not marked). See map on page 76.

Restrictions: No camping permitted at springs

Contact: Mount Baker Ranger District, Mount Baker–Snoqualmie National Forest

Finding the hot springs: From I-5 near Mount Vernon, take SR 20 about 23 miles east. Bear left at milepost 82 on Baker Lake Road and follow it up the west side of the lake. After 18 miles turn left onto FR 1130 (Marten Lake Road), which is just beyond Boulder Creek Bridge. Continue 1.5 miles and bear right at a junction, then about 2.5 miles later turn right onto FR 1144. Park after 0.5 mile at a large pullout on the left. The trailhead is across the road. A 0.3-mile path through the woods emerges into a clearing at the pool.

Note: The previous edition gave directions to the springs via FR 1144. This road has been decommissioned beyond Park Creek Campground and is closed to all motorized use. (It's a 3.0-mile walk from the campground to the hot springs).

The pool at Baker Hot Springs looks a lot cleaner and quieter than usual on a quiet winter's day. Tim Messing

Warning: The forest service discourages people from bathing at Baker Hot Springs. This is due to concerns over the water quality, which is often compromised as a result of too many soakers and not enough flow to cleanse the pool. This is one spring where it's definitely a good idea not to put your head under.

Users have dug a soaking pool at Baker out of a sandy bank. The pool is around 15 feet across and 2 feet deep. Natural mineral water slowly bubbles up from the bottom at 110°F and cools as it disperses. The pool's temperature varies with the air temperature, but it tends to hover around 100°F. The water is quite murky and has a sulfur odor, but that doesn't faze the aficionados who come for a soak. Unless you feel like sharing your cozy cocoon, try the early mornings or the off-season months.

Storms in recent years have triggered mudslides that on several occasions have filled the pools with debris. Dedicated volunteers dig them out again, but sometimes the result is a smaller and shallower pool.

Hike 34 Park Butte

General description: A day hike or backpack featuring alpine meadows and close-up views of Mount Baker, not far from Baker Hot Springs

Difficulty: Strenuous

Distance: About 7.0 miles round-trip

General location: 45 miles northeast of Mount Vernon

Elevation gain: +2,180 feet, -80 feet

High point: 5,450 feet (lookout)

Hiking quad: Green Trails Hamilton

Road map: Mount Baker–Snoqualmie National Forest

Restrictions: Northwest Forest Pass required

Contact: Mount Baker Ranger District, Mount Baker–Snoqualmie National Forest

Finding the trailhead: Follow the preceding directions and drive 12 miles up Baker Lake Road. Turn left just beyond a bridge onto FR 12 and follow signs to Mount Baker National Recreation Area and Schriebers Meadow. You'll reach a camping area and the trail sign in another 9 miles. The trailhead is a 20-mile drive from Baker Hot Springs.

The Hike

This short climb in the Mount Baker National Recreation Area is a hard one to beat for wall-to-wall alpine views. Snow-draped peaks rim the horizon, and the awesome sight of Mount Baker's Easton Glacier steals the foreground. Lush meadows and tiny lakes are cupped between rocky knolls, and tumbling streams carve clefts between ridges and glacial moraines.

Park Butte Trail (603) begins by bridging Sulphur Creek and undulating through Schriebers Meadow, where heather and huckleberries choke the open spaces and Mount Baker glistens between scattered stands of cedar and fir. Beyond lies a moonscape of rock and rushing streams. Volcanic mudflows and meltwater from the massive

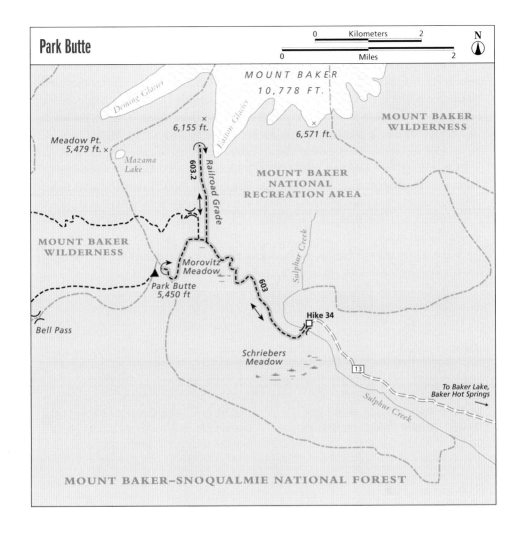

Easton Glacier have sliced freeways through the forest here; you'll probably have to boulder-hop a bit to cross the channels, especially on warm summer afternoons.

The path gradually becomes wrapped in cool woods and gains 800 feet in a long steep mile to Lower Morovitz Meadow. Western hemlock gives way to mountain hemlock en route. Western red cedar yields to a strange-looking cousin, the Alaska cedar, whose needles hang in long chains from drooping limbs. The off-white, shaggy bark peels off in long strips as though a bear had used the tree as a sharpening post for giant claws.

The grade tapers on the way to Upper Morovitz Meadow, where you'll find superb picnic sites amid alpine scenery. The main trail goes across the meadow past a junction. Spectacular panoramas increase as the trail climbs the last mile above Pocket Lake to the summit of Park Butte. A lookout cabin, maintained by Skagit Alpine Club of Mount Vernon, is available to the public on a first-come, first-served basis when not being used by its maintenance crew.

Park Butte, ringed by peaks far and near, will take your breath away just when you stop to catch it. The 10,778-foot white cone of Mount Baker dominates the view. Its satellite peaks, the Black Buttes, jut above the Deming Glacier in sharp contrast. Looking westward, you'll see the serrated crests of the Twin Sisters range. To the south are Loomis Mountain and Dock Butte, backed in the far distance by Mount Rainier. To the east and southeast rise other distant cones, including snow-clad Glacier Peak.

Returning to the junction in the upper meadow, there's another direction to go that's well worth exploring. Take Railroad Grade Trail (603.2) north toward Baker Pass and ramble 1.0 mile northeast to intersect the long rocky spine of Railroad Grade. Pick your way along the tip of this knife-edge ridge, a moraine built up by nearby Easton Glacier.

You can gaze eastward across the giant cleft to the massive glacier and barren landscape below the ice or look up to the gleaming white volcanic cone of Mount Baker. Clusters of subalpine fir speckle the high meadows west of Railroad Grade, and other cross-country routes beckon.

35 Olympic Hot Springs

Hike 35a To Olympic Hot Springs

General description: A day hike or overnighter to popular soaking pools in Olympic National Park. Skinnydippable with (much) discretion.
Difficulty: Easy
Distance: 4.8 miles round-trip
General location: 18 miles southwest of Port Angeles
Elevation gain: 260 feet
High point: 2,060 feet (hot springs)

GPS: N47.97630 / W123.69023
Hiking quad: USGS Mount Carrie (springs named)
Road map: Olympic National Park brochure
Restrictions: A Wilderness Camping Permit is required for overnight hikes.
Contact: Olympic National Park, Wilderness Information Center

Finding the trailhead: Drive 8 miles west of Port Angeles on US 101. Take Olympic Hot Springs Road 10 miles south and west on pavement, past Elwha Ranger Station, to a roadblock and parking area at the signed trailhead.

The bad news: As of 2011 the access to the springs via Olympic Hot Springs Road was closed due to the dam removal projects on the Elwha River. The shortest route to the hot springs during this period of road closure has been a 14-mile hike in over Appleton Pass from the Sol Duc Valley.

The good news: Olympic Hot Springs Road is scheduled to reopen toward the end of 2014 (check with Olympic National Park).

The Hike

Walk the last 2.2 miles of decommissioned road, a gentle grade through deep woods, and set your pack down at Boulder Creek backcountry camp. At one time this site was fully developed with flush toilets and piped water, but it has been transformed into a primitive camp for backpackers. The short path to the springs drops down to bridge Boulder Creek and then meanders downstream, passing one soaking pool after another.

A variety of side paths wriggle down the grassy bank and up into the forest. Some hit the jackpot, while others just circle around in a maze reinforced by the steady tread

Just one of the many soaking pools hidden in the rainforest at Olympic Hot Springs BLUE MEEK

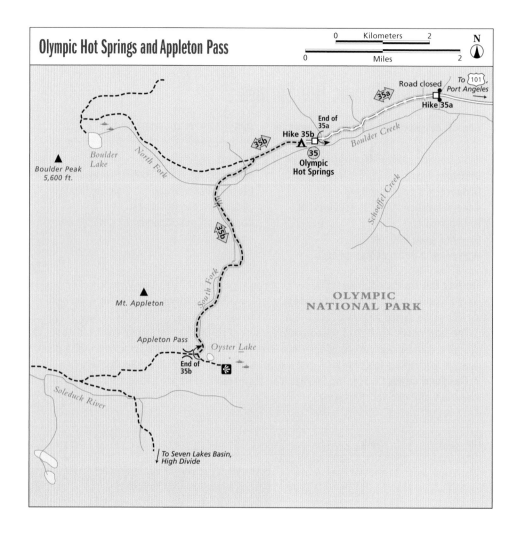

Olympic Hot Springs and Appleton Pass

0   Kilometers   2

0   Miles   2

N

Road closed   To 101, Port Angeles

35a

Hike 35a

End of 35a

Hike 35b

35b

35

Olympic Hot Springs

Boulder Creek

Schoeffel Creek

North Fork

Boulder Lake

Boulder Peak 5,600 ft.

35b

South Fork

Mt. Appleton

OLYMPIC NATIONAL PARK

Appleton Pass

Oyster Lake

End of 35b

Soleduck River

To Seven Lakes Basin, High Divide

of hopeful feet. Perseverance mixed with a dash of logic and luck will lead you to the more-secluded pools. A popular destination for day-trippers, it's also the stepping-off point for longer trips into the high Olympics (see the following hike).

The Hot Springs

Without a doubt the hot spot of the Olympics, this cluster of steaming springs and pools lies sandwiched between a lush forest of fir and hemlock and the whitewater rapids of Boulder Creek. There are a total of seven bubbly soakers in a variety of sizes and temperatures, including one by a small waterfall. The most skinnydippable pool, at the end of the trail, is an easy one to miss when unoccupied.

Hike 35b Olympic Hot Springs to Appleton Pass

General description: A day hike or overnighter from the hot springs to alpine meadows and views, in Olympic National Park
Difficulty: Strenuous
Distance: About 10.2 miles round-trip
General location: 20 miles southwest of Port Angeles
Elevation gain: +2,920 feet, -120 feet

High point: 5,050 feet
Hiking quad: USGS Mount Carrie (springs named)
Road map: Olympic National Park brochure
Restrictions: A Wilderness Camping Permit is required for overnight hikes.
Contact: Olympic National Park, Wilderness Information Center

Finding the trailhead: Follow the preceding hike to Olympic Hot Springs (check on current road access).

The Hike

Olympic Hot Springs makes a great base for a side trip to Appleton Pass. This deservedly popular route climbs up through a moss-coated primeval forest to an awesome view across High Divide. Wave after wave of snowcapped peaks recede southward to the horizon like whitecaps on a stormy sea. At 7,980 feet, Mount Olympus rides the highest crest. Airy campsites dot the pass, and a tempting extension of the route could be made from here across to Seven Lakes Basin and High Divide.

Appleton Pass Trail begins at the upper end of Boulder Creek backcountry camp and winds through twilight woods to a junction with Boulder Lake Trail at 0.7 mile. The gentle grade continues until the path bridges the North Fork of Boulder Creek. Now the work begins as the route shoots up the canyon of the South Fork of Boulder Creek. Two short spurs a short distance apart lead to cascading falls and a small campsite apiece, while the main trail bridges the creek and climbs on.

Crunch your way along a path littered with the small cones of western hemlock and Douglas fir mixed with a dash of cedar. Log walkways aid the traverse over fragile marshy areas to a large campsite at 2.5 miles. The route crosses several rockslides spaced between stands of subalpine fir and a wavy tangle of slide alder.

Cross the South Fork twice and eventually emerge into a steep meadow in a high basin just below the pass. A thick mat of summer wildflowers competes with huckleberry, willow, and other plants in the waist-deep grass. The humid fragrance is intoxicating. Watch for marmots sunbathing on rocky outcrops as you hike up the trail.

Catch your breath and prepare for the last nine switchbacks up a precipitous slope that's often deep in snow until midsummer. An ice ax is well advised for early-season hikers; a far easier snow climb from here crosses past tiny Oyster Lake up a long valley to a viewpoint 0.5 mile east of Appleton Pass.

Views from the pass itself are limited to tantalizing glimpses through the trees, so it's well worth the extra 0.5 mile and 300-foot gain to follow the ridgeline path east to the unnamed viewpoint. You can see the glaciers of Mount Olympus directly behind the foreground ridge of High Divide.

British Columbia

Beautiful British Columbia has her fair share of wild hot springs. The ones described here are concentrated in the southwest and the southeast corners of the province. The southwest area covers both Vancouver Island and the Lillooet Valley on the adjacent mainland. The southeast corner, known as the Kootenays, includes dips on both the west and east sides. The reader will find a total of eighteen hot springs, all temptingly close to the US border, marked on the British Columbia map.

The hot springs in the southwest corner see the highest use. This isn't too surprising when you consider that roughly 75 percent of British Columbia's population is located here, concentrated mainly in metropolitan Vancouver, the largest city, and in Victoria, the capital. The soaks in the Kootenays, however, remain nearly as lonesome as those in Idaho.

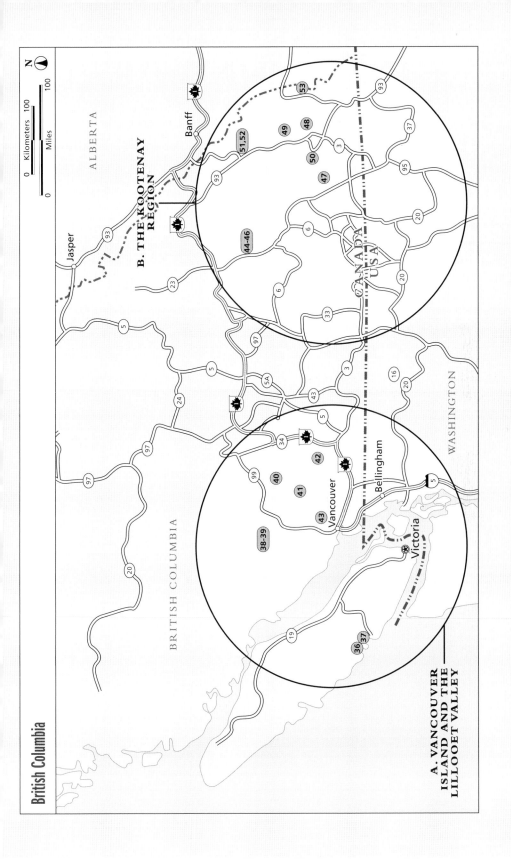

British Columbia

A. Vancouver Island and the Lillooet Valley

The west side of Vancouver Island is a maze of inlets, channels, and islands. The rugged coastline boasts two hot springs, 8 miles/13 km apart, accessible only by boat or plane. Several companies at the road-end town of Tofino offer scheduled service in addition to charters; the two springs can be combined for a double dip.

On the nearby mainland (see map on page 110), hot spring fans will find no fewer than six soaks scattered within weekend range of the greater Vancouver area. They stretch the length of the Lillooet Valley in a line northwest from Harrison Lake to the upper Lillooet River, bordered by ranges of high peaks in spectacular Garibaldi Park and the remote and sparsely developed Coast Mountains.

Hikers in these parts will discover driftwood-strewn beaches interspersed with tidal pools on the big island. In contrast, the high country on both sides of the Lillooet

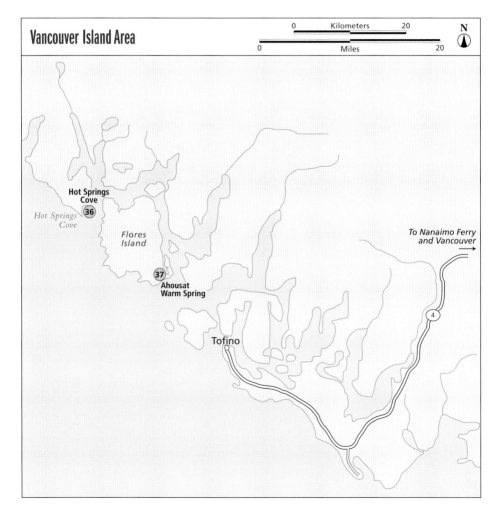

Valley offers day-trippers and backpackers alike such enticements as twilight forests and glacial streams, jagged peaks, and a broad range of alpine delights, including up-close glacier views.

Directions in this guide follow from towns on Highways 4, 99, and 7 and a variety of back roads. As a general rule, the forest roads are long and dusty from excessive use by logging trucks, some of the backwoods campsites are still undeveloped, hiking trails may be primitive outside of the parks, and the soaking pools are well used on weekends despite somewhat cumbersome access.

Hot Springs and Hikes

On the west coast of Vancouver Island, hops by sea or air will drop you at popular Hot Springs Cove (36) and little-known Ahousat (37). Back on the mainland, a remote road up the Lillooet River northwest of Pemberton reaches five-star soaks at Pebble (39) and also passes practically inaccessible Meager Creek (38). A drive southeast of town accesses a glacier hike en route down the Lillooet River to dips in St. Agnes Well (40) and Sloquet Creek Hot Springs (41). A dusty drive up the east side of Harrison Lake leads to a hike-in soak at Clear Creek (42). Last (and least known) is the spring closest to Vancouver, the elusive Pitt River Hot Springs (43), which requires a boat trip up Pitt Lake followed by a long hike or bike ride to reach.

Season

The springs on Vancouver Island can be accessed and enjoyed almost year-round thanks to scheduled transportation and a mild maritime climate. The Lillooet Valley soaks are best in early summer through fall, as winter road closures make access difficult and spring runoff buries all the streamside pools. In the coastal area you can expect cool but sunny summers and mild winters with heavy rains. The hiking season on the mainland is limited to summer months only for the higher routes, with cold winters and heavy snows on west-facing slopes.

36 Hot Springs Cove

Hike 36 To Hot Springs Cove

General description: A popular boardwalk stroll to tidal hot pools in a marine park. Swimwear is advised.

Difficulty: Easy

Distance: 2.0 miles/3.4 km round-trip

General location: West coast of Vancouver Island

Elevation: Sea level

GPS: N49.34980 / W 126.25988

Map: *Backroad Mapbook: Vancouver Island BC, Victoria & Gulf Islands* (springs marked)

Restrictions: The welcome sign states: No CAMPING, FIRES OR DOGS, NO GLASS IN SPRINGS AND NO NUDE BATHING. There is a ranger based at the marina from May to November. Bring change for the small day-use fee honesty box.

Contact: RLC Park Services (250-474-1336)

Finding the trailhead: On Vancouver Island take Highway 19 north to Parksville, then take Highway 4 west to the road-end town of Tofino (134 miles total). The springs at Sharp Point are on the tiny Openit Peninsula, 26 miles/42 km to the northwest and can only be accessed by sea or air. You can make arrangements to stop over at Ahousat Warm Spring (see following hike), halfway up the coast to Sharp Point.

Transportation: Several charter companies in Tofino offer day trips to Hot Springs Cove by boat, but the soaking time averages barely 2 hours. With money to spare, you can extend your soak by taking a boat there and a floatplane out later in the day. With time to spare, you can arrange for a next-day pickup and camp at the Hesquiat First Nation operated campground, which is located past the restrooms near the wharf (cash only). Fires are prohibited at the campground, and no drinking water is available here or at the springs. Contact the Tofino Infocentre (250-725-3414) for an update on transportation choices and general information, or visit gotofino.com. You may be able to combine a whale-watching tour with your boat trip.

The Hike

From the wharf, a boardwalk trail spans the marshy ground south to the rocky tip of the Openit Peninsula. It travels through a gorgeous rain forest, climbing up and down, twisting around huge trees and fallen logs, and undulating along beneath a thick green canopy. Many of the boards have been painstakingly engraved by sailors with the names of their ships and dates of their visits. There are pit toilets and a changing shed at the end of the boardwalk. Beyond the springs, you can explore the rocky point and observe the abundance of marine life at low tide.

The Hot Springs

Steamy 124°F/51°C water cascades over a cliff and flows through a chain of small to medium-size bedrock pools. At high tide in the lowermost one, ocean currents

The boardwalk to Hot Springs Cove, which snakes through lush rain forest, is composed of many planks donated by visiting sailors. SALLY JACKSON

swirl back and forth across the pool and create a delicious marbling of temperatures. Those whose taste runs more to solid comfort can kick back in one of the upper pools, which usually measures well over 104°F/40°C. The lower pools vary in size and temperature, depending on the tides. Magnificent Hot Springs Cove has become quite a tourist attraction in recent years. Access is no longer a major obstacle, and in

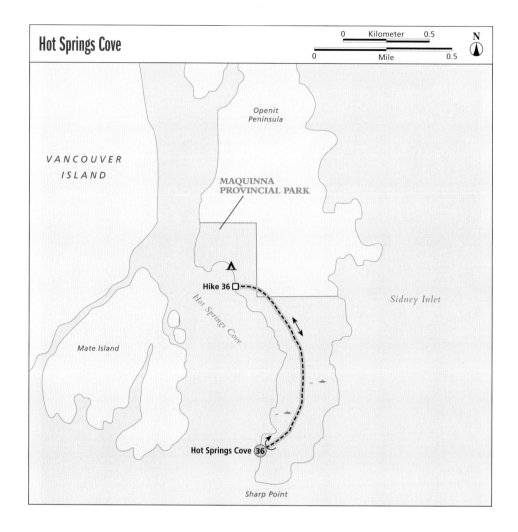

the prime summer months, July through September, as many as one hundred people or more may flock to the springs in a single day. The best odds of getting a quiet soak would be on weekdays or during the off-season.

Note: If you need to stay in Tofino for a night and don't want to blow out your budget, anymore than has been required to reach these springs, the Tofino Traveler's Guesthouse (250-725-2338) is highly recommended.

37 Ahousat (Flores Island) Warm Spring

Hike 37 To Ahousat Warm Spring

General description: A muddy stroll to a warm thermal pool on an island, not far from Hot Springs Cove. Swimwear is recommended.
Difficulty: Easy
Distance: About 2.0 miles/3.2 km round-trip
General location: Off the west coast of Vancouver Island
Elevation: Sea level
GPS: N49.26992 / W 126.07535

Map: *Backroad Mapbook: Vancouver Island BC, Victoria & Gulf Islands* (spring marked but in wrong location—likely to be amended in their next edition)
Restrictions: There have been incidents involving wolves killing dogs in this park. BC Parks is strongly advising visitors not to bring their dogs. Keep food out of reach of wildlife when camping.
Contact: BC Parks, West Coast Region

Finding the trailhead: On Vancouver Island, take Highway 4 west to the road-end town of Tofino. The warm spring is located at the south end of Flores Island, 12 miles/19 km northwest, and can be accessed only by sea or air. Hot spring fans can get in a double dip by arranging to stop here en route to Hot Springs Cove (see preceding hike).

    Transportation: From Tofino to Ahousat, it's a scenic kayak paddle, 10-minute seaplane flight, or 30-minute boat-taxi (usually departing from the First Street Dock). Visit gotofino .com, or contact the Tofino Infocentre (250-725-3414) for an update on transportation choices and general information. BC Parks has information on Flores Island and Gibson Marine Park at env.gov.bc.ca/bcparks/explore/parkpgs/gibson.html.

The Hike

Planes or boats to Flores Island drop people off at Ahousat, where there's a dock and a tiny general store. Trails are poorly defined, but you can follow the BC Hydro power poles south from the shoreline of Matilda Inlet to the spring. Skirt or cut across a small bay, depending on the tide. Private boats can cruise right by Ahousat and head for the dock, if it's still afloat, on the tidal flat by the pool.

    You can also disembark at Marktosis, but you'll have to ask around for clues on where to pick up the faint trail that heads south through a dense groundcover of salal, salmonberry bushes, and ferns toward a line of power poles at Matilda Inlet. At the halfway point it reaches the small bay mentioned above and follows the poles and shoreline west to the spring. At low tide the water is only 6 inches/15 cm deep, and you can cut across the head of the inlet. The distance from Marktosis is 3 miles/5 km round-trip. The Wild Side Trail also offers access to the springs from Marktosis via Whitesand Cove—there is a fee to walk this private trail. For more information on the Wildside Trail plus transportation options to Flores Island, visit wildsidetrail.com.

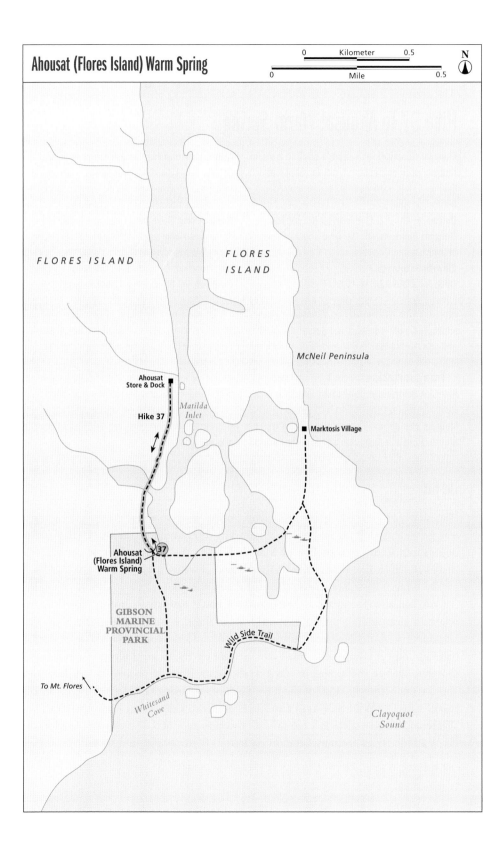

Ahousat (Flores Island) Warm Spring

0 ——— Kilometer ——— 0.5

0 ——— Mile ——— 0.5

N

FLORES ISLAND

FLORES
ISLAND

McNeil Peninsula

Ahousat
Store & Dock

Hike 37

Matilda
Inlet

Marktosis Village

Ahousat
(Flores Island)
Warm Spring

37

GIBSON
MARINE
PROVINCIAL
PARK

Wild Side Trail

To Mt. Flores

Whitesand
Cove

Clayoquot
Sound

The ruins of a concrete swimming pool, 8 × 20 × 4 feet deep (2.4 × 6 × 1.2 m deep), collect the meager flow of sulfur-tinged water. The pool has a magnificent setting on a beach at the southwest tip of Matilda Inlet in tiny Gibson Marine Park. The drawback is a soaking temperature that hovers around 77°F/25°C, well below the optimum range except during hot weather.

If you have a little time to spare, there's an outstanding side trip nearby. As you near the spring, an old boardwalk path branches south. The unmaintained scenic route leads to a sandy beach on the south end of the island at Whitesand Cove. Tiny islands dot the ocean view, and Vargas Island is visible to the southeast across Clayoquot Sound.

Note: Many maps show the village of Ahousat being located on the eastern side of Matilda Inlet. Satellite imagery courtesy of Google Earth reveals a dock and buildings on the western side that corresponds with the map on page 108.

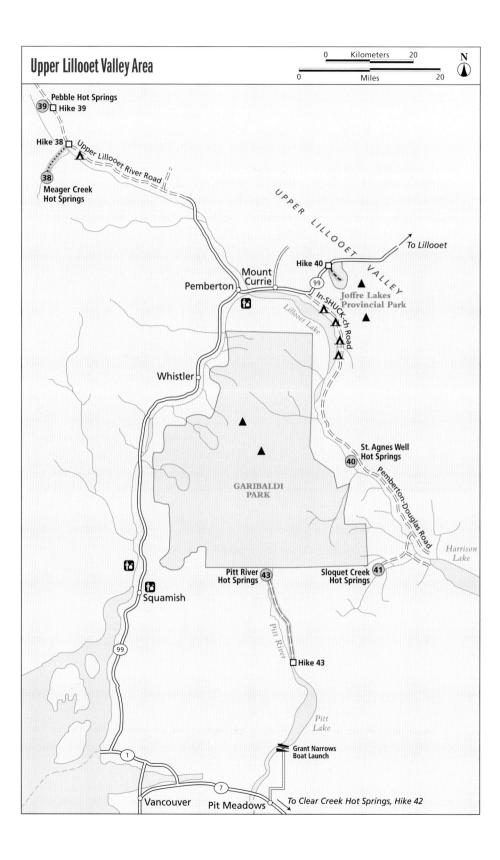

Upper Lillooet Valley Area

0 Kilometers **20**

0 Miles **20**

N

Pebble Hot Springs
39 ☐ Hike 39

Hike 38 ☐
Upper Lillooet River Road

38
Meager Creek
Hot Springs

UPPER LILLOOET VALLEY

To Lilloet

Hike 40 ☐
99
In-SHUCK-ch Road

Mount Currie

Pemberton

Joffre Lakes
Provincial Park

Lillooet Lake

Whistler

St. Agnes Well
Hot Springs

40
Pemberton-Douglas Road

GARIBALDI
PARK

Harrison Lake

Pitt River
Hot Springs **43**

Sloquet Creek
Hot Springs **41**

Squamish

Pitt River

☐ Hike 43

99

Pitt Lake

Grant Narrows
Boat Launch

1

7

Vancouver Pit Meadows

To Clear Creek Hot Springs, Hike 42

38 Meager Creek Hot Springs

Hike 38 To Meager Creek Hot Springs

General description: This was once the Shangri-la of soaking pools, but Mother Nature has been wreaking havoc on the access, making the pools inaccessible to all but the most tenacious and adventurous hot springers. Swimwear is the least of your worries.

Difficulty: Extremely difficult—impossible for most until a new road is built

Distance: About 11 miles/17 km round-trip for both options

General location: Upper Lillooet Valley, about 39 miles/63 km from Pemberton

Elevation gain: 500 feet/150 m, route from bridge washout; -1,050 feet/-320 m, route from south side of Lillooet River

Elevation: 1,900 feet/580 m (hot spring)

GPS: N50.57554 / W123.46495 (estimate)

Map: *Backroad Mapbook: Vancouver, Coast and Mountains* (springs named but marked on the wrong side of the river). See map on page 110.

Restrictions: The springs are officially closed to protect people as well as the fragile ecosystem. This is likely to remain the case until such time as a new road is built and the springs' use can once again be monitored. This is best attempted later in the season, when the river and creeks are running lower.

Contact: BC Forests, Squamish Forest District. The Pemberton Visitor Centre (604-894-6175) is also a good source of information.

Finding the trailheads: From Vancouver take scenic Highway 99 north past Whistler and on to Pemberton. Turn left at the traffic lights onto Portage Road and drive though the town, turning left at the roundabout then right at the three-way stop onto Pemberton Meadows Road (set trip odometer to 0 at this junction). After 1.1 miles/1.8 km turn left at the T junction. At 15.5 miles/25 km either proceed straight at the junction to access the south-side trailhead (high clearance required) or turn right onto Lillooet River FSR. This road soon crosses the Lillooet River and becomes unpaved (watch for industrial traffic). At 20.7 miles/33.3 km take the left fork, and at 27.6 miles/44.4 km take another left fork, remaining on Lillooet River FSR. At 39.2 miles/63.1 km turn left and park by the mound of dirt. This is where the bridge to Meager Creek was washed out; it is now one of the very unofficial trailheads for reaching the springs.

A Volatile History

This geologically active area has a history of massively destructive landslides. On Thanksgiving weekend of 1984, heavy rains brought down a monstrous mudslide that covered the valley floor and flooded areas as far away as Pemberton. The hot springs were demolished, vehicles were buried, and stranded bathers were evacuated by helicopter. After years of hard work mending the damage, the Squamish Forest District developed the area into a designated recreation site.

These improvements soon led to a massive influx of visitors (30,000 in 1994 alone), as well as to many of the overuse/abuse problems so common at popular hot springs. In response, the Canadian Forest Service (CFS) began to limit the number of vehicles allowed on the site and imposed a camping fee. In 1995–96 the pools were shut down due to health concerns. New pools had to be built to conform to Health Authority Pool Regulations and camping moved away from the hot springs source.

Flooding and washouts continued to be a seasonal problem both at the springs and along Meager Creek Road. Storms in October 2003 washed away the road bridge that spanned the Upper Lillooet River and accessed the Meager Creek Valley. This bridge wasn't replaced until 2008, costing almost a million dollars. Then, in 2010, one of Canada's largest recorded landslides occurred off the flanks of Mount Meager, sweeping a path of destruction down Capricorn Creek into Meager Creek and the Lillooet River. Mud and debris obliterated the bridge and much of the Upper Lillooet Road.

The road has been bulldozed out of the rubble, but there are no plans to rebuild the bridge. Prolonged periods of hot weather create snowmelt off the Mount Meager glacier that trickles over unstable volcanic ash, leading to large landslides, the largest and most recurring happening in the Capricorn drainage.

The challenge: There are plans for a new access road to the springs to be built via the south side of Meager Creek "sometime in the future," but until that happens the only alternatives to visiting Meager Creek vicinity are as follows: One route involves hazardous river and creek crossings and also traversing extremely unstable ground. The other possible route requires a high-clearance vehicle and good navigational skills to negotiate a maze of forestry roads and subsequent off-trail hiking.

Hiking Options

There are two possible routes; both options involve approximately 5.5 miles/8.6 km of challenging hiking. The most obvious route—but not the safest—begins with trying not to drown as you ford the Lillooet River; a kayak and whitewater skills could be put to good use here. This route then involves heading up the northwest side of Meager Creek and facing a second problematic ford at Capricorn Creek. Continue 3.7 miles/6 km and bear left at the fork to cross a large concrete bridge. The short foot trail to the springs takes off into the woods to the right, immediately after crossing the bridge. This extremely unstable valley should definitely not be entered during times of snowmelt or after heavy rain.

Another route that has been used occasionally and sounds like it could be the somewhat saner option, involves driving up the south side of the Lillooet River in a high-clearance vehicle. A GPS unit is going to be essential for locating the "trailhead" and the subsequent off-trail hiking. Follow the logging roads that lead to the GPS coordinates N50.60000 / W123.40760 (a bend in the road just before it dead-ends; check Google Earth). From here, look for flagging tape marking a route that heads southwest through the forest high above Meager Creek. After about 2.2 miles/3.5 km of bushwhacking, you will hopefully reach an old logging road that leads to the hot springs.

The Hot Springs

There are whispers, rumors, and the occasional Internet posting with tantalizing photographic evidence of people still hiking to Meager Hot Springs and finding intact soaking pools at Meager Creek. The three boulder-lined pools weren't damaged by the 2010 landslide. The larger one measures a good 20 feet/6 m across. You might also find a rock-lined seasonal pool or two at the edge of the creek. Algae buildup can be a problem at infrequently visited hot pools. An age-old forest spreads a green canopy above the trail, and ferns border the causeways that were built to help protect the delicate ecosystem around the springs.

Warning: The accessibility of these springs is forever changing. Be sure to ring the Squamish Forest District and also scout around online for any recent trip reports.

Hike 39 To Pebble (Keyhole Falls) Hot Springs

General description: A long drive plus a short but challenging hike to reach a series of pools nestled in a dramatic canyon setting. Swimwear is first come, first served.

Difficulty: Challenging in 2012; proposed new trail access is likely to be a longer but flatter route (see Note).

Distance: About 1.0 mile/1.5 km round-trip

General location: Upper Lillooet Valley, about 43 miles/69 km from Pemberton

Elevation gain: -390 feet/-120 m

High point: 2,120 feet/650 m (at the car park)

GPS: N50.66690 / W123.46016

Map: *Backroad Mapbook: Vancouver, Coast and Mountains* (springs not marked). See map on page 110.

Contact: BC Forests, Squamish Forest District. The Pemberton Visitor Centre (604-894-6175) is also a good source of information.

Note: There's a proposed hydroelectric project in the Upper Lillooet Valley. If this goes ahead, the current trail to Pebble Hot Springs will become inaccessible for three years during a construction phase. An alternative trail would be built, starting at about "45 km" on the left-hand side of the Lillooet River FSR. Check with the Squamish Forest District or the Pemberton Visitor Centre for updates on road and trail conditions. This project will involve diverting water around both Pebble Hot Springs and the impressive Keyhole Falls (located upstream of the springs). Check out friendsofkeyholefalls.wordpress.com for more information about other likely impacts.

Finding the trailhead: Follow the preceding directions to the turnoff to where the bridge to Meager Creek was washed away (63 km marker), proceed up Lillooet River FSR for 4.4 miles/7.1 km, ignoring turnoffs to the right, to reach a ford. Park here, or drive across and up the hill 500 feet/150 m to the small turnout on the left. (You've gone too far if you see a yellow 44 KM sign). The last 30 miles/48 km of this scenic drive from Pemberton are unpaved. During summer and fall it should be fine to travel in a standard car, so long as there's been no recent heavy rain.

The Hike

As of August 2012 there was no signage at the turnout trailhead and only a faint trail leading to the springs. The path was flagged with an assortment of discarded swimwear and beer cans that led us to believe we were probably on the right track. After 600 feet/180 m the route starts its first steep descent toward the river, followed by a sidle to a cliff. The trail is very steep and loose.

Bear right and keep sidling before plunging farther, sometimes with the assistance of volunteer-installed ropes, through a magnificent stand of old-growth forest. You're almost there when you to arrive at an informal campsite boasting an elaborate food cache platform. From here, pick up the faint trail heading upstream toward the river. About 0.4 mile/0.7 km from the turnout you'll reach the first signs of geothermal activity, which stretches for more than 300 feet/90 m upstream.

Two of the cleverly constructed "swallows nest pools" at Pebble Hot Springs JOHN HERCHENRIDER

These springs aren't located on Pebble Creek, which is crossed about 1.0 mile after passing the Meager Bridge washout—this is part of the package of misinformation swirling around about these springs, probably designed to keep the would-be soaker at bay.

The Hot Springs

There were four small pools in summer 2012, each one large enough to accommodate two or three soakers. The first pool is located among large boulders away from the main flow of the river. It's a shallow, silty affair built directly over a small source and was registering 106°F/41°C. The next pool was a rock-and-mortar "swallows nest" perched on bedrock right on the river's edge. It was a scalding 115°F/46°C, but thankfully there was a bucket on hand to regulate the temperature with a few scoops of icy river water. The last set of pools features two more side-by-side "swallows nests" that have some simple plumbing for temperature regulation. The pools are likely to be inundated by the river during spring melt and after heavy rain.

With the closure of Meager Creek Hot Springs to all but an intrepid few, Pebble Hot Springs have been promoted locally as an alternative destination, resulting in a dramatic increase in visitor numbers over a few short years. Please do your part to keep this area as pristine as possible.

40 St. Agnes Well (T'sek Hot Spring / Skookumchuck)

General description: Roadside hot tanks near the Lillooet River, seasonally frequented by locals and man-eating mosquitoes. Keep swimwear handy.
Elevation: 400 feet/122 m
General location: Lillooet Valley
GPS: N49.96536 / W122.43170

Map: *Backroad Mapbook: Vancouver, Coast and Mountains* (spring named). See map on page 110.
Restrictions: Dogs must be leashed. Fees apply for use of the springs and for the adjacent campsites (cash only).
Contact: None available. The Pemberton Visitor Centre (604-894-6175) will have updated information on the Lillooet Valley.

Finding the hot spring: From Vancouver take Highway 99 north to Pemberton and east to Lillooet Lake. About 11 miles/18 km east of Pemberton, bear right onto the gravel In-SHUK-ch Forest Road. Keeping an eye peeled for logging trucks, follow the road for the length of the lake and down the east side of the Lillooet River, bearing left at 19 miles/30.6 km and crossing Rogers Creek at 28 miles/45 km. After a total of 30 miles/48 km down this good logging road, there's a driveway on the right with all three names of the springs on a carved sign. This short driveway to the springs heads past an information board, a self-registration box, and the turnoff to the wooded camping area. St. Agnes Well is located about 40 miles/64 km from Pemberton.

A galvanized cattle trough provides just one of the many and varied soaking tubs at St. Agnes Well. John Herchenrider

The Hot Spring

The spring bubbles up at 129°F/54°C and feeds into an assortment of seven tubs of various shapes and sizes made of cedar, fiberglass, plastic, and metal. Each has a cold water source, allowing for easy temperature control. One of the large fiberglass tanks is squeezed inside an A-frame shelter. There's an outhouse, a changing area, and an interesting interpretive panel about the springs with both scientific and cultural information.

The name Skookumchuck means "strong water" in Chinook. These springs are said to be one of the most important spiritual sites of the In-SHUCK-ch people. Their elders refer to the healing properties of the springs and use it in traditional ceremonies. Those suffering from rheumatism and a wide range of other ailments have sought relief in these pools.

Note: Members of the Skatin (Skookumchuck) community manage the hot springs. This small First Nation village is located on a loop road 2.4 miles/3.8 km south of St Agnes Well. It has a striking triple-spire Gothic church that has been designated a National Historic Site of Canada. The Church of the Holy Cross was built in 1908, and services are still held there.

Hike 40 Joffre Lakes

General description: A day hike or overnighter to glacier-fed lakes and alpine views, on the way to St. Agnes Well

Difficulty: Moderate

Distance: About 7.0 miles/11 km round-trip

General location: Lillooet Valley

Elevation gain: 1,200 feet/366 m

High point: 5,300 feet/1,615 m

Hiking quad: NTS Duffey Lake 92J/8

Road map: *Backroad Mapbook: Vancouver, Coast and Mountains*

Restrictions: No campfires permitted. Pets must be kept on a leash.

Contact: BC Parks, Squamish Office; or visit env.gov.bc.ca/bcparks/explore/parkpgs/joffre _lks/. The Pemberton Visitor Centre (604-894-6175) is also a good source of information.

Finding the trailhead: Follow the preceding directions to Duffey Lake junction, located 11 miles/18 km east of Pemberton or 29 miles/47 km north of St. Agnes Well. Signed to Lillooet, Highway 99 climbs to tiny Joffre Lakes Provincial Park in another 8 miles/13 km. The signed trail, not shown on the NTS quad, starts off from the parking lot.

The Hike

Good things come in small packages, and the short climb to Upper Joffre Lake opens into a world of tiny wildflowers against a backdrop of snow and ice. Hikers' tents are dwarfed by the broad snout of the Matier Glacier hanging over the blue-green surface, and white peaks cast shimmering reflections on the water.

Joffre Lakes Trail begins in deep woods but soon emerges to a magnificent view of the glacier from the lower lake. Continuing in forest through a thick growth of ferns and berry bushes, the trail does its best to skirt muddy areas around the lake.

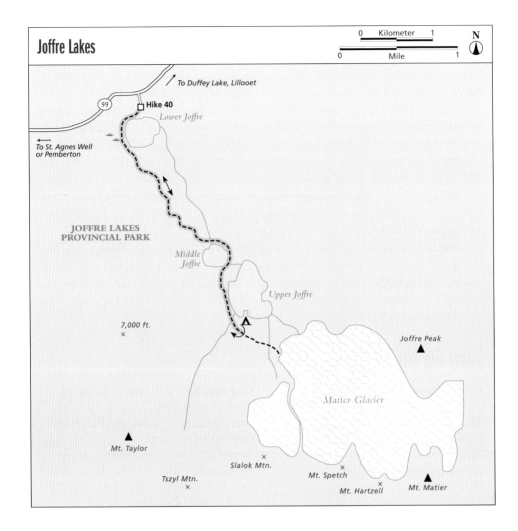

Beyond the lake the route climbs steeply for the next 1 mile/1.6 km, zigzagging high above Joffre Creek in the shade of tall cedars and Douglas fir. Next comes a boulder field to cross before the path drops to bridge the creek and circle the small middle lake.

A final short pitch brings you to beautiful Upper Joffre. The size of the two lower lakes combined, Upper Joffre's roughly triangular shape is convoluted with tiny inlets and peninsulas. Clusters of subalpine fir dot the rocky slopes, and a wall of scree and talus rises above the far shore to the ragged tongue of the glacier, backed by Mount Matier.

For a close confrontation with glacial magnificence, take the rocky path beyond the lake and follow the inlet stream to a twenty-four–site camping area. A cairned route climbs over talus to a ridge overlooking the lake and mountains beyond; the short climb adds a gain of around 700 feet/213 m to the hike. Look directly across the lake to Joffre Peak. A few more steps brings you face to face with the icefalls of the Matier Glacier.

41 Sloquet Creek Hot Springs

General description: A long but scenic drive to remote creekside hot pools in the Coast Mountains. Swimwear is advised if others are present.
Elevation: 650 feet/198 m
General location: Lower Lillooet Valley

GPS: N49.72990 / W122.32660
Map: *Backroad Mapbook: Vancouver, Coast and Mountains* (springs named). See map on page 110.
Contact: BC Forests, Squamish Forest District

Finding the hot springs: Follow the preceding directions to St. Agnes Well. From the entrance set your trip odometer to 0 and continue southeast down the Lillooet River, bearing left at 2.4 miles/3.8 km and then right at 16.3 miles/26.2 km (the left goes to Port Douglas). At 18.7 miles/30.1 km cross the Lillooet River and turn left at the four-way junction. Just before a bridge, turn right at 21.7 miles/34.9 km, ignoring an immediate right fork, and at 25.4 miles/40.9 km take the left fork, which crosses a bridge. After 27.1 miles/43.6 km (just past the 76 km marker), bear left at the signed entrance and proceed up the hill for 0.3 mile/0.5 km; park near the campsites. It's then a 330 yard/300 m plunge down a well-defined trail to reach the springs. The basic campsites above the springs have picnic tables and pit toilets. They are managed by the local Douglas First Nation—bring cash to pay the camping fee.

The Hot Springs

The main spring, one of the hottest in British Columbia at 154°F/68°C, cascades gracefully down a mossy cliff-face toward the soaking pools. Downstream, steamy water flows through a chain of shallow pools in the bedrock bank. Closest to the source, the upper pool registers nearly 113°F/45°C; then the temperature drops to a toasty 105°F/40.5°C in the large middle pool. There are usually a few small creekside pools where the cold water can be admitted for a cooler dip. There's a changing shed beside the pools, but the nearest bathrooms are back up at the campsites.

The soaking pools are enclosed on one side by a tangle of undergrowth and overhanging trees and hemmed in on the other by the rushing torrent of Sloquet Creek. Shafts of sunlight filter through the treetops, and the stream ripples right past your nearly submerged nose. How close to heaven can you get?

Sloquet Creek Hot Springs offer the ultimate in secluded soaking close to nature. SALLY JACKSON

42 Clear Creek Hot Springs

Hike 42 To Clear Creek Hot Springs

General description: A four-wheel drive or a long day hike or mountain bike ride to hot tubs on the east side of Harrison Lake. Swimwear is anyone's guess.
Difficulty: Moderate
Distance: About 15 miles/24 km round-trip
General location: Lower Lillooet Valley
Elevation gain: Around 1,900 feet/580 m

Elevation at hot spring: 2,130 feet/650 m
GPS: N49.68594 / W121.74200
Maps: *Backroad Mapbook: Vancouver, Coast and Mountains;* or *Backroad Mapbook Recreation Map: Chilliwack and Merritt British Columbia* (springs named as a small reserve on both maps)
Contact: BC Forests, Chilliwack Forest District

Finding the trailhead: From Vancouver take Highway 7 east to the Kent district. Go north on Highway 9 and turn onto Hot Springs Road to reach the resort town of Harrison Hot Springs. From here, turn your trip odometer to 0. Turn left onto Lillooet Avenue and follow it around the lake as it turns into Rockwell Drive and passes Sasquatch Provincial Park. At about 4 miles turn left at a fork onto Harrison East Forest Road. Beware of logging trucks as you continue on this gravel road up the east side of Harrison Lake.

After passing a logging camp, stay on the main road, which veers left at Cogburn Creek. The turn-off to Clear Creek Road is reached 28 miles from Harrison Hot Springs—a yellow Forest District sign on a tree states that the road is closed at 12 km to traffic (where the springs are). It's now decision time—to park at the Clear Creek Road turnoff or continue driving. There are few places to turn around and even fewer to park as the road steadily deteriorates. If you don't have four-wheel drive along with high clearance, then definitely park here and continue on foot for 7.5 miles/12 km.

The Hike

The 7.5 miles/12 km along Clear Creek Road is subject to seasonal closures. (Check the road status with the local BC Forests website or with their Chilliwack office.) The road is bordered by stately trees and is a pleasant hike, although some may find the abandoned vehicles and wooden crosses on the roadside somewhat disconcerting. There are a couple of streams to navigate. Camping is rustic and unmanaged, so pack out your garbage.

The Hot Springs

Clear Creek has three principal soaking tubs. Two, made of tongue-and-groove cedar boards, are 6 feet/1.8 m in diameter. Beside them sits a recessed wood-and-plastic soaking box big enough for half a dozen cozy bodies to enjoy. There's a small changing shelter and a bench seat; such amenities are periodically vandalized, so they may or may not be there when you visit. The hottest source (109°F/43°C) feeds the round tubs via a tangle of pipes, while the adjacent soaking box runs several degrees cooler. Take your pick!

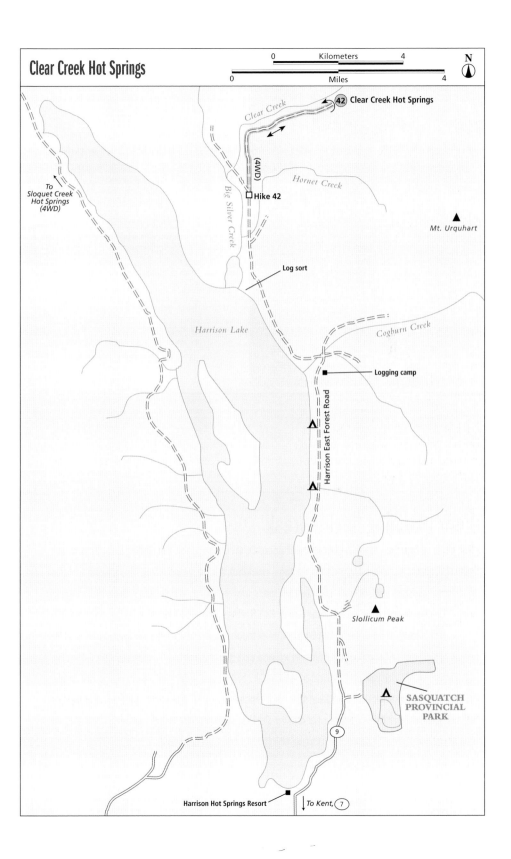

Clear Creek Hot Springs

0 Kilometers 4

0 Miles 4

N

Clear Creek

42 Clear Creek Hot Springs

(4WD)

Hornet Creek

Hike 42

Big Silver Creek

To
Sloquet Creek
Hot Springs
(4WD)

Mt. Urquhart

Log sort

Harrison Lake

Cogburn Creek

Logging camp

Harrison East Forest Road

Slollicum Peak

SASQUATCH
PROVINCIAL
PARK

9

Harrison Hot Springs Resort

To Kent, 7

Nearby, there's the remains of a swimming pool built of cedar logs by a woman prospector back when the road was first opened. The pool wastes away, collecting silt and algae. Although the woman still has mining claims, the land is publicly owned.

You'd expect this far-flung spot to be one of the quieter soaking grounds in the province, but unfortunately that isn't the case. Remote as it may be, Clear Creek is still one of the closest wild dips to the metropolitan Vancouver area. It's normally accessible and usable from April through September, but visitors on summer weekends must come prepared to wait awhile for a tub.

The wooden tubs at Clear Creek Hot Springs have plugs, allowing them to be drained and scrubbed of algae buildup for a crystal-clear soak.
SALLY JACKSON

Poor planning/lucky break

Our party of four had made a plan to meet up and visit Clear Creek Hot Springs the first weekend of August, not realizing this was a long weekend. As we drove along the shores of Lake Harrison, passing wall-to-wall clusters of tents and vehicles, we couldn't help but wonder about the scene awaiting us at Clear Creek Hot Springs. We also passed a traffic checkpoint.

After a long, slow drive in the trusty Chevy truck, we arrived at the springs close to midnight and to our utter amazement found no one else there! How could this be? The following day some locals arrived and informed us that a large avalanche had come down the creek at the last major ford. This had kept the road closed well into the early summer, and people must have thought the road was still closed. Driving out a couple of days later in daylight, we could still see piles of snow debris near the ford in the creek. (Sally)

43 Pitt River Hot Springs

Hike 43 To Pitt River Hot Springs

General description: A boat trip, followed by a long walk or bike ride, ending in a short and scary drop into a gorge to reach two relatively unknown hot pools. Swimwear is first come, first served.

Difficulty: Moderate

Distance: 27 miles/44 km round-trip from the head of Pitt Lake

General location: Northeast of Vancouver

Elevation gain: 360 feet/110 m

Elevation at hot springs: 380 feet/116 m

GPS: N49.69625 / W122.70887

Map: *Backroad Mapbook: Vancouver, Coast and Mountains* (springs not marked). See map on page 110.

Restrictions: Trailhead accessible only by boat (unless you are a mountain goat—see sidebar). Final descent to the springs is not suitable for pets, young children, or those scared of heights. Best done when the river level is low.

Finding the trailhead: From Vancouver take the Longheed Highway (Hwy. 7) heading southeast, crossing Pitt River. Turn left onto Harris Road (signs for Pitt Lake) and then right onto Dewdney Trunk Road and left on Neaves Road. Head north on this last road, which becomes Rannie Road, for 8 miles/12.8 km to reach Grant Narrows Regional Park boat launch. From here it's a 16-mile/25.7-km boat trip to the head of the lake to reach the trailhead (GPS: N49.54246 / W122.59511).

Earl and Bobbie, who live at the head of the lake, operate Pitt River Water Taxi (pittriverwater taxi.com; 778-373-6325 or 604-526-0140). You can arrange in advance to have them ferry you and up to five others across the lake and back again—the same day or a day or two later. Earl charges a flat fee, so the larger your group, the less the taxi fare is going to sting! Van City Sea-planes (604-716-0536; vancityseaplanes.com) also do charter flights to the northern end of the lake. See the Pitt Meadows Regional Airport website (pittmeadowsairport.com) for other operators who may also charter flights in that direction.

The Hike

The next stage involves hiking (or biking) a relatively straight and flat section of logging road through an overhanging tunnel of lush forest. At the 13-mile/21 km mark, bear left at a junction. Continue about 0.5 mile/0.8 km down to the bridge that crosses Pitt River where the springs sit just out of sight some 260 feet/80 m upstream. Immediately after crossing the bridge, turn right to start the faint 330-foot/100 m trail through the forest to reach the springs. Nailed high in a tree is a large PRIVATE PROPERTY sign, informing visitors that the landowners accept no liability. A tiny clearing near the river is soon reached. From here the trail sidles away from the river before descending sharply back down to the edge of a small canyon, where the two pools will be visible below. The remaining 33 feet/10 m requires a near-vertical

An intrepid explorer is rewarded with a sublime soak at Pitt River Hot Springs. SALLY JACKSON

descent down the canyon wall. There are usually several ropes installed at this spot—check them over carefully before deciding on which ones to entrust your life.

The Hot Springs

A modest flow of 136°F/58°C water issues from a cleft in the canyon wall. Thirteen feet/4 m below, two pools have been built utilizing the natural shape of the bedrock, with the addition of a small cement wall to keep the ice-cold river water at bay. The pools are usually flooded during spring melt and after heavy rain (which occurs frequently in this neck of the woods). The upstream pool is shallower and is the first to be inundated by rising river levels. The pools' temperatures can be regulated by placing gravel-filled socks in the hot spring channels to divert the flow.

The nearest flat spots for camping are reached by following the road over the bridge for about 0.2 mile/0.3 km uphill and turning right at an overgrown logging road. Be aware that brown bears and mountain lions frequent this area.

A precarious climb down to the pools—the last of several hurdles faced to get to Pitt River Hot Springs SALLY JACKSON

Four hardy folk have apparently avoided the lake and hiked to the springs from Crawford Creek Forest Road. Check out trippin.ca, which gives a colorful trip report. It took them four attempts over five years to successfully reach the springs via this route!

B. The Kootenay Region

The Kootenays encompass an area of fertile river valleys and narrow, glacially carved lakes sandwiched between mountain ranges, with Kootenay Lake running north to south down the center. To the west, three hot springs are clustered above a long lake in the rugged Selkirk Range; to the east, seven more are spread out across the southern Rocky Mountain Trench (see map on page 134). All are tucked away in sylvan settings, yet most are accessible by short walks.

Hikers enjoy trails that meander through age-old forests to the many scenic lakes in the area or climb to high overlooks. In addition to the routes in this guide, national parks such as Glacier and Banff and a variety of provincial parks offer a wide range of alpine destinations.

Directions follow out of Nakusp on Highways 6 and 23 and out of Cranbrook on Highways 95A, 93/95, and 3. Back roads and hiking routes run the gamut from short and well maintained to long and poorly defined. Campsites vary from developed to primitive, and the bubbly soaking pools generally have room to spare.

Hot Springs and Hikes

In the West Kootenays, Highway 23 north of Nakusp leads to easily accessed yet secluded soaks at St. Leon and Halfway River (44–46) near Upper Arrow Lake; hiking options include a climb to an overlook of the lake. In the East Kootenays, the remaining seven springs fan out north of Cranbrook. A remote road northwest of town accesses a trek to Dewar Creek Hot Springs (47) in the Purcell Wilderness. North of town are shorter but still dusty drives to roadside soaks at Ram Creek (48) and popular Lussier (49) with a hike in a nearby park. A remote roadside soak at Buhl Creek (50) is followed by easy-access dips at Indian Tubs (51) and Fairmont Warm Waterfall (52). To the northeast, logging roads access a stroll to Fording Mountain Warm Springs (53).

Season

Although early summer through fall is the best time, the soaks in the West Kootenays are accessible in winter from the highway by cross-country skiers. They shouldn't be affected by the spring runoff. In the East Kootenays, access to all but Lussier, Indian Tubs, and Fairmont Warm Waterfall hinges on seasonal road closures. The hiking season is normally late July through mid-September for high routes such as Saddle Mountain. Summer weather generally brings hot days with occasional thunderstorms. Expect cold nights at higher elevations.

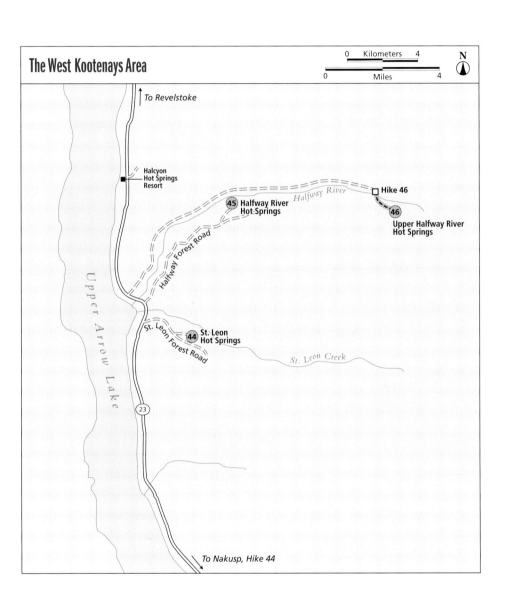

The West Kootenays Area

0   Kilometers   4

0   Miles   4

N

To Revelstoke

Halcyon
Hot Springs
Resort

Halfway River

Hike 46

45 Halfway River
Hot Springs

46

Upper Halfway River
Hot Springs

Halfway Forest Road

Upper Arrow Lake

St. Leon Forest Road

44 St. Leon
Hot Springs

St. Leon Creek

23

To Nakusp, Hike 44

44 St. Leon Hot Springs

General description: A unique soak in a cedar forest well hidden below a dirt road. Keep swimwear handy.
Elevation: 2,410 feet/735 m
General location: The West Kootenays

GPS: N50.43407 / W117.85376
Map: *Backroad Mapbook: Kootenay Rockies BC* (springs named)
Contact: BC Forest Service, Selkirk Forest District

Finding the hot springs: From Nakusp take Highway 23 north 14 miles/23 km up the east side of Upper Arrow Lake. Turn right 1.5 miles/2.4 km past a rest area onto gravel St. Leon Forest Road (south of the bridge over St. Leon Creek). Stay right, climb 0.8 mile/1.3 km to a fork, then go left for 1.4 miles/2.3 km. After the road levels out, look for a narrow pullout on the right. A path plunges downhill and reaches the pool in 0.25 mile/0.4 km.

In summer 2012 an alternative access to the springs provided better parking and an easier, though longer, walk to the springs. This involves bearing left at a nearly invisible turnoff 1.4 miles/2.25 km from Highway 23, driving carefully down a rough stretch of track for 0.4 mile/0.6 km, and then parking in a large clearing near the creek. From here, it's just under a 0.5-mile/0.7 km stroll up a gentle gradient through the trees on an old forest road to reach the springs. There are a lot of thimbleberry bushes near both parking areas—in early summer watch for bears, which like to snack on the bright red fruit.

The Hot Springs

A small clearing in the forest reveals a concrete pool with free-flowing curves and a smooth and sloped bottom. The kidney-shaped pool is a good 20 feet/6 m long and 3 feet/1 m deep in the center. The springs emerge from fractures in nearby rocks and are piped into the pool to provide a blissful soak averaging 103°F/39°C, although the temperature can be adjusted by moving the pipes. There are also three small pools in the rocks above, which usually run a bit hotter. A triangular shaped changing shelter has been erected beside the largest pool.

St. Leon Hot Springs is on private property but is open to the public. A hotel dating back to gold rush days once stood nearby, as at nearby Halcyon, but it burned down in 1968; no trace remains today. The forest is magnificent, and the gourmet sampler of wild dips would be hard pressed to improve on the present user-built pool.

Potentially bad news: In 2012 this private parcel of land was sold, and it's unknown what the new owners have planned for the hot springs. For updates check savethehotsprings.org.

The unique pool at St. Leon Hot Springs, with curves in the shape of a guitar, sets a new standard in creative design. SALLY JACKSON

Hike 44 Saddle Mountain Lookout

General description: A day hike to a lookout with sweeping views of the Arrow Lakes and surrounding mountains, not far from St. Leon Hot Springs
Difficulty: Strenuous
Distance: About 6.0 miles/9.7 km round-trip
General location: The West Kootenays

Elevation gain: 2,243 feet/684 m
High point: 7,643 feet/2,330 m
Hiking quad: NTS Nakusp 82K/4
Road map: *Backroad Mapbook: Kootenay Rockies BC*
Contact: BC Forest Service, Selkirk Forest District

Finding the trailhead: From Nakusp drive 12 miles/20 km south on Highway 6 and take the ferry across Arrow Lake. Turn right onto Saddle Mountain Road and drive 6 miles/10 km up the far shore. Take a left on the lookout road and climb 5 miles/8 km to the road-end parking area. The trailhead is 23 miles/37 km from Nakusp.

The Hike

Saddle Mountain Trail begins near the top of a large clear-cut but is soon wrapped in a forest of hemlock and cedar as it climbs the east-facing flank. You'll pass an old cabin on the way, then travel past stands of spruce and balsam, and eventually reach alpine meadows dotted with tiny wildflowers, giving way to rocky slopes near the summit.

The lookout is a great spot to enjoy the sight of Upper and Lower Arrow Lakes stretched out below. Look west to views of the Monashee Range and east to the southern Selkirks. Scalping Knife Mountain looms across the lake canyon to the south. But don't lose track of time, or you'll find yourself watching the last ferry of the day depart without you.

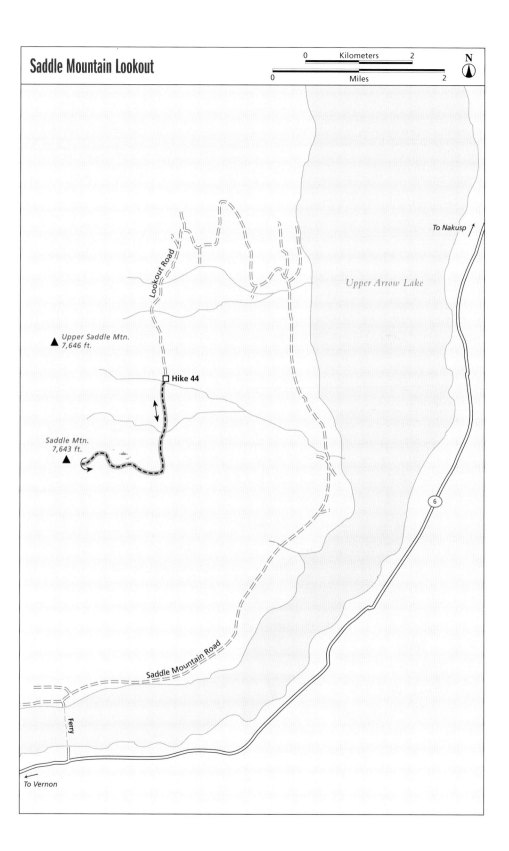

0   Kilometers   2

0   Miles   2

N

To Nakusp

Upper Arrow Lake

Lookout Road

▲ Upper Saddle Mtn.
7,646 ft.

□ Hike 44

Saddle Mtn.
7,643 ft.
▲

6

Saddle Mountain Road

Ferry

To Vernon

45 Halfway River Hot Springs

General description: Steamy soaks hiding in the woods below a dirt road. Skinnydippable with discretion.
Elevation: 2,400 feet/730 m
General location: The West Kootenays
GPS: N50.50467 / W117.78638

Map: *Backroad Mapbook: Kootenay Rockies BC* (springs named but not accurately located; the current edition marks them more than half a mile too far upstream). See map on page 127.
Contact: BC Forest Service, Selkirk Forest District

Finding the hot springs: From Nakusp drive 16 miles/26 km north along the east side of Upper Arrow Lake on Highway 23. Turn right onto gravel Halfway Forest Road, ignoring a turnoff to the right at 6.7 miles/10.8 km, and go a total of 7 miles/11.2 km uphill to a junction. The left fork is a four-wheel-drive shortcut that plunges over the edge to a flat area and short path down to the springs. The right fork continues 0.2 mile/0.3 km to a junction.

Go left to a campsite, then walk a short path down to the flat area and on down the precipitous slope to the springs. Once you reach level ground, follow one of the faint paths, starting near the outhouse, downstream for 330 feet/100 m to the pool, taking care to avoid contact with the heavy covering of poison ivy in this vicinity. There is another outhouse near the start of this flat section of trail.

The Hot Springs

In the forest, just above the riverbank, you'll find an assortment of tarp-lined plywood soaking boxes. Pipes channel water from the 141°F/60.5°C spring, and valves regulate the flow. The recommended technique is to leave the flow at just a trickle; otherwise it gets far too hot. A bucket is usually on hand for adding river water. A small wooden shelter offers a dry spot for clothes.

The primary soaking box at Halfway River Hot Springs sits above the level of most spring flooding.
SALLY JACKSON

A path leads to the nearby river, where those so inclined can take an ice-cold plunge between soaks. Just over 150 feet/50 m downstream, there's a separate source and a rock/sand hot pool or two at the river's edge that surface after spring runoff subsides. A lush cedar forest wraps the area in total privacy.

In September 2012 we stumbled across a third set of springs at Halfway. Follow a faint trail downstream from the riverside springs for about 0.25 mile/0.4 km to find some shallow seasonal pools near the upper end of a small gorge.

46 Upper Halfway River Hot Springs

Hike 46 To Upper Halfway River Hot Springs

General description: A short but challenging hike to an elusive soak in a rugged river canyon. Swimsuits are superfluous.

Difficulty: Moderate; a major creek crossing to contend with and not much of a trail up to the springs

Distance: About 2.0 miles round-trip (depends on where you ford the river)

General location: The West Kootenays

Elevation gain: 650 feet/200 m (estimate)

High point: 3,800 feet/1,160 m (estimate)

GPS: N50.49883 / W117.65472 (estimate)

Map: *Backroad Mapbook: Kootenay Rockies BC* (springs not marked). See map on page 127.

Restrictions: Attempt only when the river is running low.

Contact: BC Forest Service, Selkirk Forest District

Finding the trailhead: Second-hand reports indicate that the best way to access these springs is to drive 13.6 miles/22 km up the logging road on the north side of the Halfway River (high clearance recommended).

Just for the record: In 1973 forest service employees were fighting a forest fire and discovered this second hot spring on the Halfway River. It is reported to lie another 7 miles/11 km upstream in a rocky gorge on the south bank. The terrain isn't conducive to making a pool, as the spring flows down a rockslide of boulders. Yet where there's a will there's usually a way, and dipping diehards sometimes succeed.

The Hike

There's no obvious trailhead, but at GPS: N50.50539 / W117.66319 there's a narrow 660-foot/200 m trail leading down to the river where the footbridge was washed away in 2012 (there are no plans for it to be replaced). It's a challenging section of river to ford. Most people wait until autumn to attempt it and usually cross farther downstream, around the 14-mile/21-km mark. It's less than 1.0 mile to the springs from the washed-out bridge. Expect a 45-minute bushwhack upvalley before arriving at an eroded area where the springs are perched well above the river (about 0.3 mile/0.5 km).

The Hot Springs

The springs have a good hot source of at least 120°F/49°C, so the potential is there. Whatever volunteer-built pool(s) you may luck out and find, or end up building yourself, would certainly offer spectacular mountain views.

Note: Driving up the south side road beyond Halfway River Hot Springs to access Upper Halfway Hot Springs is not advised unless you're keen for a 3-hour bushwhack.

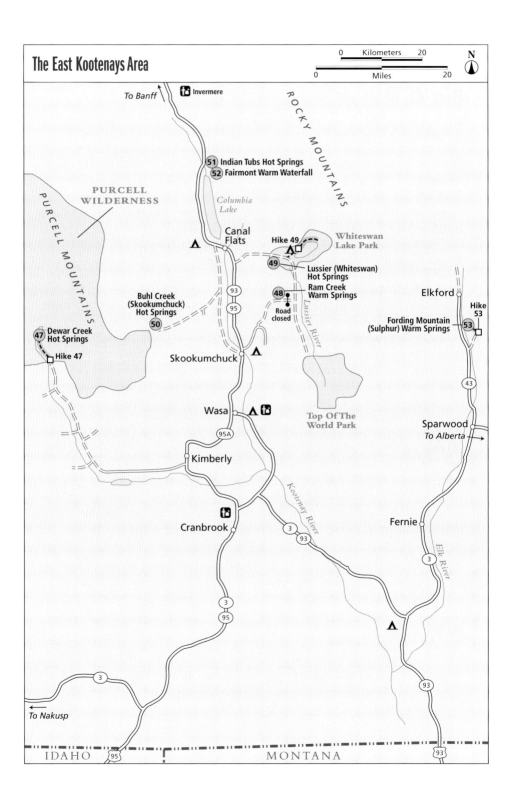

The East Kootenays Area

0 Kilometers 20
0 Miles 20

N

To Banff

Invermere

ROCKY MOUNTAINS

51 Indian Tubs Hot Springs
52 Fairmont Warm Waterfall

PURCELL
WILDERNESS

Columbia
Lake

PURCELL MOUNTAINS

Canal
Flats

Hike 49

Whiteswan
Lake Park

49 Lussier (Whiteswan)
Hot Springs

Ram Creek
Warm Springs

Buhl Creek
(Skookumchuck)
Hot Springs

93

95

48

Road
closed

Lussier River

Elkford

Hike
53

Fording Mountain
(Sulphur) Warm Springs

53

50

47 Dewar Creek
Hot Springs

Hike 47

Skookumchuck

Top Of The
World Park

43

Wasa

Sparwood

To Alberta

95A

Kimberly

Kootenay River

Cranbrook

3

93

Fernie

Elk River

3

3

95

To Nakusp

3

95

IDAHO

MONTANA

93

47 Dewar Creek Hot Springs

Hike 47 To Dewar Creek Hot Springs

General description: A remote overnighter to geothermal wonders and a dicey dip in the Purcell Wilderness. Extremely skinnydippable.
Difficulty: Moderate
Distance: 12 miles/19.3 km round-trip
General location: The East Kootenays
Elevation gain: 720 feet/220 m
High point: 5,150 feet/ 1,570 m (hot springs)

GPS: N49.95534 / W116.51636
Hiking quads: NTS Kaslo 82F/15 and Dewar Creek 82F/16
Road map: *Backroad Mapbook: Kootenay Rockies BC* (springs named)
Restrictions: No camping is permitted near the springs.
Contact: BC Parks, Kootenay Regional Office

Finding the trailhead: From Cranbrook take Highway 95A north to Marysville, which is one stop before Kimberly. Turn left onto St. Mary Lake Road and head west past the lake, where pavement turns to good gravel after 10.8 miles/17.4 km. The road is maintained to 16.1 miles/ 25.9 km and becomes a slower, bumpier surface after this. Pass the turnoff to Grey Creek at 19 miles/30.6 km and ignore a logging road to the right at 24.6 miles/39.6 km before crossing a bridge at White Creek at 24.9 miles/40.1 km. A junction with St. Mary West Fork Road is reached at 25.2 miles/40.5 km, where you bear right onto Dewar Creek Road. Ignore several turnoffs to the right. After 38.3 miles/61.6 km the road condition deteriorates dramatically—care is required if you are in a regular car. At 39.7 miles/63.9 km, bear left and proceed 0.4 mile/0.6 km to the grassy clearing where the trailhead sign is located, a total of 40.1 miles/64.5 km from Highway 95A. The hiking trail isn't shown on the maps.

The challenge: The geothermal display at Dewar Creek is guaranteed to take your breath away. Both the steaming springs and the wild setting are visually stunning. But the access to this remote fairyland can be a different story. Both the roads and the trail are subject to spring washouts, and visitors should check the BC Parks website before setting out. The roads get progressively rougher even when intact; it's also a bit of a navigational challenge to follow them. The path isn't too difficult in dry weather but becomes a quagmire when damp.

The Hike

The Dewar Creek Trail into the Purcell Wilderness Conservancy can be found west of the clearing. The path plunges into a twilight forest of Douglas fir and Engelmann spruce dotted with stands of aspen and birch. You'll soon cross a major stream on a footbridge, then continue through woods above the east bank of Dewar Creek. Many small side streams intersect the route, and the ground tends to stay damp. Huge puddles of ankle-deep mud alternate with meadows laced with blue lupine and pale pink paintbrush. These open meadows have been created by avalanches; there were still snow remnants across the track in August from where an avalanche had blocked the track in the springtime. After 3.2 miles/5.2 km, take the right fork at a

These two local families hiked into Dewar Creek Hot Springs with their packhorse and were making the most of their amazing geothermal backyard. SALLY JACKSON

junction—the left is the wet-footed option for those with pack animals. Take the left fork at the 4.6-mile/7.5-km junction, and at 5.7 miles/9.2 km there's a DOGS ON A LEASH BEYOND THIS POINT sign on a tree. A few steps later you will see a large outcrop of rock. The trail skirts around a bright geothermal display to a signed junction. To the left it's 300 feet/90 m down to the riverside bathing and 0.25 mile/0.4 km straight ahead to the campsites at Bugle Basin, which offer more magnificent views as well as bear-proof food lockers and a pit toilet. Both the hot springs and campsites are good spots to observe wildlife in the early mornings.

The Hot Springs

The bluff is shrouded by billowing clouds of steam. Tendrils of 180°F/82°C water issue from a multitude of fractures in the travertine and drop over the rocky bank into the creek. Despite the abundance of superheated water, there are usually only one or two modest seasonal soaking pools, located at the upstream end of the huge rock mound. This is partly because BC Parks encourages the existence of only one small seasonal pool. Rangers have been known to tear out the occasional cement creation that has cropped up here over the years. According to a sign at the trailhead, THE INTRINSIC VALUE OF THE SPRINGS FOR WILDLIFE USE FAR OUTWEIGHS MODIFICATIONS OF THE SPRINGS FOR RECREATIONAL BATHING.

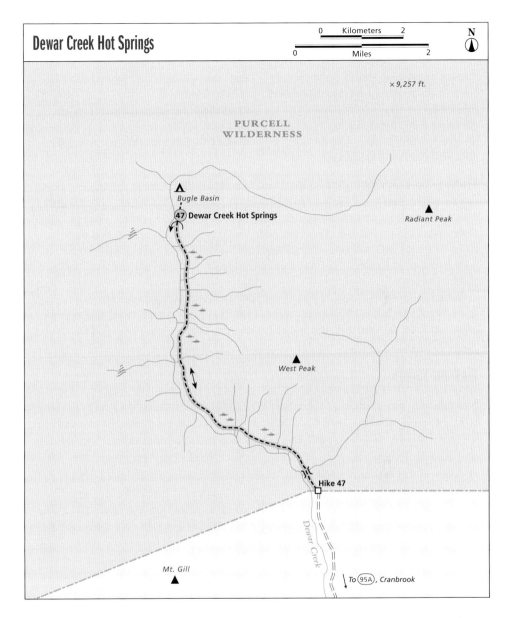

In winter, thermal heating around the springs creates a hole in the surrounding blanket of deep snow, and special plants and lichen keep the area green year-round. The springs also provide important mineral licks for elk, moose, goats, and deer. The springs are spectacular any time of year, but the prime time for a soak is late summer into early fall.

Note: Past visitors have trampled the hillside above the springs and destroyed rare habitat. To allow these areas to regenerate, do not camp above the springs or trample the bog areas.

48 Ram Creek Warm Springs

General description: Possible warm pools on a mountainside above a dirt road. Swimwear is advised.
Elevation: 4,800 feet/1,463 m
General location: The East Kootenays
GPS: N50.03290 / W115.59260

Map: *Backroad Mapbook: Kootenay Rockies BC* (springs named)
Restrictions: No camping or campfires are permitted.
Contact: BC Parks, Kootenay Regional Office

Finding the warm springs: From Cranbrook take Highway 93/95 north to Skookumchuck and continue 0.6 mi/1 km. Turn right on the paved road signed to Premier Lake Provincial Park. Bear right a short way up and continue just under 5 miles/8 km to a T junction, where the right fork goes to Premier Lake. Take the left fork north. You'll soon bridge a river and pass some farms. Where the pavement ends, the road becomes the White-Ram Forest Road. Continue uphill a total of 13.2 miles/21.2 km to a pullout on the left at a sharp turn. Follow a short path uphill to the pools.

Note: This area is an Ecological Reserve that contains several at-risk species of flora and fauna. Please take care to minimize your impact on this fragile area. Visiting during or after heavy rain events is not recommended; this is when further debris flows are most likely to occur.

The Warm Springs

News flash: A large thunderstorm in July 2012 triggered a massive debris flow that covered both pools at Ram Creek Warm Springs. These springs have been used for bathing for many decades, and before BC Parks could stop them, volunteers got busy and dug out some small replacement pools. Geologists have determined that more debris flows are likely in this area, and therefore BC Parks is discouraging public use of this site.

Here's the information on the two large pools that existed prior to June 2012. The springs emerged from several fissures along the bank and fed each pool separately. The upper pool was around 92°F/33.3°C; the lower one averaged 88°F/31°C. Daisies carpeted the landscape, and poison ivy thrived on the slopes above the springs.

Road note: At the time of printing, a loop drive from Ram Creek Warm Springs to Lussier Hot Springs was no longer possible. White-Ram Road has been closed to all through traffic about 328 feet/100 m east of the springs as an environmental protection measure. It has yet to be decided whether this will be a permanent or temporary closure. Check with the Cranbrook Forest District on the current road status. If the road is reopened, it would be possible to reach Lussier by continuing east down White-Ram Road to the Lussier River Road. You could turn left and follow the gravel logging road 9.5 miles/15.2 km north to Whiteswan Lake Road and then go left for 2 miles/3.2 km to Lussier.

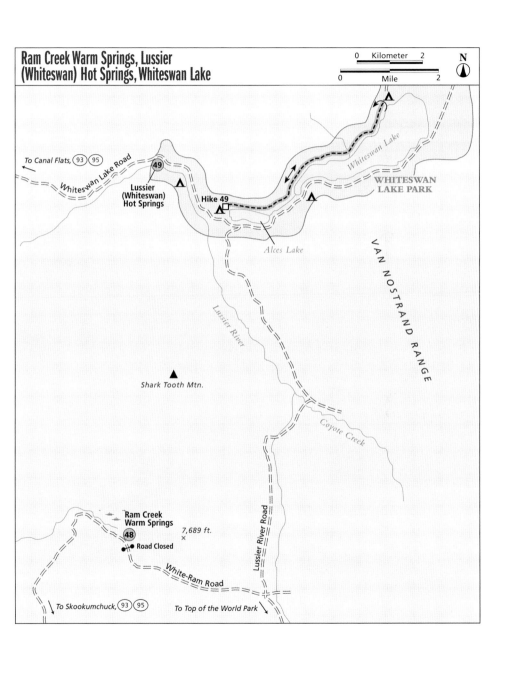

Ram Creek Warm Springs, Lussier (Whiteswan) Hot Springs, Whiteswan Lake

0   Kilometer   2

0   Mile   2

N

To Canal Flats, 93 95

Whiteswan Lake Road

49

Lussier
(Whiteswan)
Hot Springs

Hike 49

Whiteswan Lake

**WHITESWAN
LAKE PARK**

Alces Lake

Lussier River

V A N   N O S T R A N D   R A N G E

Shark Tooth Mtn.

Coyote Creek

Lussier River Road

**Ram Creek
Warm Springs**

7,689 ft.
×

48
● Road Closed

White-Ram Road

To Skookumchuck, 93 95

To Top of the World Park

49 Lussier (Whiteswan) Hot Springs

General description: Easy-access riverside soaks in Whiteswan Lake Park. Swimwear is required.
Elevation: 3,600 feet/1,100 m
General location: The East Kootenays
GPS: N50.13539 / W115.57688

Map: *Backroad Mapbook: Kootenay Rockies BC* (springs named). See map on page 139.
Restrictions: Nudity, dogs, and alcohol are prohibited at the springs.
Contact: BC Parks, Kootenay Park Services, or Kootenay Regional Office

Finding the hot springs: The most direct route to Lussier is to take Highway 93/95 north from Cranbrook to Whiteswan Lake Road, which is located 3 miles/4.8 km south of Canal Flats. Drive a dusty 11.3 miles/18.3 km east into tiny Whiteswan Lake Park. The signed turnout is just inside the park boundary, and a 660-foot/200 m ramp drops down the steep bank to the riverside pools.

Note: At the time of printing, the route between Lussier and Ram Creek via Lussier River Road was closed; it has yet to be decided whether this will be a permanent or temporary closure. See road note for Ram Creek Warm Springs (48).

A busy summer afternoon at popular Lussier Hot Springs SALLY JACKSON

The Hot Springs

Visitors will find a chain of rock-lined soaking pools along a gravel beach on the scenic Lussier River. All have comfortable sandy bottoms and are kept clean by the ample flow of the springs. The popular pools are accessible year-round thanks to the logging trucks, and the uppermost pool should be abovewater even during spring runoff. Sulfur-infused springwater issues out of a rocky crevice at 110°F/43.3°C, then flows into a large and very toasty soaking pool. The outflow fills another large rock-lined soaker just below. Succeeding pools, each slightly cooler than the one above, emerge as the river recedes through the summer.

Hike 49 Whiteswan Lake

General description: A day hike in a tiny park in the Rocky Mountains near Lussier Hot Springs
Difficulty: Easy
Distance: Up to 7 miles/11.2 km round-trip
General location: The East Kootenays

Elevation gain: Minimal
High point: 4,000 feet/1,219 m
Map: *Backroad Mapbook: Kootenay Rockies BC.* See map on page 139.
Contact: BC Parks, Kootenay Regional Office

Finding the trailhead: Follow the preceding directions to Lussier and drive 2 miles/3.2 km east to the junction of Whiteswan Lake and Lussier River Roads. The trailhead is located in nearby Alces Lake Campground.

The Hike

Whiteswan Lake is nestled in a small but popular park that offers pleasant mountain scenery and excellent fishing. The 2.5-mile/4 km-long Whiteswan Lake, along with tiny Alces Lake, are both stocked annually with rainbow trout. Several family campgrounds accommodate the weekend crowds, and an angler's path skirts the north shores of both lakes.

The lakeshore route begins at the west end of Alces Lake and hugs the rocky shore to a picnic site at the far end, then follows the meadowed inlet stream to the larger lake. You can look back past Alces to rugged Shark Tooth Mountain and other peaks across the Lussier Valley.

Whiteswan Lake sits just below White Knight Peak, but the upper slopes can't be seen from the trail. Looking south, the route offers increasing glimpses of the Van Nostrand Range. Pass a boater's camp about midway along; the path ends at Home Basin Campground, at the northeast tip of the lake.

50 Buhl Creek (Skookumchuck) Hot Springs

General description: Warm pools in a remote and scenic valley near a dirt road. Swimwear is superfluous.
Elevation: 4,070 feet/1,240 m
General location: The East Kootenays

GPS: N49.96411 / W116.02682
Map: *Backroad Mapbook: Kootenay Rockies BC* (springs named). See map on page 134.
Contact: BC Forest Service, Kootenay Boundary Region

Finding the hot springs: From Cranbrook take Highway 93/95 about 50 miles/80 km north to Canal Flats. Go 3.2 miles/5.1 km past the bridge and then hang a left onto Findlay Creek Road. Continue for 3.6 miles/5.8 km and turn left onto Skookumchuck Forest Road. Drive 6.1 miles/9.8 km to reach the turnoff to Torrent Road (a rougher road that isn't recommended as a route in from the south). Stay right at this junction; then ignore several turnoffs to the right including the Bradford turnoff.

The road bridges Findlay Creek canyon and heads south, eventually dropping into the valley of Skookumchuck Creek. It winds westward along the creek, getting progressively rougher, and reaching Skookumchuck Creek Recreation Site (only two campsites). Continue 1.4 miles/2.2 km; turn left immediately after crossing a bridge and drive 330 feet/100 m to the springs, a total distance of 27.4 miles/44.1 km from Highway 93/95. With care, regular cars can usually make it to these springs in summer and fall.

The Hot Springs

Buhl Creek has a cluster of small, shallow pools plus one much larger one, actually a warm pond. At the time tested, none were very hot, ranging from 87°F/30.5°C to 96°F/35.5°C. Some of the pools lie along the creek and submerge during spring runoff. Other pools border the pond. The nicest pools can be found just upstream from the old bridge abutment. Warm water seeps in and around the whole area, and the temperature is said to rise as the creek level recedes over the summer months. The setting is a small open meadow bordered by wooded slopes. Buhl Creek Recreation Site provides a small camping area across the road near the last bridge and is a pleasant spot to rest between soaks.

The warmest pools at Buhl Creek Hot Springs are usually by the old bridge site. John Herchenrider

51 Indian Tubs Hot Springs

General description: Free hot soaks on the property of Fairmont Hot Springs Resort. Swimwear is advisable.
Elevation: 3,250 feet/990 m
General location: The East Kootenays

GPS: N50.32976 / W115.84216
Map: Any BC road map (resort named). See map on page 134.
Contact: Fairmont Hot Springs Resort, BC; (250) 345-6070

Finding the hot springs: Anyone can point you to Fairmont Hot Springs Resort. It's right on Highway 93/95 between Canal Flats and Invermere and just north of Columbia Lake. Turn east off the highway at the main entrance and continue uphill. When you reach the upper parking area, go left uphill. You can't miss it.

The Hot Springs

Visitors venturing up this hill will find an old stone building with three small, doorless rooms. Within each room is a concrete bathtub. Pipes fill the tubs from nearby springs at a variety of temperatures. Just outside sits a giant travertine mound. Hot water emerges at the top, and steamy rivulets run down the sides, gradually building the mound ever higher as the water evaporates and leaves mineral deposits behind. Up on top are two small, shallow pools carved out of the travertine; one is set up as a foot soaker with a handy bench. Both run around 111°F/44°C during the warmer months. These toasty little treats offer fine 360-degree views of the mountains and valley. Indian Tubs is part of Fairmont Resort but is open to the public free of charge.

The dramatically situated bathhouse at Indian Tubs Hot Springs SALLY JACKSON

52 Fairmont Warm Waterfall

General description: Free warm pools at the base of the outflow waterfall on the property of Fairmont Hot Springs Resort. Swimwear is advisable.
Elevation: 3,180 feet/970 m
General location: The East Kootenays

GPS: N50.32684 / W115.84457
Map: Any BC road map (resort named). See map on page 134.
Contact: Fairmont Hot Springs Resort, BC; (250) 345-6070

Finding the hot springs: See previous directions to Fairmont Hot Springs Resort. From the resort's RV park, follow the path that leads down into the gully below the commercial pools. After less than 10 minutes, you'll come to a cliff comprising many layers of travertine over which pours the outflow from the resort's mineral-rich springs—some 1.5 million gallons daily.

The Hot Springs

At the base of the powerful waterfall is a large travertine pool over 3 feet deep and full of turquoise-blue water that is usually 90°F to 95°F/32°C to 35°C. Several smaller mineral-lined pools fan out below the main pool, forming a low terrace.

With its huge flow and scalloped pools, it's easy to forgive Fairmont Warm Waterfall for its tepid temperature. JOHN HERCHENRIDER

53 Fording Mountain (Sulphur) Warm Springs

Hike 53 To Fording Mountain Warm Springs

General description: A day hike to a thermal pond in the Elk River Valley. Swimwear is likely to be optional.
Difficulty: Easy
Distance: About 2.0 miles/3.2 km round-trip
General location: The East Kootenays
Elevation gain: Minimal

High point: 4,100 feet/1,250 m (warm springs)
GPS: N49.9695 / W114.8980 (estimate)
Map: *Backroad Mapbook: Kootenay Rockies BC* (springs not marked). See map on page 134.
Contact: BC Forest Service, Kootenay Boundary Region

Finding the trailhead: From Cranbrook take Highway 3 about 78 miles/125 km to Sparwood and continue north on Highway 43. Make a right turn midway between Sparwood and Elkford and bridge the confluence of the Elk and Fording Rivers. The final approach up the Elk River Valley is via a series of active and inactive logging roads. Contact the forest service in Cranbrook or the logging camp in Sparwood regarding the current route. The maps can't keep pace with the changing roads.

The Hike

The last 1.0 mile/1.6 km is over an old road that's now closed to motor vehicles. It leads through an evergreen forest to meadowed slopes above the Elk River. The route emerges near the springs at the upper end of a clearing. There is a small campground just beyond the springs and a view across the river valley to mountain ranges farther west.

The Warm Springs

One spring emerges from at least two outlets at the bottom of a large oval-shaped pond. Unfortunately, the temperature hovers around 76°F/24.4°C, but the pond looks like a classic swimming hole and even sports a diving board. The outflow snakes across the meadow, and a second spring bubbles to the surface at 78°F/25.5°C a couple of bends downstream.

Fording Mountain Warm Springs has a very high sulfur content and the associated smell of rotten eggs. The highly mineralized water attracts a variety of wildlife, and you can sometimes see moose, deer, and elk grazing nearby. The poplar-lined meadow, a pleasant spot to pitch a tent, doesn't see many visitors.

Idaho

The state of Idaho contains more than twice the number of geothermal gems than the fifty-three described in Oregon, Washington, and British Columbia combined! This is truly an amazing fact. The 109 hot springs shown on the Idaho map are all located in prime hiking areas in national forests. Nearly a third lie either near the edge or well within the boundaries of protected wilderness areas. Still, surprisingly few backcountry buffs visit the "Potato State." Even the spectacular Sawtooths, congested by Idaho's standards, seem deserted to hikers accustomed to fighting the summer crowds in the Cascades or Olympics.

Compared to Oregon and Washington, the backcountry of Idaho is far less developed. Few forest roads are paved, many involve the time-consuming process of skirting rocks and potholes, and most cover vast distances in an endless cloud of dust.

Free campgrounds are a thing of the past, but persistent purists will have no trouble finding dispersed campsites. The hikes often involve wading, log balancing, or rock hopping. But Idaho's hot springs make up for any minor inconvenience.

Access Areas A through K

Nearly all of Idaho's best hot springs are located in the central mountain ranges. They're grouped here by similar road access into the eleven areas shown on the Idaho A–K Area Map (see page 149). These areas are grouped according to approach routes instead of political or wilderness boundaries so that the greedy soaker with limited time may sample several on the same trip. Only four leftover hot springs lie scattered outside this region. It's called Area L: All by Themselves.

A tiny north-central area, covered in the first section of text (A), is located between Lewiston and Missoula, Montana, via US 12. It lies along the Lochsa River in Clearwater National Forest. One of the springs here is tucked away in the Selway-Bitterroot Wilderness.

A west-central region, described in the next six areas (B through G), is accessed north and northeast of Boise via SR 55 and SR 21, and northeast of Mountain Home by US 20. It includes the backcountry west of the Sawtooth crest and extends north to the Salmon River and into the southwestern quarter of the Frank Church–River

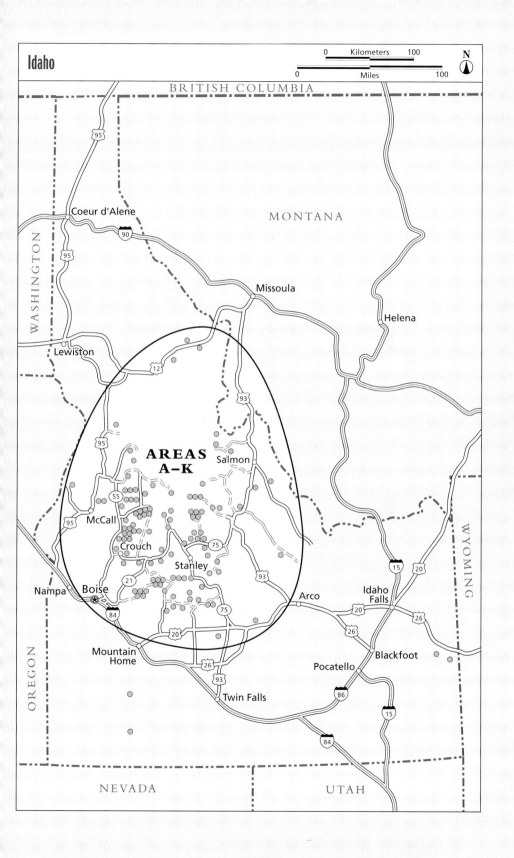

of No Return Wilderness. Outside of the two wildlands, the hot soaks and hikes are located in the rolling mountains of Payette, Boise, and Sawtooth National Forests.

An east-central region, covered in the final four areas (H through K), is accessible north of Twin Falls via SR 75 and northwest of Pocatello and Idaho Falls by US 26 and 93. It consists mainly of the eastern side of the Sawtooths and the Sawtooth National Recreation Area (NRA) plus the eastern half of the Frank Church Wilderness and adjacent mountains. This rugged country is administered by Sawtooth and Salmon-Challis National Forests and the Bureau of Land Management.

At the beginning of each area, you'll find a summary of the hot springs, hikes, and the best season for soaking. You'll also find an area map marking hot springs and hikes as well as back roads, campgrounds, ranger stations, and land features.

Wilderness Hot Springs and Hikes

Central Idaho is composed of a mountainous mass, fully 100 miles wide and 300 miles long, etched by deep river canyons. The Selway-Bitterroot Wilderness forms the northern third of this spine, and the vast Frank Church Wilderness fills in most of the remainder. The combined wildland is one of the most pristine areas left in the lower forty-eight states. Whitewater float trips are the primary attraction for tourists. Hiking trails are scarcely touched outside of hunting season. The scenery, for the most part, is subtle compared to the jagged Sawtooths to the south. The canyons are dotted with sagebrush and ponderosa pines up to about 7,000 feet, while forests of spruce and fir dominate the higher elevations.

The Selway-Bitterroot Wilderness, with more than 1.3 million acres, covers four national forests. From the adjacent Frank Church Wilderness to the south, it stretches north almost to US 12.

The 2.3-million-acre Frank Church Wilderness spreads out through six national forests and forms the largest designated wildland in the lower forty-eight states. Near the northern boundary, the mountains are bisected by the Salmon River Canyon—the second-deepest gorge in North America (Hells Canyon is the deepest). It was dubbed "The River of No Return" by a *National Geographic* party in 1935 because of its steep walls and many rapids. Farther south, the 100-mile-long Middle Fork of the Salmon River carves the third-deepest gorge, bisecting the wilderness in its journey northward to the Main Salmon.

A surprising number of practically unknown hot springs lie concealed along the Middle Fork and its many tributaries. As the few access roads are far apart, this guide groups the trips here into separate areas for the traveler's convenience. Only one of these far-flung gems is located near a road; the other fourteen are accessed by hiking trails. With few exceptions they exact their toll in the form of long dusty roads and lengthy "upside-down" treks that start on top of a mountain and wind up at the bottom.

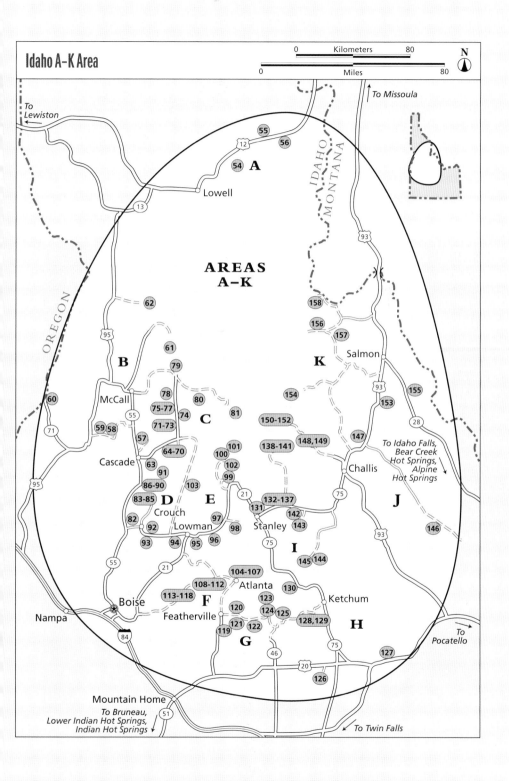

Just south of the canyon country of the Frank Church Wilderness rise the alpine peaks of the Sawtooth Wilderness, filling 217,000 prime acres of the Sawtooth NRA. The Sawtooths draw hikers along 300 miles of well-tended paths through an intricate landscape of colorful granite shaped into countless needle-edged spires, peaks, and ridges. Small lakes and streams are fringed with postage-stamp meadows lush with wildflowers and forests of spruce, fir, and pine. The area boasts more than forty-two peaks reaching more than 10,000 feet.

The Sawtooths contain only one known hike-in hot spring. But they also offer several roadside springs not far from major trailheads. On the east side of the range, hot dips located in the Sawtooth NRA may be alternated with popular hikes into the high country. On the west side, trailhead soaks and less-congested paths out of Grandjean and Atlanta do much to make up for the extra mileage on both tires and boots.

A chain of delightful pools awaits the weary hiker at Stanley Hot Springs. SALLY JACKSON

A. Out of Kamiah

Hot Springs and Hikes

US 12 bisects north-central Idaho between Lewiston and Missoula, Montana, following the Lochsa River through lush Clearwater National Forest to an area spanning the 65 miles between Lowell and Powell Junction. A quiet trail in the Selway-Bitterroot Wilderness leads to hot soaks at Stanley (54). Twenty miles up the highway comes a toasty soak at Weir Creek (55). And 10 miles farther east up the road comes a stroll to the ever-popular Jerry Johnson (56).

Season

Hot soaks at Stanley are best on cooler days from late summer through fall. The streamside path to Weir Creek limits access during spring runoff. Jerry Johnson, however, has easy access on packed snow through the winter, and the uppermost pools are usable year-round. Summer tends to be hot, and thunderstorms are fairly common.

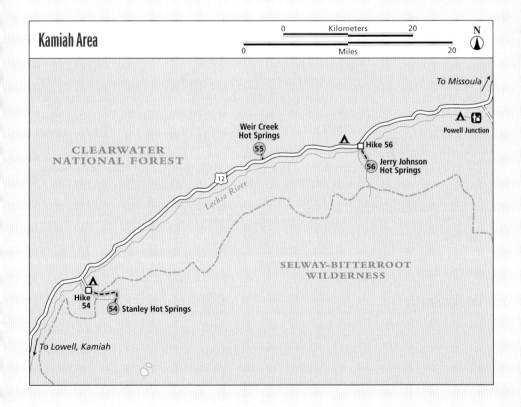

54 Stanley Hot Springs

Hike 54 To Stanley Hot Springs

General description: A steep day hike or overnighter to soaks in an age-old forest, in the Selway-Bitterroot Wilderness. Swimwear is optional.
Difficulty: Strenuous
Distance: 10 miles round-trip
General location: 54 miles east of Kamiah
Elevation gain: +1,620 feet, -120 feet
High point: 3,600 feet (hot springs)

GPS: N46.31609 / W115.25869
Hiking quad: USGS Huckleberry Butte (springs marked)
Road map: Clearwater National Forest (springs not marked)
Restrictions: Should be done when the creeks aren't running too high
Contact: Lochsa Ranger District, Clearwater National Forest

Finding the trailhead: From Kamiah take US 12 about 28 miles east to Lowell and continue 26 miles to Wilderness Gateway Campground. Go past Loops A and B and the amphitheater, and drive across the bridge to the Trail 211 parking area. (The trailhead is visible on the left as you cross the bridge.)

The Hike

Trail 211 climbs a few switchbacks and then traverses a hillside well above Boulder Creek to enter the Selway-Bitterroot Wilderness at 2.0 miles. The elevated route lacks shade but provides a number of pleasant views up and down the wide valley. Bracken fern and thimbleberries line the path and cover the surrounding slopes between islands of Douglas fir and pines.

At a signed trail junction at 4.5 miles, take the right fork (2210), marked to Seven Lakes. From here it's 0.6 mile to the springs. The path drops downhill to cross Boulder Creek and enters a dark forest with a plush green carpet. Continue south along the edge of Huckleberry Creek; you'll find the soaking pools in a large clearing above the trail.

Warning: There's no longer a footbridge spanning Boulder Creek, so you must now ford the broad stream on foot. Don't try it when the water level is high.

The Hot Springs

Water steams out of a canyon bank at 120°F, tumbles through a chain of hot pools, then continues past the trail to the creek below. Each pool is lined with logs and rocks, and, as is usually the case, the lowest ones are the coolest. Enjoy your stay, but please treat the fragile ecosystem around the springs with the respect it deserves. Remember to practice low-impact camping techniques.

Stanley Hot Springs

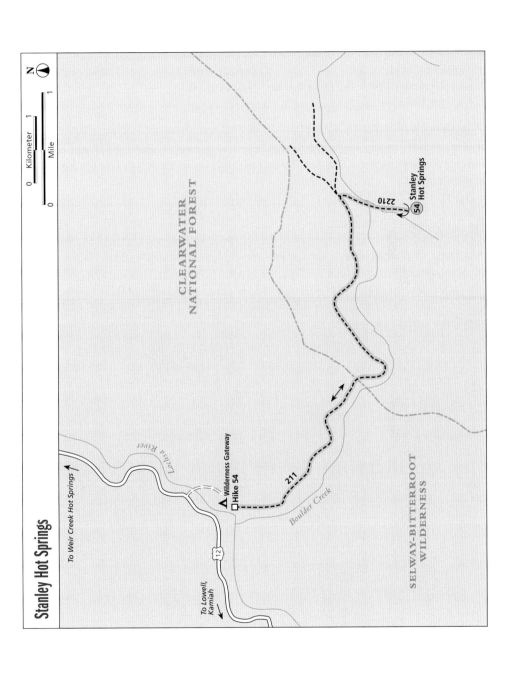

55 Weir Creek Hot Springs

General description: A popular pool cloaked in greenery at the end of a faint 0.5-mile creekside path. Swimwear is first come, first served.

Elevation: 2,900 feet

General location: 73 miles from either Kamiah or Missoula, Montana

GPS: N46.46288 / W115.03572

Map: Clearwater National Forest (springs named). See map on page 151.

Contact: Powell Ranger District, Clearwater National Forest

Finding the hot springs: From Kamiah take US 12 about 28 miles east to Lowell and continue 45 miles. Park in a pullout along the Lochsa River just east of milepost 142. Parking can be a problem on summer weekends. Follow a slippery path up the west bank of the creek to reach the pools.

The Hot Springs

A very toasty pool sits under a canopy of evergreens above a lively creek. It's bordered by split logs and features a slab rock/sand bottom. The water is constantly cleaned by the ample flow from the 117°F springs. Beside it sits a smaller, slightly cooler pool. Cooler yet is the outflow piped from the main pool into a tiny one that's directly below but tough to reach.

56 Jerry Johnson Hot Springs

Hike 56 To Jerry Johnson Hot Springs

General description: A short hike to popular soaks in a scenic valley. Swimwear is common—it's a mixed bag.
Difficulty: Easy
Distance: 2.0 miles round-trip
General location: 83 miles northeast of Kamiah; 62 miles southwest of Missoula, Montana

Elevation gain: 150 feet
High point: 3,200 feet (hot springs)
GPS: N46.46193 / W114.87205 (upper spring)
Map: Clearwater National Forest (springs named)
Restrictions: Day use only
Contact: Powell Ranger District, Clearwater National Forest

Finding the trailhead: Take US 12 about 55 miles northeast of Lowell (or 10.5 miles southwest of Powell Junction) to Warm Springs Pack Bridge, which spans the Lochsa River 0.5 mile west of milepost 152. There's ample parking nearby.

The upper "meadow pool" at Jerry Johnson Hot Springs SALLY JACKSON

Jerry Johnson Hot Springs

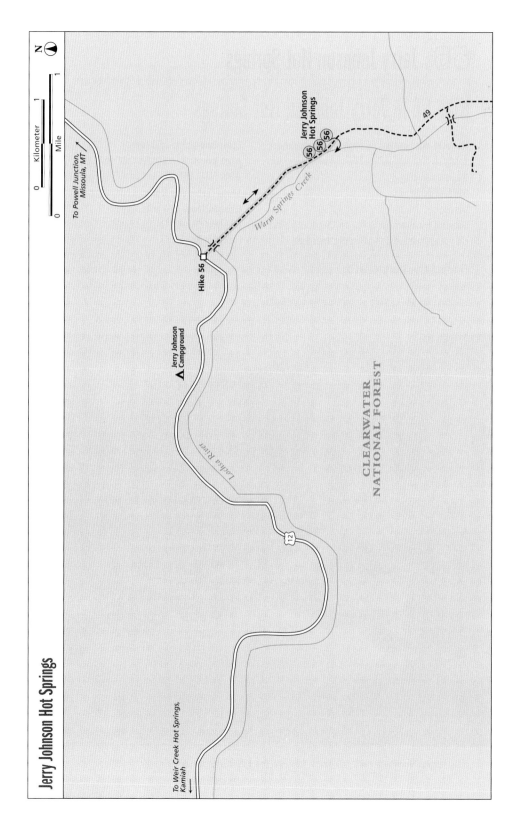

Enjoying an autumn soak in the "waterfall pool" at Jerry Johnson Hot Springs SALLY JACKSON

The Hike

Three separate hot springs lie near a creek in a broad valley forested with stately old-growth cedar and grand fir. Cross the pack bridge to the sign for Warm Springs Creek Trail (Trail 49). Follow the sneaker-worn path a short mile upvalley to the springs.

The Hot Springs

The first boulder-lined soaking pool, known to many as "the waterfall pool," is down the steep bank from the trail and right at waterline by the end of summer. This late-season pool is easy to miss if unoccupied. It needs the creek water mix to drop into the comfort zone, as 115°F water gushing from holes in the bank pours directly into it.

You can't miss the next user-friendly group of pools. The broad outflow from the second spring crosses right over the trail en route to the creek. The largest and hottest pool sits just above the path, and steamy rivulets lead over the rocks to more dips by the creek. These rocky pools vary in size and temperature; it isn't hard to find one that's just right.

The third spring, a short way beyond the others in a meadow just above the trail, has a single rock-and-mud soaking pool that is over knee-deep and large enough to float several cozy bodies; it averages 100°F to 104°F without a mix from the creek.

Nighttime closure: Due to a variety of overuse and abuse problems arising from the year-round popularity of the springs, the forest service has been forced to turn Jerry Johnson into a day-use area, 6 a.m. to 8 p.m.

B. Out of McCall

Hot Springs and Hikes

SR 55, the Payette River Scenic Biway, runs south from McCall to Donnelly. To the south a dirt road reaches Bernard (57). To the west a seasonal road along the Weiser River passes roadside baths at White Licks (58) and accesses a hike-in soak at Council Mountain (59). Farther west, a paved road on the Snake River passes Oxbow Hot Springs (60) en route to Hells Canyon. And north of McCall, back roads past Burgdorf lead the more adventurous hiker trekking to Secesh (61) and Cable Car Hot Spring (62). This area is mostly in Payette National Forest.

Season

Winter road closures are the limiting factor on most of these springs. Soaks at Council Mountain, Oxbow, and Cable Car are definitely best in cooler weather. Bernard and White Licks have a longer use season. Wait until late summer to ford the river to Secesh. The hiking season varies with elevation; summer weather is generally warm to hot, with scattered thundershowers.

The bad news: Krigbaum (Last Chance) Hot Springs was closed to the public in the fall of 2000. This site has since been posted with No Trespassing signs, and people ignoring them have been fined. This sad closure stems from a history of problems that run the gamut from littering and vandalism to crimes, including drugs and physical violence. The property has been on the market for several years. It's possible that the Krigbaum family or subsequent owners might one day allow the public back (certain conditions would likely apply, such as a fee along with nighttime closure). It would be a terrible loss if Krigbaum were closed forever due to a few irresponsible users.

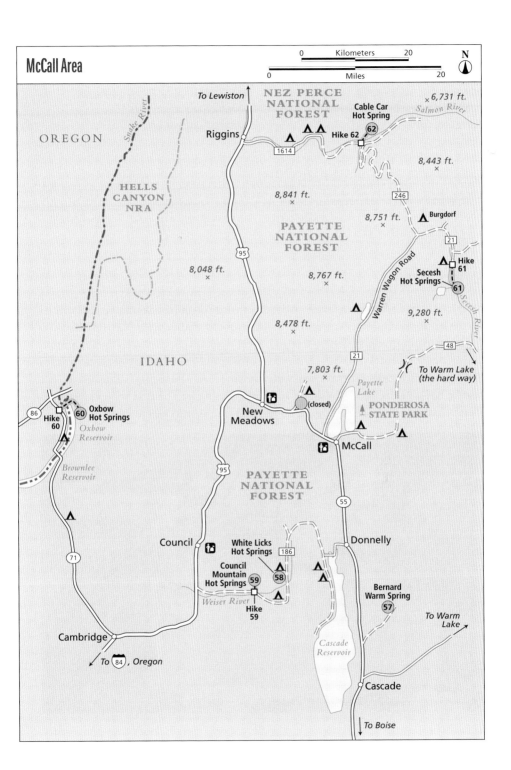

McCall Area

Kilometers 0 — 20

Miles 0 — 20

N

OREGON

Snake River

To Lewiston

NEZ PERCE NATIONAL FOREST

× 6,731 ft.

Salmon River

Cable Car Hot Spring

Riggins

Hike 62 — 62

1614

8,443 ft. ×

HELLS CANYON NRA

8,841 ft. ×

246

8,751 ft. × — Burgdorf

PAYETTE NATIONAL FOREST

21

8,048 ft. ×

95

8,767 ft. ×

Warren Wagon Road

Hike 61 — 61

Secesh Hot Springs — 61

Secesh River

8,478 ft. ×

9,280 ft. ×

21

48

7,803 ft. × — To Warm Lake (the hard way)

IDAHO

Payette Lake

PONDEROSA STATE PARK

86 — Hike 60

60 — Oxbow Hot Springs

Oxbow Reservoir

New Meadows

(closed)

McCall

Brownlee Reservoir

55

95

PAYETTE NATIONAL FOREST

71

Council

White Licks Hot Springs

186

Donnelly

Council Mountain Hot Springs — 59

Hike 59

58

Weiser River

Bernard Warm Spring — 57

To Warm Lake

Cambridge

Cascade Reservoir

To 84, Oregon

Cascade

To Boise

57 Bernard (Badley) Warm Spring

General description: A lukewarm soak in the remains of an old swimming pool, near a dirt road. Skinnydippable with discretion.
Elevation: 5,360 feet
General location: 30 miles south of McCall; 8 miles north of Cascade

GPS: N44.61540 / W115.98495 (estimate)
Map: Boise National Forest (spring not marked). See map on page 159.
Contact: None available

Finding the warm spring: Drive 25 miles south of McCall on SR 55 to the bottom of a hill. The turnoff is midway between mileposts 118 and 119, and it's 3 miles north of Cascade. Make a very sharp left turn onto Smalley Road and follow it on dirt, bearing right at a fork in 5 miles. Bernard will be off to your left at mile 5.6.

The Warm Spring

What you'll find is the crumbling foundation of what was once a swimming pool owned by the Badley family. Water emerges from nearby rocks at just over 100°F and flows into a free-form pool, roughly 7 × 10 feet and 2 feet deep, that lies between the foundation and an outcrop of rock. The pool is dammed by logs and an abundance of plastic tarp. It's just lukewarm, but the water is clean, with a healthy flow. The setting is attractive except for the tarp, but the pool is in site of any traffic passing by. The land is now owned by Boise Cascade, but the site isn't posted. Please do your part to keep it clean.

Bernard Warm Spring flows into the ruins of an old swimming pool. We used a tarp to install this temporary green pool closer to the source for a cleaner and slightly warmer soak. SALLY JACKSON

58 White Licks Hot Springs

General description: A small roadside bath-house and some riverside soaks in a camp on the Middle Fork Weiser River. Wear what you normally bathe in.
Elevation: 4,900 feet

General location: 27 miles southwest of McCall
GPS: N44.68140 / W116.22961
Map: Payette National Forest, West Half (springs named). See map on page 159.
Contact: None available

Finding the hot springs: From McCall take SR 55 south to Donnelly, where seasonal roads cross the mountains to US 95. Head west on Roseberry Road, signed to Lake Cascade State Park, then left on Norwood and right on Tamarack Falls Road. Cross a bridge at Cascade Reservoir at 4 miles. Turn right on West Mountain Road, where pavement soon ends, then left in 1 mile on No Business Road. Bear left in another 6 miles on the Middle Fork Weiser River Road (Road 186) and reach White Licks 4 miles later. The springs are a total of 15 miles from Donnelly. Council Mountain is 9 miles farther, and US 95 is a total of 18 miles to the west.

The Hot Springs

Two recessed concrete tubs, one in a small shack and the other in open air, sit 100 feet apart in a grassy flat bordered by riverside woods. The tubs are about 2.5 feet x 7 feet and 1.5 feet deep. Each has an inlet pipe fed by the sulfur springs located in the meadow above. The temperatures are said to vary depending on the outside air—the outdoor pool filled to a perfect 106°F on a cool autumn evening. Drain the tubs after use, and be prepared to pick up some trash left by less considerate visitors. The rustic tubs and primitive camp, on a parcel owned by Boise Cascade, are free of charge and maintained by users.

White Licks Hot Springs still has one dilapidated bath-house, but the other has been removed, which now allows for riverside soaking under the stars. SALLY JACKSON

59 Council Mountain Hot Springs

Hike 59 To Council Mountain Hot Springs

General description: A day hike climbing to hidden hot pools in a wooded ravine. Swimwear is superfluous.
Difficulty: Moderate
Distance: About 4.0 miles round-trip
General location: 36 miles southwest of McCall via SR 55; 50 miles via US 95
Elevation gain: 720 feet

High point: 4,480 feet (hot springs)
GPS: N44.66913 / W116.30575
Hiking quad: USGS Council Mountain (springs marked)
Road map: Payette National Forest, West Half (springs not marked)
Contact: Council Ranger District, Payette National Forest

Finding the trailhead: The quickest route from McCall is to go south on US 95, 5 miles past Council, then hang a left at milepost 130 onto the Middle Fork Road. Go 9 miles east on gravel to the trail sign at Warm Springs Creek. For those coming from White Licks (see preceding springs), continue west another 9 miles on the Middle Fork Road. The hot springs are located 24 miles west of SR 55.

The Hike

Warm Springs Trail (203) is a steep and steady climb above the east bank of Warm Springs Creek. One of Idaho's all too common forest fires swept through this area, so

Enjoying the Jacuzzi effect at Council Mountain Hot Springs SALLY JACKSON

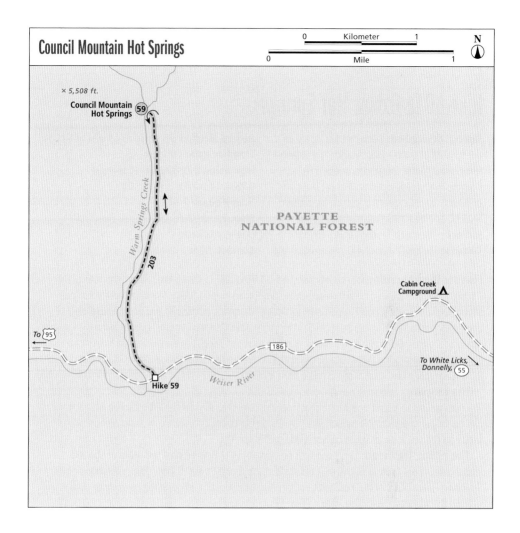

there's no longer a canopy of ponderosa pine and Douglas fir shading the way.

A large trailhead signs reads: WARNING: THIS TRAIL ENTERS BURNED AREA. EXPECT HAZARDS SUCH AS FALLING TREES AND UNSTABLE TRAIL AHEAD. Keep an eye out for rattlesnakes in the summertime. The creek forks 2.0 miles upstream, where the path drops to the water. The hot springs, with a telltale border of orange algae, cascade down the rocky bank.

The Hot Springs

Copious amounts of superhot water issue out of the rocky bank at temperatures approaching 150°F. A few yards downstream, the combined flow of hot and cold currents swirls down a slick waterslide into a bubbly whirlpool scoured out of solid rock. The pool temperature rises through the summer months as the creek flow diminishes; you'll have to head farther downstream to find (or build) a cooler pool.

60 Oxbow Hot Springs

Hike 60 To Oxbow Hot Springs

General description: Secluded hot pools on the far side of Oxbow Reservoir on the Snake River, close to the Oregon border and Hells Canyon. Two access options: a short boat trip or a long day hike dodging poison ivy, rattlesnakes, and bears! Swimwear is optional.

Difficulty (by trail): Moderately strenuous

Distance (by trail): About 4.0 miles round-trip

General location: 95 paved miles west of McCall

Elevation gain: 100 feet

High point: 1,880 feet (hot springs)

GPS: N44.94428 / W116.83387

Hiking quad: Oxbow

Map: Payette National Forest, West Half (spring marked)

Contact: None available

Finding the hot springs: From McCall take US 95 south to Cambridge. Turn right onto SR 71, signed to Hells Canyon. You'll reach Brownlee Reservoir and follow the east bank north past Brownlee Dam. The highway drops down to Oxbow Reservoir, crosses to the Oregon side, and continues north. At 3.3 miles past the bridge, you'll pass Carter's Landing, a boat ramp with some shady campsites. Go another 4.7 miles (8 miles past the bridge) to another small boat ramp with a cinderblock restroom. This is the last launch site before reaching Oxbow Dam, 37 miles from US 95 at Cambridge and a total of 95 miles from McCall.

The crossing: Oxbow Reservoir is a good 300 yards wide, so you'll need a boat to get across. Any type will make it, but one with a motor would sure help. Aim for the little canyon with a white cliff directly across from the launch site. There's a small beach to pull up on, and a short path winds up around a bend in the canyon walls to the springs.

The hiking trailhead: For those with no boat, drive 2.7 miles past the aforementioned launch site. At the bottom of the hill, turn right at the Idaho Power/Oxbow Dam operations onto Spillaway Road. Stop by their office to confirm the best location to park. This is likely to be 0.4 mile up the road near a locked gate.

The Hike

Follow the unpaved road for 1.0 mile over a low saddle to reach the Oxbow Dam. Cross over the dam and head upstream for another mile before leaving the unpaved road to start following game trails that skirt the edge of the reservoir. Don't be fooled into following any roads that start to climb away from the water. At a quarter of a mile before reaching the springs, you should start smelling sulfur from small seeps at the water's edge and also be able to see the boat launch on the other side. The springs are located 400 feet up a small gully from the reservoir.

The Hot Springs

Users have built a first-class soaking pool out of travertine rock, nestled in the bushes beneath a travertine cliff. The pool is 5 × 8 feet and 2 feet deep, with a nice deck on

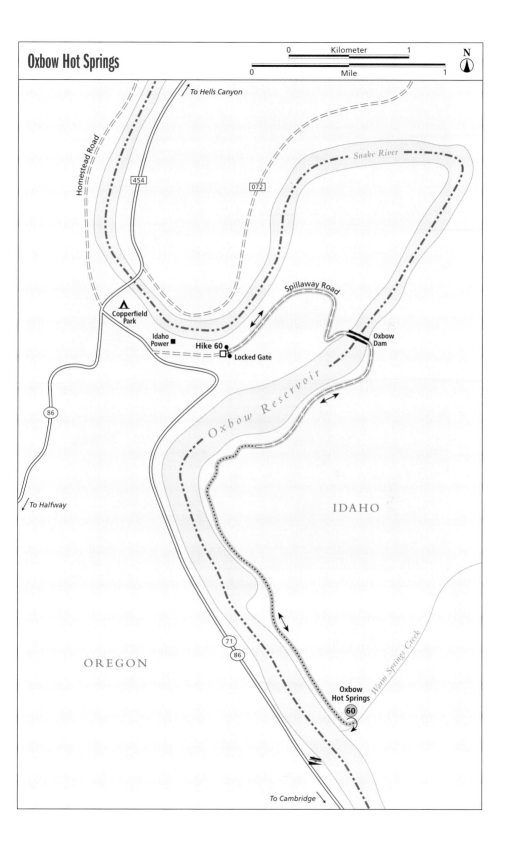

Oxbow Hot Springs

To Hells Canyon

Snake River

Homestead Road

454

072

Spillaway Road

Copperfield Park

Idaho Power

Hike 60

Locked Gate

Oxbow Dam

86

Oxbow Reservoir

To Halfway

IDAHO

71

86

OREGON

Warm Springs Creek

Oxbow Hot Springs

60

To Cambridge

N

0   Kilometer   1

0   Mile   1

The primary soaking pool at Oxbow Hot Springs is located at the base of a tower-ing travertine cliff. SALLY JACKSON

one side. One pipe feeds hot water into the pool from the spring; a second pipe brings in the cold. You'll enjoy total privacy and all the comforts of home, except one—no air-conditioning. Hells Canyon is one place that could use it about ten months of the year.

If you're game, clamber up and around the downstream side of the cliff. You'll be rewarded not only with stunning views but also another spring. It issues from a small circular pool, large enough for one person to easily achieve full-body immersion. It was registering 106°F in late September 2012.

Oxbow Hot Springs are privately owned but open to the public as long as the privilege is not abused. Be sure you leave the site at least as clean as you found it.

61 Secesh Hot Springs

Hike 61 To Secesh Hot Springs

General description: A late-season day hike or mountain bike ride to a lonesome hot springs on the wrong side of the Secesh River. Swimwear is superfluous.

Difficulty: Easy except for a major stream ford

Distance: About 8.0 miles round-trip

General location: 36 miles northeast of McCall

Elevation gain: 140 feet

High point: 5,700 feet (trailhead)

GPS: N45.16295 / W115.80848 (estimate)

Hiking quad: USGS Loon Lake (springs not marked)

Road map: Payette National Forest, East Half (springs not marked)

Restrictions: Should be done when the river is low

Contact: McCall Ranger District, Payette National Forest

Finding the trailhead: From the west side of McCall, take the Warren Wagon Road (FR 21) 28 miles northeast to a junction where the pavement ends. The left fork reaches Burgdorf Hot Springs Resort, a worthwhile stop, in 2 miles and continues on to Cable Car Hot Spring (see following hike). To reach Secesh, continue straight for 6.7 miles, then turn right and continue 1.3 miles to Chinook Campground and the road-end trailhead.

The Hike

The Secesh River Trail (80) is a gentle descent through a deep canyon. The first 3.5-mile stretch reaches a bridge where most hikers cross to Loon Lake (a popular 10-mile round-trip hike or mountain bike ride). Don't cross the bridge; instead continue 0.5

It's quite a scramble to reach these upper pools at Secesh Hot Springs. Tim Messing

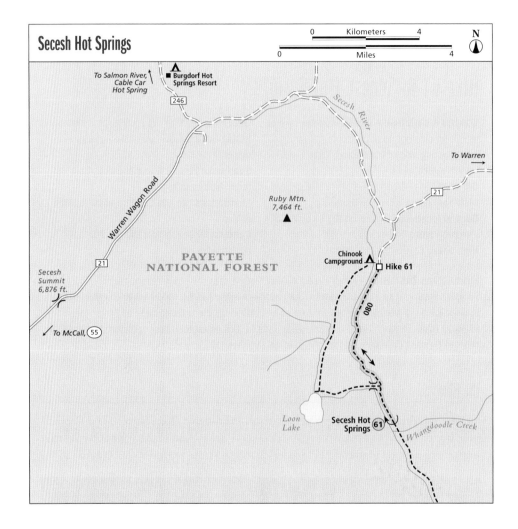

0   Kilometers   4

0   Miles   4

N

To Salmon River,
Cable Car
Hot Spring

■ Burgdorf Hot
Springs Resort

246

To Warren

Ruby Mtn.
7,464 ft.

Warren Wagon Road

21

PAYETTE
NATIONAL FOREST

Secesh
Summit
6,876 ft.

21

To McCall, 55

Secesh River

Chinook
Campground

Hike 61

080

Loon
Lake

Secesh Hot
Springs 61

Whangdoodle Creek

mile south. Just before reaching the Whangdoodle Trail turnoff, look across the river for two rocky chutes clear of foliage. That's your goal, but don't attempt a ford until late summer, when the water is lower and slower.

The Hot Springs

Two small streams of steamy water tumble down to the river from source springs located high up the mountainside. Each channel cuts a broad swath through the forest, and each twists through a steep landslide of boulders. The best pools are usually found after a stiff climb to the top of this area. As these springs don't see much use, it might be a good idea to bring along a small tarp for building or patching up a pool. There have been reports of red spider mites at these springs (see page 6 for information and advice on dealing with spider mites).

62 Cable Car (French Creek) Hot Spring

Hike 62 To Cable Car Hot Spring

General description: A major crossing plus a short climb to a one-of-a-kind hot spring, above the opposite side of the Salmon River. Requires a raft and life jackets, but there's no need for a swimsuit.

Difficulty: Problematic and strenuous

Distance: About 2.0 miles round-trip

General location: 58 miles north of McCall via Burgdorf; 63 miles via Riggins

Elevation gain: 600 feet

High point: 2,520 feet (hot springs)

GPS: N45.43142 / W116.01530

Map: Payette National Forest, East Half; Nez Perce National Forest (spring not marked)

Contact: Salmon River Ranger District, Nez Perce National Forest

Finding the trailhead: The trail to this spring is located 18.7 miles east of Riggins on the far bank of the Salmon River. The fastest way to get there from McCall is to go west to New Meadows, take US 95 north to Riggins, then follow the Salmon River Road east to the mouth of French Creek. There are several informal camping options along this road; at 10.5 miles east of Riggins you'll pass Spring Bar Campground. The road crosses French Creek 18.5 miles from Riggins, and there's a T junction. Turn left and park 0.2 mile on the left in a narrow turnout. This is a total of 63 miles from McCall, with all but the last 6 miles on pavement.

There's an alternate route for anyone coming by way of either Burgdorf or Secesh Hot Springs (see map on page 159). Via Burgdorf, it's 58 miles from McCall, but only the first 28 miles are paved. Burgdorf Hot Springs, though commercial, is so delightfully funky that it makes a perfect stopover between Secesh and Cable Car Hot Springs. Follow the preceding directions to Burgdorf and proceed 26 miles on a surface that deteriorates as the scenery improves. The final switchbacks down to the river are awesome. The road ends at the mouth of French Creek on the Salmon River. Continue straight at the French Creek junction for 0.2 mile; park in the narrow turnout on the left.

A crude tramway was built at the mouth of French Creek back in the 1930s. This cable car was the principal access to the hot spring until it was finally condemned and torn down in 1995.

The crossing: The Salmon is the mighty "River of No Return." There's no fording or swimming this one. You'll need a good raft and life jackets to get across safely. Check with the outfitters in Riggins on current water level and choice of put-ins. The usual spot, just upstream of the old cableway, requires a rocky scramble down to the river. August into October is usually the best time to do the river.

The Hike

From the beach on the north side of the river (GPS: N45.42628 / W116.02644), head for the large area of brambles, interspersed with a few fruit trees, to pick up the main trail that heads to the hot spring. The trail curves in through a stretch of midsummer blackberries and crosses Robbins Creek drainage before commencing

Cable Car (French Creek) Hot Spring

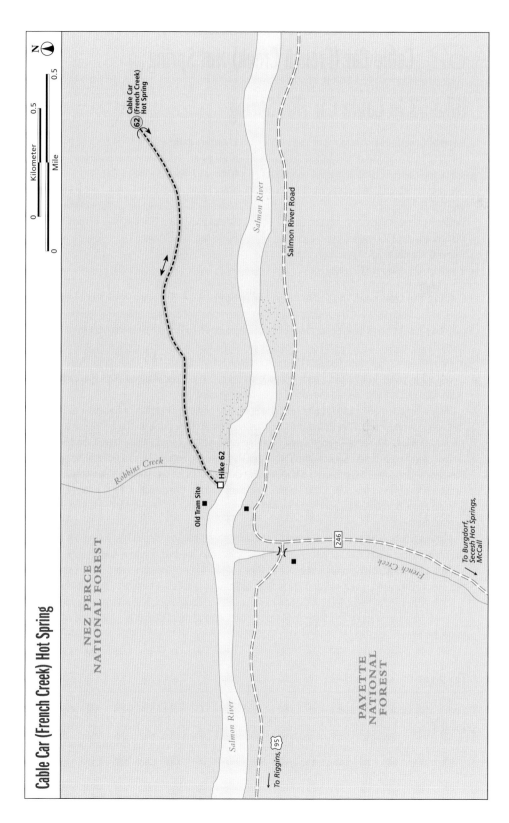

The first stop at Cable Car Hot Spring is an old mine shaft full of warm water. SALLY JACKSON

a steady climb. Keep an eye peeled for poison ivy and rattlesnakes. One more long shadeless stretch takes you around a bend and into a small ravine, where you'll find what you've come this far to discover.

The Hot Spring

First, you'll find a rocky tunnel filled with 98°F water. A concrete wall constructed at the entrance dams a 2.5 foot deep pool of clear warm water. (Warning: Small bats commonly roost on the ceiling, so heading deeper into the shaft is not recommended.)

Second, a log bathhouse straddles the spring 100 feet farther up the trail. A wide entrance and windows let in light, while the roof keeps out the hot sun. (In 2012 it was showing signs of decay, with rotting roof beams starting to give way.) Inside, you'll find a giant ponderosa pine log hollowed out into a tub. Steamy 102°F water enters through a pipe; the tub can be drained like a whirlpool through a large hole in the bottom. The slick surface makes for a most comfortable soak.

C. Out of Cascade

Hot Springs and Hikes

The Warm Lake Highway leads northeast from Cascade to a variety of easy-access soaks (63–73) on the South Fork Salmon River, all in the Warm Lake area of Boise National Forest. To the north are three easy-access hot pools (75–77), as well as three that require hikes (74, 78, 79) in Payette National Forest. East of this area, a hike near Yellow Pine climbs to Hubcap (80), and a mad expedition into the Frank Church Wilderness plunges down a canyon to Kwiskwis Hot Spring (81).

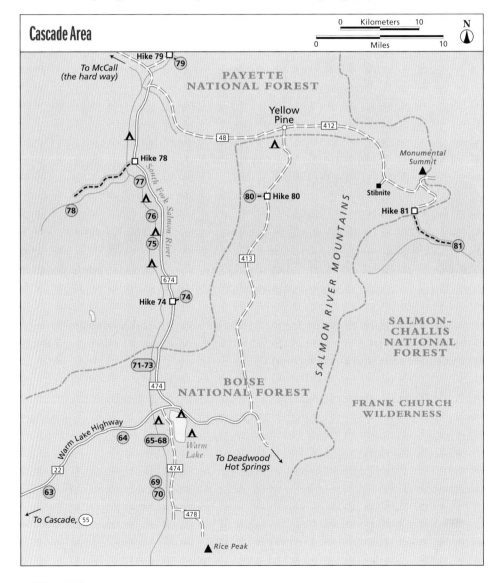

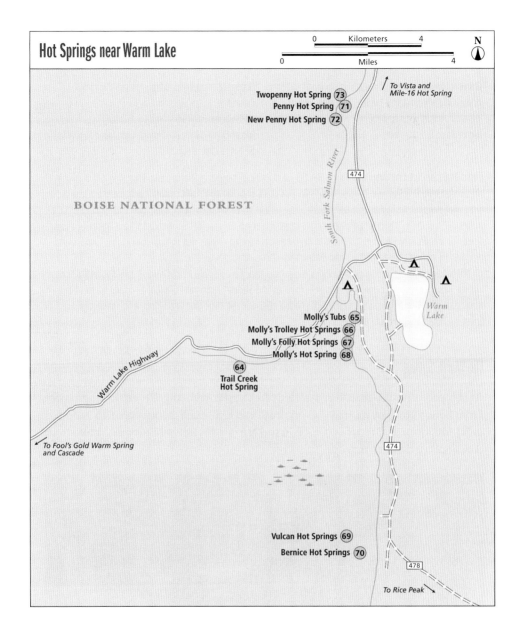

Hot Springs near Warm Lake

0   Kilometers   4

0   Miles   4

N

To Vista and
Mile-16 Hot Spring

Twopenny Hot Spring (73)
Penny Hot Spring (71)
New Penny Hot Spring (72)

South Fork Salmon River

474

BOISE NATIONAL FOREST

Warm Lake

Molly's Tubs (65)
Molly's Trolley Hot Springs (66)
Molly's Folly Hot Springs (67)
Molly's Hot Spring (68)

Warm Lake Highway

(64)
Trail Creek
Hot Spring

To Fool's Gold Warm Spring
and Cascade

474

Vulcan Hot Springs (69)

Bernice Hot Springs (70)

478

To Rice Peak

Season

Vulcan and Vista have the longest season of use, followed by Mile-16. The streamside pools all submerge during the runoff, but Penny is best before the river is too low. Hubcap and Fool's Gold are good in hot weather. Several of these springs require a late-season ford. The hiking season stretches from mid-July through mid-October. Summer weather is generally hot, with occasional thunderstorms.

63 Fool's Gold Warm Spring

General description: A large warm pool in a grassy clearing near a paved highway. Swimwear or not is your choice.
Elevation: 5,200 feet

General location: 11 miles northeast of Cascade
GPS: N44.58456 / W115.87404
Map: Boise National Forest (springs not marked). See map on page 172.

Finding the warm spring: From SR 55 at Cascade, take the Warm Lake Highway 10.8 miles northeast keeping an eye out for the Gold Fork L.O. sign on the right (south) side of the road. Seventy feet beyond this sign, on the same side, is a high-clearance spur that leads for just over 0.1 mile to the spring. It's best to park in the large clearing on the left at the Gold Fork Turnoff (often used for informal camping). Cross the highway on foot to check out the spur and the turnaround options in case other folk are already parked at the spring.

Note: Despite its close proximity to a paved road, few people know about this delightful warm spring. It's located on private land very close to the Boise National Forest Boundary. At the time of writing, there was no gate or signs, but please respect the landowner's rights and leave the area at least as tidy as when you arrived.

The Warm Spring

At the end of the spur road is a secluded campsite with Big Creek flowing nearby. From here, ford what is usually a very small creek to reach a pool about 15 × 30 feet and 1 foot deep. It runs around 93°F in the warmer months and probably a lot cooler during other times of the year.

A warm day is required to fully enjoy the below-body-temperature soak at Fool's Gold Warm Spring. Matt Rosenthal

64 Trail Creek Hot Spring

General description: Peekaboo pools in a wooded canyon below a highway. Keep swimwear handy.
Elevation: 5,600 feet
General location: 19 miles northeast of Cascade

GPS: N44.62747 / W115.75051
Map: Boise National Forest (spring not marked). See map on page 173.
Contact: Cascade Ranger District, Boise National Forest

Finding the hot springs: From SR 55 at Cascade, take the Warm Lake Highway just over 19 miles northeast (3 miles past Big Creek Summit). Watch for a large pullout on your right. If you pass Clear Creek Road (FR 409), you've gone too far. Slide down a slippery 60-yard path from the west end to the canyon floor and across Trail Creek to the soaking pools.

Thanks to some elaborate rock work and plumbing, a five-star soak is easy to attain in the upstream pool at Trail Creek Hot Spring. SALLY JACKSON

The Hot Springs

The first pool sits in the creek at the base of a slab of rock. Hot water streams down from the spring above at 122°F, coating the slab with colorful algae patterns. Cold water is gravity-fed into the pool by pipe. The pool is visible from the west end of the pullout but invisible to passing motorists. Upstream a short distance and even harder to spot from above, there's a second soaker. This little gem has hot water trickling in from the edge and also has creek water piped in. It measures a good 8 × 12 feet and 2 feet deep. The rock border is reinforced with mortar. Both pools submerge during spring runoff.

The simpler downstream pool at Trail Creek Hot Spring STEPHANIE ENSIGN

65 Molly's Tubs

General description: A seasonal riverside soak on the South Fork Salmon River below a dirt road. The name remains, but the forest service has removed the bevy of bathtubs. A swimsuit/birthday suit mix.
Elevation: 5,200 feet

General location: 24 miles northeast of Cascade
GPS: N44.64155 / W115.69446
Map: Boise National Forest (spring not marked). See map on page 173.
Contact: Cascade Ranger District, Boise National Forest

Finding the hot spring: From SR 55 at Cascade, take the Warm Lake Highway 23 miles northeast to graded FR 474, located between mileposts 56 and 57 (3.7 miles past Trail Creek Hot Springs). It's the westernmost of two roads signed to Stolle Meadows. Drive south for 1.3 miles to a pullout on your right and follow a a steep 200-foot path down to the springs.

The Hot Springs

The site sure looks different without the motley assortment of bathtubs! Water at a temperature of 138°F issues out of a low rock embankment, forming a small hot stream. You're likely to find a seasonal rock pool or two where this meets the river. As the river level recedes, pools are built near the waterline so cold water can be mixed with the hot to achieve a comfortable temperature.

Molly's Tubs sans tubs. They used to sit at the base of the dark outcrop. SALLY JACKSON

66 Molly's Trolley Hot Springs

67 Molly's Folly Hot Springs

General description: A pair of late-season, handyman specials on the far side of the South Fork Salmon River. Swimwear is advised when standing up.
Elevation: 5,200 feet
General location: 24 miles northeast of Cascade

GPS: Molly's Trolley, N44.63793 / W115.69406; Molly's Folly, N44.63688 / W115.69402
Map: Boise National Forest (springs not marked). See map on page 173.
Contact: Cascade Ranger District, Boise National Forest

Finding the hot springs: Follow directions to FR 474 given for Molly's Tubs (65). Continue 0.3 mile past Molly's Tubs to a narrow pullout. The springs are 0.1 mile apart on the far side of the river. They sit below a craggy knoll between Molly's Tubs and Molly's Hot Spring and can be spotted from the road by the telltale orange algae. Both require some scratchy bushwhacking and a river ford, but for true diehards the end justifies the means—especially when the other Mollys have customers. Don't attempt to cross before at least midsummer or you'll wash up back at Molly's Tubs!

Walk the road 150 yards south to a point where the bank has a gradual slope with few trees but dense, low bushes. Molly's Trolley rides down a boulder into the river directly across. Beat your way through the brush and cross over to it. Molly's Folly lies around the bend upstream, but bushwhacking the far bank looks like "folly" to me. Best to retrace your steps and walk the road to a gap in the woods across the river that extends uphill. You'll spot the spring 30 yards up the damp slope. It trickles over an alcove in a rock slab, then fans out below. Work your way down a short but steep drop to the river; then cross over and scramble up the bank.

The Hot Springs

Molly's Trolley putters down a granite slab into the remnants of a rock-lined pool that's exposed at low water. The quality of the soak depends on the skills of the (re)builder. Because the nearby spring is 140°F, the flow must be premixed with cold before reaching the pool. This calls for some creative plumbing after the digging is done.

Another challenge awaits the dipping diehard at Molly's Folly. Because the river is out of reach, the would-be user not only has to build a pool far enough down from the source (130°F) to air-cool the water but also must find a way to channel in the meager flow and keep it from leaking out. The solution would be a tub with a hot-water pipe that can be diverted. And there actually is an aging bathtub sans plumbing up there, tipped on its side in the rubble below the source—a monument to what lengths some folks will go to get a bath!

68 Molly's Hot Spring

General description: A sadly neglected pool above the South Fork Salmon River 0.3 mile from a dirt road. Bathing suits are optional.
Elevation: 5,260 feet
General location: 25 miles northeast of Cascade

GPS: N44.63351 / W115.69614
Map: Boise National Forest (spring not marked). See map on page 173.
Contact: Cascade Ranger District, Boise National Forest

Finding the hot spring: Follow the directions to FR 474 given in Molly's Tubs (65) and go south 1.9 miles (nearly 0.6 mile past Molly's Tubs) to a pullout. Park here and walk west on a road (FR 490), closed to motor vehicles, that leads to the river and bridges it in 0.2 mile. Immediately past the bridge, hang a right onto an overgrown path that meanders for 0.1 mile back downstream and up a slippery slope to the pool.

The Hot Spring

Molly is perched far enough above the river to escape the runoff. Her 129°F spring still streams down the hillside past a log-lined soaker built directly over the flow. A hodgepodge of pipes and hoses carries water down the steep slope from several sources into a shallow pool. You can control the pool temperature by diverting or combining pipes with a hotter or cooler flow. Molly has great potential; she just needs a helping hand.

Note: Keep an eye out for the red spider mites that sometimes frequent this spring (see page 6 for information and advice on dealing with spider mites).

The wall of evergreens that once provided shade and privacy at Molly's Hot Spring is no more, a result of forest fires that have swept through the area. The silver lining is a more expansive view. SALLY JACKSON

69 Vulcan Hot Springs

General description: A popular creek-wide soaker in the South Fork Salmon River Valley on a 1.0-mile path. Swimwear is first come, first served.
Elevation: 5,500 feet
General location: 30 miles northeast of Cascade

GPS: N44.56754 / W115.69400
Map: Boise National Forest (springs named). See map on page 173.
Contact: Cascade Ranger District, Boise National Forest

Finding the hot springs: Follow the directions to FR 474 given in Molly's Tubs (65). Drive south 6.5 miles, 4.7 miles past Molly's Hot Spring and shortly beyond Stolle Meadows. Park by the toilets on the left. The trail begins on the other side of the road, soon crosses a pack bridge, and then reaches a second bridge after 0.3 mile. Cross the bridge and then turn left at the T junction, continuing 0.7 mile to the first signs of pools built in a warm creek littered with fallen trees. The main pool is usually about 500 feet below the spectacular source area.

The Hot Springs

Many bubbling springs, at temperatures up to 190°F, join forces to form a hot creek that cools as it flows down a fire-charred hillside toward the South Fork Salmon River. The creek has been dammed with logs at a point just beyond optimum soaking temperature (106°F) to form a soaking pool 30 feet across with a sand-and-mud bottom. There should be other smaller and cooler dammed spots downstream for quite a ways. You can almost guarantee an abundance of red spider mites at Vulcan's pools (see page 6 for information and advice on dealing with spider mites).

70 Bernice (Spock) Hot Springs

General description: A practically unknown spring reached via 0.4 mile of off-trail hiking from Vulcan Hot Springs. Swimwear is optional.
Elevation: 5,500 feet
General location: 30 miles northeast of Cascade

GPS: N44.56424 / W115.68894
Map: Boise National Forest (springs not marked). See map on page 173.
Contact: Cascade Ranger District, Boise National Forest

Finding the hot springs: Follow the preceding directions. From the source area at Vulcan Springs, head southeast (there's no trail) up and over a low hill for about 0.4 mile to reach a small stream.

The Hot Springs

On the western bank is a rock ledge about 6 feet above the creek from which numerous small, but very hot (up to 153°F), springs issue. In fall 2012 there was a newly constructed soaking box made of logs that measured 4 × 8 feet and 2.5 feet deep located just downstream from the springs. It looked as if a large tarp and at least two long lengths of hose would be required to turn this into a viable soak. Alternatively, just bring a tarp and attempt a do-it-yourself pool at the base of the ledge when the creek is at normal or low flow.

71 Penny Hot Spring

General description: A secluded spring in the South Fork Salmon River Canyon on a 0.4-mile path. Keep swimwear handy.

Elevation: 4,900 feet

General location: 28 miles northeast of Cascade

GPS: N44.71041 / W115.70031

Map: Boise National Forest (spring area named but not marked). See map on page 173.

Contact: Cascade Ranger District, Boise National Forest

Finding the hot spring: From Cascade, take the Warm Lake Highway 24 miles northeast (a mile past FR 474 south) and turn left onto the paved South Fork Road (FR 474/674) signed to Krassel, Yellow Pine, and McCall. Drive 3.6 miles north, then turn left at a sharp right bend into a parking area. Park here and follow a path that shows increasing use. Unfortunately for hot springers, this has become a very popular fishing access. The route curves north around a hill, traverses a steep slope well above the river, then drops sharply down the downstream side of a cliff to the pools at the bottom.

The Hot Spring

Steaming 144°F springwater flows down the side of a cliff into a few rock-and-sand pools along a scenic bend in the river. You can spot other hot springs both downstream and on the opposite bank by the telltale orange algae (see following hot springs description). The fragile pools swamp during high water but get landlocked and far too hot once the river is low. There's plenty of hot water just waiting for some energetic soul to rebuild a proper soaking pool, so if you're intent on a bath, bring a shovel and plenty of elbow grease—and be prepared for company.

The pools at Penny Hot Spring are built seasonally between the river and springs that issue from this cliff.
SALLY JACKSON

72 New Penny Hot Spring

73 Twopenny Hot Spring

General description: Two more pennies to add to the jar, near Penny Hot Spring. Keep swimwear handy.
Elevation: 4,900 feet
General location: 28 miles northeast of Cascade

GPS: New Penny Hot Spring, N44.70928 / W115.70001; Twopenny Hot Spring, N44.71070 / W115.70068
Map: Boise National Forest (spring area named but not marked). See map on page 173.
Contact: Cascade Ranger District, Boise National Forest

Finding the hot springs: Follow the preceding directions to the trail to Penny Hot Spring and follow it around the big bend northward. To find New Penny, watch for a stairway in 0.25 mile that goes halfway down the bank. The final plunge is steep and slippery. The spring sits a few yards downstream. Once the water is low, the pool can be spotted from the trail above. To reach Twopenny, continue on to Penny and ford the river if it's low. Keep these Pennys in mind for times when the more popular Penny is occupied.

The Hot Springs

The spring at New Penny flows from a tiny source pool over a granite slab coated with bright algae into the remnants of a rock-lined pool that should surface by midsummer. It needs some rebuilding and patchwork every year, so if you're the first arrival, you get the honors. Blending the hot and cold is a challenge, because the spring is 130°F, and there's not much space for premixing. You may end up stirring while you soak.

Twopenny Hot Spring streams down a cliff into the river right across the canyon from the popular Penny. Colorful orange and green algae borders the site and makes it easy to spot. Once the river is down and safe to ford, there should be room beneath the cascade to (re)build a small pool. This spring runs a bit cooler than the other Pennys, so premixing shouldn't be too hard. The problem is more likely to be keeping the hot and cold separated!

New Penny Hot Spring provides the potential. The user supplies the pool. SALLY JACKSON

74 Vista Hot Springs

Hike 74 To Vista Hot Springs

General description: A stiff little off-trail hike that climbs 600 feet to reach a small sulfur spring. Skinnydippable for sure.
Difficulty: Moderately strenuous
Distance: About 1.2 miles round-trip
General location: 35 miles northeast of Cascade
High point: 5,470 feet

GPS: Trailhead, N44.77077 / W115.67881; hot spring,N44.77404 / W115.66939
Map: Boise National Forest or Payette National Forest, East Half (spring not marked). See map on page 172.
Contact: Krassel Ranger District, Payette National Forest

Finding the hot springs: Follow the directions to FR 474/674 given in Penny Hot Spring (71). Drive north for 8.8 paved miles (5.2 miles beyond the Penny Trailhead) and look for a narrow pullout on the right by a small drainage (Sister Creek on maps). **Note:** You're unlikely to find these springs if you don't take a GPS unit and the coordinates.

Vista Hot Springs before . . . SALLY JACKSON

The Hike

Set off upstream in a northeasterly direction for 0.6 mile to reach the springs. A tip or two: After 0.25 mile of following the creek on its northwestern side, cross over and head toward a shallow side gully that has one of the area's few live trees located just to the left of it. The springs are located below a rocky outcropping on the right. You'll be weaving through scrubby bushes and burnt logs to reach them.

The Hot Springs

There are two small 107°F sources issuing out of a small rock outcrop, below which a 4 × 6-foot, 1-foot-deep depression has been dug out and dammed up with a drain installed. It's likely that you'll have to dig out some accumulated debris and clear the drain before laying down your tarp and waiting about 30 minutes for the modest flow to fill your two-person pool. For the few who will venture to Vista Hot Springs, the views and the special sulfur water make all this effort worth it.

Note: Prior to publication of this edition, probably fewer than ten people had ever visited this spring. Many thanks to the Idaho Dippers for finding it, naming it, and giving clearance for its top-secret status to be lifted so that others can enjoy and help maintain this little gem.

. . . Vista Hot Springs an hour later. If you want a decent soak, be sure to take along a shovel and a 6 × 8-foot tarp. MATT ROSENTHAL

75 Mile-16 Hot Spring

General description: A classic soak in the South Fork Salmon River Canyon hidden below a paved road. Keep swimwear handy.
Elevation: 4,150 feet
General location: 40 miles northeast of Cascade

GPS: N44.84655 / W115.69759
Map: Payette National Forest, East Half (spring not marked). See map on page 172.
Contact: Krassel Ranger District, Payette National Forest

Finding the hot spring: Follow the directions to FR 474/674 given in Penny Hot Spring (71). Drive north past Penny into Payette National Forest and on to Poverty Flat Campground, a total of 13.5 paved miles. Continue 1.6 miles north to a very narrow pullout. For southbound travelers, the spring is 1.2 miles past Fourmile Campground. Peer over the edge; you'll spot a stairway followed by a short path winding down the steep bank to the riverside pool.

The Hot Spring

A crystal-clear soaking pool, well concealed from the nearby road, sits at the base of a steep bank on the river's edge. It's enclosed by attractive chunks of stream rock mortared tightly in place. A large slab at one end makes a backrest for enjoying the view up the tree-studded canyon. Springwater, cooling from 115°F as it trickles down the bank, spills into the opposite end of the pool from a long overhead pipe. For the past few years, there's been no easy way to divert the pipe, so the resulting toasty soak feels best on a nippy day (there's no cold water supply unless you bring along a bucket). As with all well-constructed pools, this one has a drain to make cleaning and refilling

This solidly built pool at Mile-16 Hot Spring has changed little over the years and remains a favorite for many hot springers. SALLY JACKSON

a more viable proposition. There's sometimes a bathtub-size pool just a stone's throw upstream of the main pool; it might be your cup of tea if you're after a solitary soak.

Locals refer to this spot as Mile-16 because of its strategic location on the road, which dates back to the days before the road was rerouted and paved. Back then there were more mileposts, including a Mile-16 at the pullout. The rerouting shortened the distance by nearly a mile, so forget about mileposts as clues. Whatever it's called, this is a tastefully designed pool in a great setting. Please don't abuse the privilege of using it—remember, no soap or shampoo.

76 Darling's Cabin Hot Spring

General description: A disappearing hot tub on the opposite side of the South Fork Salmon River. Skinnydippable whenever dippable.
Elevation: 4,100 feet
General location: 43 miles northeast of Cascade

GPS: N44.87327 / W115.70337
Map: Payette National Forest, East Half (spring not marked). See map on page 172.
Contact: Krassel Ranger District, Payette National Forest

Finding the hot spring: Follow the directions to FR 474/674 given in Penny Hot Spring (71). Drive north about 18 paved miles (2.5 miles past Mile-16 Hot Spring or 2.2 miles south of Camp Creek Campground). Watch for a grassy flat by the river, and park in the closest turnout. In late season you can ford nearby and follow a faint path by a small thermal stream for just over 0.1 mile up the bank.

The Hot Spring

Springwater may or may not be piped into a stock tank hidden in the woods. The soaking temperature runs around 96°F. The spring is located on an unpatented mining claim. The miners also hold the claim on the tub—and carry it away when they leave! The hike is so short that you may want to carry in a small Rubbermaid tub to guarantee a soak.

This fall soak at Darling's Cabin Hot Spring was perfectly timed, as the miners had carried the tub in the previous day. They told us they would be carrying it out again in a few days time.
SALLY JACKSON

77 Teapot Hot Spring

General description: A hot spring sandwich spread between a forest road and the South Fork Salmon River. Swimwear is vital when standing up.
Elevation: 3,950 feet
General location: 47 miles northeast of Cascade

GPS: N44.91370 / W115.72263
Map: Payette National Forest, East Half (spring not marked). See maps on pages 172 and 190.
Contact: Krassel Ranger District, Payette National Forest

Finding the hot spring: Follow the directions to FR 474/674 given in Penny Hot Spring (71). Drive north about 22 paved miles (2 miles north of Camp Creek Campground or 1 mile south of the Buckhorn Bridge) and squeeze into a narrow pullout at the south end of a long straight stretch. The spring is located just below the road.

The Hot Spring

Water issues from the riverbank at 140°F and flows or seeps into a string of small pools at the river's edge. These shallow soakers get submerged during runoff, but when the river is down, they can be cooled by shifting the rocks enclosing them. There are three strikes against Teapot that keep it in the minor leagues: lack of privacy, lack of shade, and lack of a decent soaking pool.

78 Buckhorn Hot Spring

Hike 78 To Buckhorn Hot Spring

General description: A day hike or mountain bike ride to a former easy-access soak. It's highly skinnydippable.

Difficulty: Moderate

Distance: About 10 miles round-trip

General location: 49 miles northeast of Cascade

Elevation gain: 1,000 feet

High point: 4,900 feet

GPS: N44.89696 / W115.81432

Map: Payette National Forest, East Half (spring not marked); note that the hiking trail is shown as a decommissioned road.

Restriction: As this edition went to print, there was no motorcycle access from this trailhead due to washouts over the first mile, and care is required for those on foot. Check with Krassel Ranger District on the status of the track.

Contact: Krassel Ranger District, Payette National Forest

Finding the trailhead: Follow the directions to FR 474/674 given in Penny Hot Spring (71). Drive north about 23 paved miles to Buckhorn Bridge and Trail (1 mile past Teapot). Cross the river bridge to the trailhead.

The main pool at Buckhorn Hot Spring, with the clearing beyond, makes for a good camping combo. SALLY JACKSON

Teapot Hot Spring, Buckhorn Hot Spring

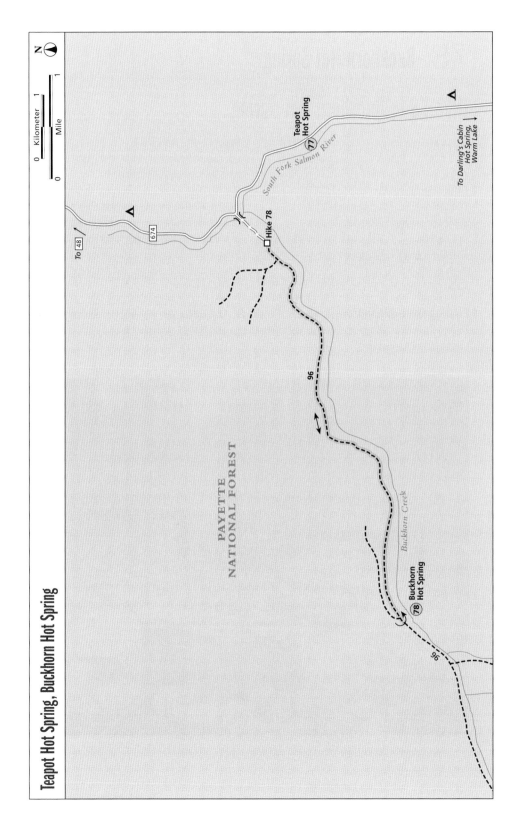

PAYETTE
NATIONAL FOREST

South Fork Salmon River

Buckhorn Creek

Teapot
Hot Spring
77

Hike 78

674

To 48

Buckhorn
Hot Spring
78

96

96

To Darling's Cabin
Hot Spring,
Warm Lake

N

0   Kilometer   1

0   Mile   1

The Hike

Go straight at the first trail junction in 0.5 mile, then bear right before the third bridge at 0.9 mile, following the main branch of Buckhorn Creek up the hill. At 5.0 miles you'll reach the signed junction with Buckhorn Cutoff. Turn around and retrace your steps about 150 yards. Look for a faint path in the woods going down to the creek. Cross on a nearby log and head 60 yards upstream across a grassy clearing to the spring. This is not a heavily frequented spring, and once you depart the main trail for the last 0.25-mile stretch, there's not much of a track. Taking along a GPS unit with the hot spring coordinates is highly recommended for first-time visitors.

The Hot Spring

Steamy water flows through a long hose and splashes into a nice pool lined with rocks in a mountain meadow above Buckhorn Creek. The temperature drops from 124°F at the source to a still toasty 106°F to 112°F in the main pool, and there's no easy way to lower it (you just have divert the flow and wait for it to cool). Nearby there's usually a smaller pool or two and also a clever shower arrangement fed by either pipe or wooden gutter over a ledge that pours on anyone standing below.

79 Cluster Hot Springs

Hike 79 To Cluster Hot Springs

General description: A short but challenging trek to an almost unknown and uncharted cluster of hot springs hidden above the opposite bank of the South Fork Salmon River. Swimwear? You gotta be kidding!

Difficulty: Strenuous and problematic

Distance: About 3.0 miles round-trip

General location: 60 miles northeast of Cascade

Elevation gain: 300 feet

High point: 3,660 feet

GPS: N45.04817 / W115.64177

Hiking quad: USGS Williams Peak

Road map: Payette National Forest, East Half (springs not marked on any map)

Restrictions: Best done when the river is low. Requires a raft and life jackets.

Contact: Krassel Ranger District, Payette National Forest

Finding the trailhead: Follow the directions to FR 474/674 given in Penny Hot Spring (71). Drive 31 paved miles to the upper end. Turn left onto the East Fork Road (Road 48) and drive 0.9 mile; then go right on FR 340 (also referred to as FR 673 or FR 674, depending on which map you're using). Drive 3.2 miles to the road-end trailhead.

Warning: This rugged little expedition is for hot spring fanatics only. What starts off as an easy stroll winds up a nearly vertical bushwhack. In between is a river crossing that's daunting even in midsummer. It shouldn't be attempted before August and could therefore be combined with the Yellow Pine Harmonica Festival (see following hike).

The Hike

Follow the South Fork Trail downstream through a narrow and scenic canyon. The path stays fairly high on the north bank all the way. You'll pass a 1-mile marker on a tree. Next, watch for a game trail in exactly 1.33 miles that plunges down the bank on soft, loose dirt. If you miss it, you'll soon spot a gravel bar below you on a left turn and can backtrack. Slip-slide down the path to the river.

The Crossing

The river is quite deep here but smooth. By midsummer a strong swimmer could make it, but a portable raft is safer and can carry your pack and shovel. Paddle directly across, aiming for a tangle of tilted logs on the bank.

The Bushwhack

Now comes the hard part. A GPS unit would come in very handy. Your goal lies 200 yards straight uphill, and the terrain is rugged and brushy. The only landmark is an olive-green patch of yew trees (visible from the main trail) that conceals the springs.

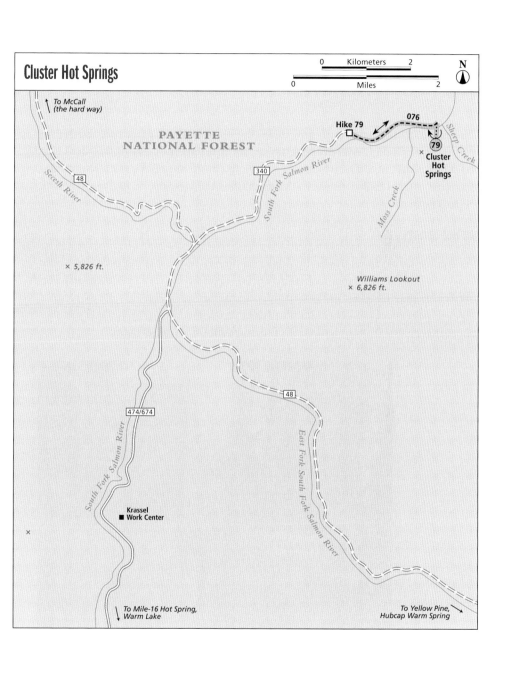

Cluster Hot Springs

0   Kilometers   2
0   Miles   2
N

To McCall
(the hard way)

PAYETTE
NATIONAL FOREST

Secesh River

48

340

South Fork Salmon River

Hike 79

076

79

Sheep Creek

Cluster
Hot
Springs

Moss Creek

× 5,826 ft.

Williams Lookout
× 6,826 ft.

48

474/674

South Fork Salmon River

East Fork South Fork Salmon River

Krassel
Work Center

×

To Mile-16 Hot Spring,
Warm Lake

To Yellow Pine,
Hubcap Warm Spring

Three separate thermal streams flow down the slope, and faint game trails work their way up, crisscrossing between them. Try a path that starts just east of the tilted logs, and when paths cross, take whichever leads you a bit to the right (west). The streams heat up as you get higher. Once you've established the locations of all three, stay with the middle one.

The Hot Springs

The middle spring flows down the slope and funnels into a soaking pool that's been dug out and lined with large rocks. The site has a panoramic view. A 4-inch-diameter pipe with a plug has been installed at the base of the dam and makes it easy to drain out even large pieces of debris. It's 5 to 6 feet across and as deep as you feel like digging; the temperature runs around 97°F. Bring a shovel for repair work.

Fall hiking to Hubcap Warm Spring SALLY JACKSON

80 Hubcap (Hot Creek) Warm Spring

Hike 80 To Hubcap Warm Spring

General description: A day hike to a tub on a hill above a backwoods airstrip; near Yellow Pine. Wear what you normally bathe in.

Difficulty: Moderate

Distance: 4.0 miles round-trip

General location: 75 miles northeast of Cascade

Elevation gain: 660 feet

High point: 5,600 feet (warm spring)

GPS: N44.89928 / W115.50540

Hiking quads: USGS Caton Lake and Yellow Pine

Road map: Frank Church Wilderness, South Half; Payette National Forest, East Half (spring marked on both maps)

Contact: Cascade Ranger District, Boise National Forest

Finding the trailhead: Follow the directions to FR 474/674 given in Penny Hot Spring (71). Drive 31 paved miles to the upper end. Turn right on the East Fork Road (Road 48) and continue 15 dusty miles to Yellow Pine. Turn right on Johnson Creek Road (FR 413) and go 4.3 miles south. Take the turnoff to the airstrip and park by the outer gate.

Worthy of note: Yellow Pine hosts an annual harmonica festival every August. There's free camping, and folks pour in days ahead to enjoy impromptu jam sessions. The place gets packed by the weekend, when the contest gets into full swing. The tiny backwoods town offers only pit-stop supplies to hungry travelers, but once a year it puts on a performance that sure feeds the soul.

The Hike

The Bryant Ranch owns a chunk of property around the airstrip. Trail access to the spring has been rerouted to bypass the ranch house, as shown on the accompanying map. (It's incorrectly marked on the USGS quad.) Walk north past the office and hangar; there's usually a caretaker around who can update you on any changes to the access. Cross the grass runway halfway down its length to a yellow sign on a tree on the far side that explains the access rules to the spring. The trail is easygoing except for the last 0.3 mile. The route heads into the woods, then winds south in a gradual climb. After a side trail forks left, the grade gets steeper and rougher. The path ends on a talus slope above Hot Creek near the base of a cliff.

The Warm Spring

High on a hillside overlooking mountains across the valley, visitors will find a bathtub nestled between boulders. Water, smelling faintly of sulfur, pours through a pipe fed from a small 99°F source 20 yards uphill. The temperature in the tub is just 95°F, but it's a soothing soak on a hot day, with acres of solitude and an unobstructed view. Hubcap may not be worth the long drive by itself, but it makes a grand finale to the Yellow Pine Harmonica Festival.

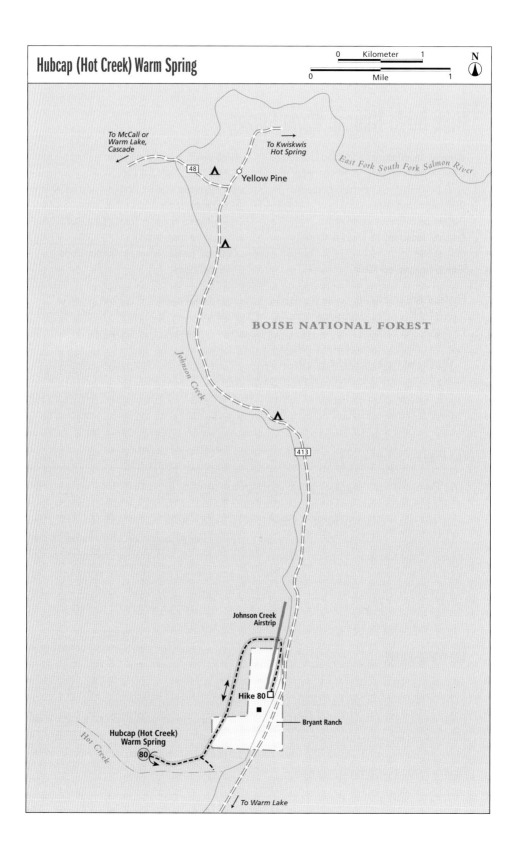

Hubcap (Hot Creek) Warm Spring

0 — Kilometer — 1

0 — Mile — 1

N

To McCall or
Warm Lake,
Cascade

To Kwiskwis
Hot Spring

East Fork South Fork Salmon River

48

Yellow Pine

Johnson Creek

BOISE NATIONAL FOREST

413

Johnson Creek
Airstrip

Hike 80

Bryant Ranch

Hubcap (Hot Creek)
Warm Spring

Hot Creek

80

To Warm Lake

Rumor has it that the bathtub at Hubcap Warm Spring was airlifted in rather than hauled by hand up the hill. MATT ROSENTHAL

Lame names

The state geothermal map labels this spring "Hot Creek," which seems like a poor choice because there are so many Hot Creeks in Idaho. Besides, this one runs pretty cold. As I lay in the tub pondering this, I glanced up at a plane taking off. The name Plane View came to mind but was soon discarded. There must be a better name out there. Then I remembered the old Chevy hubcap my tubmate once found here. Well, why not? It's a bit of a stretch, but it beats the alternatives. (Evie)

81 Kwiskwis Hot Spring

Hike 81 To Kwiskwis Hot Spring

General description: A wild and woolly overnight trek to a hot spring buried in the Frank Church Wilderness. Swimwear is nonfunctional except for sun protection.

Difficulty: Strenuous

Distance: 15.6 miles round-trip

General location: 97 miles northeast of Cascade

Elevation gain: +340 feet, -2,780 feet

High point: 8,120 feet (near trailhead)

Low point: 5,600 feet (hot springs)

GPS: N44.83095 / W115.21513

Hiking and road map: Frank Church Wilderness, South Half (spring named)

Contact: Middle Fork Ranger District, Salmon-Challis National Forest

Finding the trailhead: Follow the directions to FR 474/674 given in Penny Hot Spring (71). Drive north 31 paved miles to the upper end. Turn right onto the East Fork Road (Road 48) and proceed 15 dusty miles to Yellow Pine. This is your last chance to buy gas or anything else you might need and to check with locals on the status of Thunder Mountain Road. Continue the grind east for almost 14 miles on FR 412 to the Stibnite turnoff. Bear left, followed by a quick right onto FR 375. Climb 5.8 rocky miles toward Monumental Summit, which is open from July 1 to November 15 (if you reach the summit, you've gone about 0.25 mile too far). Watch for a primitive high-clearance road, unsigned Thunder Mountain Road (FR 640), on your right.

The ridge road winds out 3.9 miles to the trailhead on Mule Hill. Park here and walk back to the woods. Search for Trail 219 on your right (south); you'll find an overgrown path by a wooden register box and small wooden sign nailed to a tree with KIWAH MDW. AND INDIAN CR. etched into it. This is it—last chance to change your mind!

Warning: This rugged expedition is for wilderness buffs and hot springs fanatics only. The trailhead at Mule Hill, on the brink of the vast Frank Church Wilderness, is more than 70 miles from Warm Lake. The final 23 teeth-jarring miles of corrugated and rocky dirt from the closest town, Yellow Pine, are enough to test the mettle of the most determined adventurer, not to mention his or her vehicle. The primitive trail plunges downhill to a creek valley that reaches a hot spring few folks have ever heard of and fewer still have visited. If you decide to brave the trip in, you'll be rewarded with views of undulating mountains and gentle valleys, acres of solitude in a lovely creekside meadow with idyllic camping, and a guarantee that you won't have to wait in line for a soak at Kwiskwis Hot Spring.

BYO tarp: On a fall visit in 2012 there were no signs of any bathing pools. Thankfully we'd brought along a lightweight 6 × 8-foot tarp that enabled us to build a toasty two-person pool at the river's edge. Because this is a designated wilderness area, the forest service asks that you carry tarps back out again so that they don't get washed downstream come the next flood.

Kwiskwis Hot Spring spreads out a feast of hot water, and Indian Creek supplies the cold. The rare guest must furnish the only thing missing: a proper soaking pool. SALLY JACKSON

The Hike

The crude track drops down the flank of Mule Hill then plunges in earnest down a twisting ridge. In one or two places, it snakes down sloping meadows with wall-to-wall views, but for most of the 3.0-mile, 2,000-foot drop, the route is engulfed in virgin forest. After numerous lazy switchbacks, the path finally comes to rest in a peaceful valley at the junction of Indian Creek Trail (225). The creek flows southeast to join the Middle Fork Salmon River in 15 miles; Kwiskwis, at 5,600 feet, lies 4.5 miles downstream.

You'll soon reach broad Kiwah Meadow, a delightful spot to settle down for a lunch break. The path is hard to see through the knee-high grass but picks up more clearly beyond the meadow. After crossing the first side creek (Little Indian), the route climbs high above the north bank to traverse a series of precipitous talus slopes for

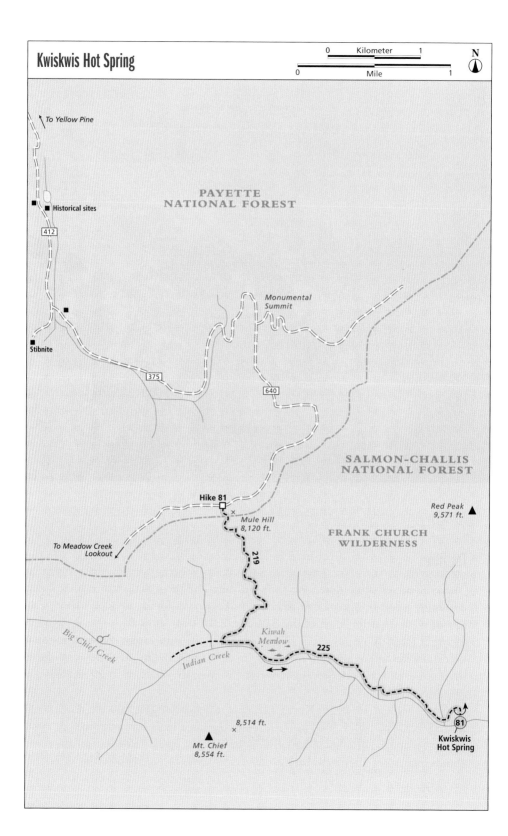

0   Kilometer   1

0   Mile   1

N

↑ To Yellow Pine

PAYETTE
NATIONAL FOREST

■ ○
■ Historical sites

412

■

■
Stibnite

Monumental
Summit

375

640

SALMON–CHALLIS
NATIONAL FOREST

Hike 81
□
×
Mule Hill
8,120 ft.

Red Peak
9,571 ft. ▲

To Meadow Creek
Lookout

219

FRANK CHURCH
WILDERNESS

Big Chief Creek ○

Kiwah
Meadow

225

Indian Creek

↔

81
Kwiskwis
Hot Spring

8,514 ft.
×

▲
Mt. Chief
8,554 ft.

the next 2.0 miles. There are also dramatic outcrops of ignimbrite rock along the way, which are the result of ancient volcanic activity. At 6.7 miles the trail crosses Indian Creek and after 0.1 mile crosses back again. It's possible to avoid these crossings by a short bushwhack down the north side of the creek. Kwiskwis Creek is 7.3 miles from the trailhead; from here it's hard to be sure of the official trail because a maze of game paths crisscross at varying heights above Indian Creek. Most are badly eroded and hard to cling to, but all lead in the same direction—downstream. After a long 7.6 miles (and it's going to seem a whole lot longer on the way out!), the trail crosses an expansive rocky slope where the primary source of Kwiskwis Hot Spring discharges more than 60 feet above the creek.

The Hot Spring

Scalding water emerges from the ground at up to 156°F but drops into the comfort zone by the time it reaches Indian Creek below. More springs appear as you follow the broad flow downhill. If you're lucky, there might be some remnants of shallow rock-lined pools where the springs meet the creek, but most likely you'll be starting from scratch—that's the price you pay for "the wilderness experience" and a steamy soak at the end of the trail. There's a small campsite across the creek, but you may prefer to camp back at Kwiskwis Creek.

Note: An element that adds even more spice to the adventure is the fact that the forest service has little firsthand information to help you. This remote area is a slice of the Frank Church "wilderness pie" held by Boise National Forest but administered by Salmon-Challis National Forest. However, the district office sits roughly 70 air miles across the state map from Mule Hill. By a series of roundabout roads, a trail crew based in Challis would have to drive a staggering 180 miles to reach the trailhead, and only 115 of them would be on pavement. The final 40 miles of dirt get progressively worse as the route travels over potholes and rock. As a result, this is one piece of wilderness that seems more than likely to remain just that!

D. Out of Crouch

Hot Springs and Hikes

Midway between Boise and Cascade on SR 55, the Banks-Lowman Highway shoots 8 miles east from Banks past the short climb to Skinnydipper (82) to the tiny town of Crouch. A back road follows the Middle Fork Payette River north of town to roadside hot dips (83–85) followed by several on hiking trails upstream (86–91). East of town are Anderson (92) and Campground Hot Springs (93) en route to Lowman. This area is in Boise National Forest.

Season

Low elevation promotes a long soaking season limited only by winter road closures north of Crouch and spring runoff in the riverside pools. Fire Crew and Moondipper are best in early summer; Rocky Canyon, Boiling Springs, and Pine Burl are usable well into the fall. Skinnydipper and Anderson are best on cooler days, while the pool at Campground Hot Springs can be enjoyed year-round. Save Groundhog and Butterfly until the river is low and Bull Creek until Silver Creek Summit is open. Summer weather runs hot and dry, but thunderstorms are not uncommon.

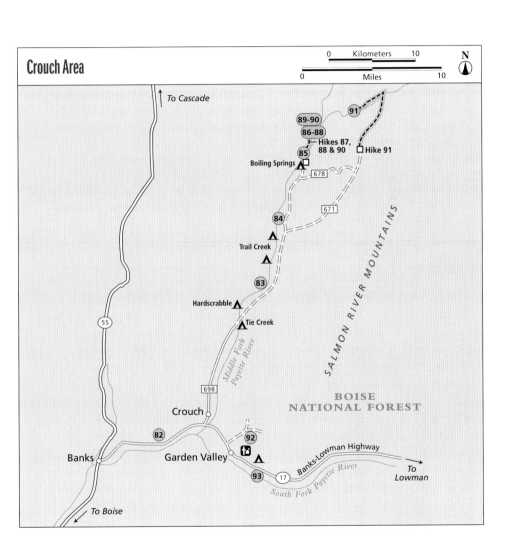

Crouch Area

Kilometers 0 — 10

Miles 0 — 10

N

To Cascade

91

89-90
86-88
Hikes 87, 88 & 90
85
Hike 91
Boiling Springs
678
671
84
Trail Creek
83
Hardscrabble
Tie Creek

55

Middle Fork Payette River

SALMON RIVER MOUNTAINS

698

Crouch

BOISE NATIONAL FOREST

82
92
Banks
Garden Valley
93   17
Banks-Lowman Highway
South Fork Payette River
To Lowman

To Boise

82 Skinnydipper Hot Spring

General description: Hot pools up a steep and hot hillside above the South Fork Payette River, reached by a 0.5-mile path that feels like a mile. Swimwear is frowned upon.
Elevation: 3,250 feet

General location: 5 miles west of Crouch
GPS: N44.09339 / W116.04920
Map: Boise National Forest (spring not marked)
Restrictions: Day use only; no fires
Contact: Boise District, BLM

Finding the hot spring: From SR 55 at Banks, take the Banks-Lowman Highway (CR 17) to a large pullout midway between Banks and Crouch at milepost 4. Walk 300 feet east and find a primitive path across the highway. Climb a short way before bearing right, which involves stepping over a cable that spans the highway. It's a brutal climb in hot weather, and the path is extremely steep and slippery. It zigzags up the hill, angles east across a dry gully, and then crosses a ridge into a wet canyon where you'll find the spring.

Note: Please stay on the path and avoid taking "shortcuts"; the trail is more vulnerable than ever to erosion after the 2012 fires swept through the area, killing most of the bushes and trees.

Nighttime closure: The BLM reports a variety of overuse and abuse problems at Skinnydipper stemming from its increasing popularity. As the problems occur mainly after dark, the milepost 4 pullout is now posted as day use only.

The Hot Spring

A waterfall cascades over a cliff and pours through a chain of pools that drops step by rocky step down the canyon floor. A complex plumbing system connects the pools. An array of pipes carries scalding water downhill from the source, while other pipes divert the excess. Custom-made valves control the flow.

At the low end of the chain is the largest pool, a good 15 feet across when filled and chest-deep if you're sitting down. It has a mortared dam, an underwater bench around one side, and two drainpipes with plugs. Cool water pours in over a ledge beside a pipe of superhot water. The temperature is fully adjustable thanks to the fancy plumbing job, although the cooler water may get scarce by summer.

Much labor went into developing this spring in the late 1990s. The entire path was user built. Heavy bags of concrete, along with everything else, had to be hauled up. The "party" pool, with its built-in ledge and drains, was dug out and dammed. Countless yards of pipe were assembled and valves fabricated. Let's thank all the contributors by taking good care of the pools and plumbing, packing out our litter, and not cutting switchbacks on the way back down.

The two upper pools at Skinnydipper Hot Spring SALLY JACKSON

83 Rocky Canyon Hot Spring

General description: Highly visible hot pools on the opposite side of the Middle Fork Payette River. Swimwear is essential when standing up.
Elevation: 3,350 feet
General location: 12.5 miles northeast of Crouch
GPS: N44.2525 / W115.8920

Map: Boise National Forest (spring marked). See map on page 203.
Restrictions: Best attempted when the river is low
Contact: Emmett Ranger District, Boise National Forest

Finding the hot spring: From SR 55 at Banks, take the Banks-Lowman Highway (CR 17) 8 miles east to Crouch (located just under a mile north of the highway). Follow FR 698 (Middle Fork Road) northeast of town. The first 8 miles are paved, but the remainder makes up for it. From Crouch go 12.5 miles (1.5 miles past Hardscrabble Campground) and park in a pullout on your left. You'll have to wade the wide river, which could be dangerous during high water.

The Hot Spring

Near the mouth of Rocky Canyon, a spring emerges at 120°F from the steep hillside and flows down to the river. Bathers have chiseled out a series of rock-lined pools well up the bank. Much cooler yet by midsummer is the shallow soaker at the river's edge. Take your pick!

The series of pools at Rocky Canyon Hot Spring provide an excellent selection of soaking temperatures. SALLY JACKSON

84　Fire Crew Hot Spring

General description: Roadside hot dips screened by woods on the Middle Fork Payette River. Keep swimwear handy.
Elevation: 3,760 feet
General location: 15 miles northeast of Crouch

GPS: N44.28188 / W115.87414
Map: Boise National Forest (spring not marked). See map on page 203.
Contact: Emmett Ranger District, Boise National Forest

Finding the hot spring: Follow the preceding directions to FR 698. Drive 15 miles (2.5 miles past Rocky Canyon Hot Spring) to a junction at Trail Creek Campground. Take the left fork (still FR 698) for 0.3 mile, then bear left on a rough spur, ending at the river in just under 0.2 mile. A loop encircles an unofficial camping area; the pools are out on a gravel bar to your right.

The Hot Spring

A few pools framed by sun-warmed rocks are concealed from the road upstream from Rocky Canyon. This site draws quite a few visitors nowadays. It's also at the river's edge, but luckily on the near side. Early in the season, the 128°F flow through the upper pools can be fine-tuned by adjusting a rock or two around the edges, but later on these pools become landlocked and get too hot for soaking. As the river drops, new pools must be built lower down the beach. It's an attractive spot and sometimes a pleasant surprise.

Some serious hot spring aficionados testing the water at Fire Crew Hot Spring
Stephanie Ensign

85 Boiling Springs

General description: Major springs and minor soaks on the Middle Fork Payette River. Nudity is a no-no if you're over age 5.
Elevation: 4,000 feet
General location: 23 miles northeast of Crouch

GPS: Upper pools, N44.36419 / W115.85670; riverside pools, N44.36249 / W115.85731
Map: Boise National Forest (springs named)
Contact: Emmett Ranger District, Boise National Forest

Finding the hot springs: Follow the directions to FR 698 given in Rocky Canyon Hot Spring (83). Drive 23 lengthy miles, past Rocky Canyon and Fire Crew Hot Springs, to the road-end campground and trailhead (0.1 mile past the campground turnoff). Stroll 0.3 mile north to find the springs flowing down a bank beside a couple of cabins. The cabins, formerly a forest service guard station, are now rented to the public for recreational use. Try to avoid the cabin area as much as possible, although it's OK to use the outhouse.

The Hot Springs

Steaming water emerges at 188°F from many fissures in a cliff just beyond the cabins, and a broad cascade streams down the hillside. One spring flows through a shallow soaking pool or two at the base. There may be some pipes diverting the hot water into the pools—remove them from the pools when you leave so that you don't create a scalding hazard for the next visitors. The water cools as it runs through a ditch across a wide meadow. A few rock-lined pools at the river's edge are usually filled on weekends with kids from the nearby campground.

Note: For information on renting the nearby cabins, check recreation.gov.

Renting a cabin at Boiling Springs for a modest fee will give you a great base for a long weekend of soaking. SALLY JACKSON

Hot Springs near Boiling Springs

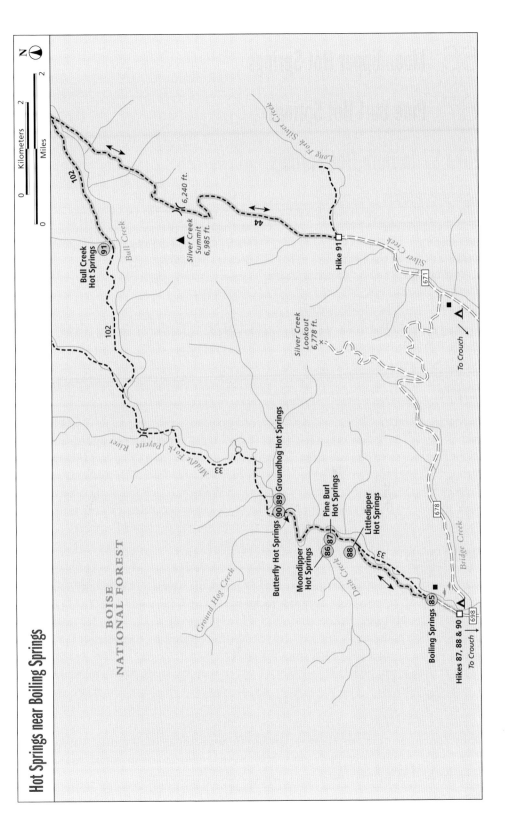

86 Moondipper Hot Springs

87 Pine Burl Hot Springs

Hike 87 To Both Hot Springs

General description: A double feature playing near the Middle Fork Payette River. A bathing suit/birthday suit mix.
Difficulty: Easy
Distance: 4.0 miles round-trip
General location: 23 miles northeast of Crouch
Elevation gain: 320 feet, -300 feet
High point: 4,120 feet (at the springs)

GPS: Moondipper, N44.38267 / W115.84072; Pine Burl, N44.38277 / W115.84151
Map: Boise National Forest (springs marked). See map on p. 209.
Contact: Emmett Ranger District, Boise National Forest

Finding the trailhead: Follow the directions given in Rocky Canyon Hot Spring (83) and Boiling Springs (85) to Boiling Springs.

The Hike

Moondipper and Pine Burl enjoy a setting worthy of their captivating names. Two separate springs at 136°F flow down the banks of a creek just above the river into a pair of scenic soakers spaced 80 yards apart along the tree-studded canyon. Both get swamped during high water but are well worth a bit of annual maintenance. The trail, steep and slippery in spots, hugs the west side of the river all the way. See following hikes for three more soaks in this catchment. **Note:** There is a low-water trail, but it's not recommended. It's overgrown, plus there are several river crossings to contend with.

The Hot Springs

When you reach Dash Creek, the first side stream on the west side, you'll find Moondipper 30 yards up the creek against a rocky bank. The large, sandy-bottomed pool can hold several happy soakers and offers a lovely view up the canyon. It's usually landlocked by midsummer and can get too hot for comfort by then without some means of transporting cold water from the creek.

Pine Burl, a gem tucked out of sight a few bends up the creek, has a pool roughly 7 to 8 feet in diameter with retaining rock walls mortared into place. The name, once inscribed on a small masonry dam at the downstream end, has eroded away, but the inspiration for it still sits up the hill on the north side. Springs perk up through the sandy bottom, but the main flow is piped in from a separate small spring. A second pipe carries stream water. Both pipes have plastic collars attached so that you can regulate the flow to easily attain your desired soaking temperature.

The soaking isn't usually as good at Moondipper Hot Springs as Pine Burl, but its setting is more picturesque. SALLY JACKSON

Hike 88 To Littledipper Hot Springs

General description: A short hike to a practically unknown rivulet of superhot water located 0.3 mile downstream from Moondipper Hot Springs. Swimwear is optional.

Difficulty: Easy

Distance: About 3.5 miles round-trip from the Boiling Springs trailhead; 0.6 mile round-trip from Moondipper

General location: 23 miles northeast of Crouch

Elevation gain: 300 feet, -280 feet

High point: 4,140 feet (at the springs)

GPS: N44.37924 / W115.84394

Map: Boise National Forest (springs not marked). See map on page 209.

Contact: Emmett Ranger District, Boise National Forest

Finding the trailhead: Follow the directions given in Moondipper Hot Springs (86) and then read on.

The Hike

A GPS is recommended to track down this hidden spring; otherwise your best bet is to backtrack downstream from Moondipper (see previous spring directions) for 0.3 mile. This is where a tiny creek, the outflow of Littledipper Hot Springs, crosses the trail. Follow this upstream as best you can for 350 feet (it's pretty brushy). The source is among the trees, and there's a large meadow nearby.

The Hot Springs

The springs issue out of an unassuming hole in the ground at an impressive 157°F. In fall 2012 there were few signs of human visitation, just some remnants of log dams and tarps in the channel of the outflow. The trick to creating a successful soak here will be to dam a pool far enough downstream from the source for the scalding water to have air-cooled, as there's no cold water nearby. You'll also need to make it watertight; the flow is not generous enough to allow for too much leakage.

89 Groundhog Hot Springs

90 Butterfly Hot Springs

Hike 90 To Both Hot Springs

General description: A very wet, late-season day hike to two lonesome soaks on the Middle Fork Payette River. Swimwear is superfluous.

Difficulty: Easy grade, but primitive path with nine river fords

Distance: About 7.0 miles round-trip from Boiling Springs

General location: 23 miles northeast of Crouch

Elevation gain: 450 feet, -300 feet

High point: 4,180 feet (at the springs)

GPS: N44.39223 / W115.83414 (Groundhog); N44.394874 / W115.83473 (Butterfly)

Hiking quads: USGS Boiling Springs and Bull Creek Hot Springs

Road map: Boise National Forest (springs marked on both maps). See map on page 209.

Restrictions: Should be done when the river is low

Contact: Emmett Ranger District, Boise National Forest

Finding the trailhead: Follow the directions in Rocky Canyon Hot Spring (83) and Boiling Springs (85) to Boiling Springs.

The Hike

This trip combines the 2.0-mile stroll to Moondipper and Pine Burl described in Hike 87 with a 1.3-mile extension upstream to access Groundhog Hot Springs and another 0.2 mile to Butterfly Hot Springs—a total of 3.5 miles. Shortly beyond Dash Creek, the Middle Fork Trail (Trail 33) crosses the river twice in quick succession. It snakes back and forth a total of nine times en route. There's little foot traffic beyond Moondipper and Pine Burl, so the route is fairly brushy. Watch for Ground Hog Creek on the west (far) bank shortly before the eighth ford. Right after this crossing, the river makes a horseshoe bend to the right. Cross one last time to find the hot springs in the center of the curve on the east bank. You may not spot the rock-lined pool(s) from the far side, but you'll see the hot water flowing down to them. Butterfly Hot Springs is another 0.2 mile upstream on the same side as Groundhog.

Note: The Middle Fork Trail is not the best way to reach Bull Creek Hot Springs, which lies another 7.7 miles upstream—it's overgrown and involves at least fifteen river crossings. On the up side, this route passes 122°F Goat Hot Springs, located by a campsite (N44.39988 / W115.82081) often used by hunters. The recommended route is via the Silver Creek Trail (see following hike).

The Hot Springs

At Groundhog, steamy water ranging up to 140°F at the source flows some 20 feet down the bank, cooling en route, into the remnants of a soaking pool or two at the river's edge that should surface by midsummer. The temperature can be fine-tuned by adjusting rocks in the dam; but as the river recedes, it gets harder to funnel in. The pool gets little use or maintenance, so come prepared to do some excavation on the floor and patchwork on the walls.

Before starting any pool construction here, you'll probably want to check out Butterfly Hot Springs upstream, which may have better soaking potential. When the river is low enough, there's sometimes a nice rock-lined pool wedged between the swift flow of the river and a hot spring showering down a rocky cliff. As is often the case, a tarp may come in handy here. There's some level ground for camping in the forest upstream. When the popular pools downstream are in use, rest assured you won't have to wait in line for a soak at Groundhog or Butterfly.

Groundhog Hot Springs is one of the more low-key set of springs out of the many that line the scenic Middle Fork Payette River. SALLY JACKSON

91 Bull Creek Hot Springs

Hike 91 To Bull Creek Hot Springs

General description: A backpack to a far-flung dip near the Middle Fork Payette River. There's no need to pack a swimsuit.
Difficulty: Strenuous
Distance: About 21 miles round-trip
General location: 26 miles northeast of Crouch
Elevation gain: +1,540 feet, -1,280 feet
High point: 6,240 feet (Silver Creek Summit)
Hot spring elevation: 5,120 feet

GPS: N44.42864 / W115.76300
Hiking quads: USGS Bull Creek Hot Springs and Wild Buck Peak
Road map: Boise National Forest (springs named on both maps). See maps on pages 203 and 209.
Contact: Emmett Ranger District, Boise National Forest

Finding the trailhead: Follow the directions to Trail Creek Campground given in Fire Crew Hot Spring (84). Bear right on Silver Creek Road (FR 671) and drive 12 miles to the road-end trail sign, 2 miles beyond the guard station. Motorcycles are allowed on the trail.

The Hike

Silver Creek Trail offers a far drier, more scenic, and slightly shorter approach to Bull Creek than the wet trek up the Middle Fork described above, but minus the hot springs en route. You'll gain an extra 1,300 feet climbing over Silver Creek Summit, but the views along the trail make up for it.

Two trails begin here. Be sure to take Silver Creek Trail (44) and not the one branching off to your right. Follow the route over Silver Creek Summit at 6,240 feet, enjoy the broad views, then drop down the far side to reach Bull Creek at 7.8 miles, a pleasant spot to spend the night. Cross the creek and watch for the Bull Creek Trail (102). Turn left and follow it 2.7 miles downstream above the north bank of Bull Creek. As you zero in, the trail drops steeply to bridge a small stream, then reaches another with no bridge. Look 30 feet uphill to spot your target, and scramble up to reach the springs (at 5,200 feet) on a granite bluff overlooking the canyon.

The Hot Springs

These remote springs located high above Bull Creek may or may not have a bather-friendly pool to greet you just when you need a hot soak. Immediately above the trail is a hump of exposed bedrock with water running over it from several 128°F sources. In the center is a small ledge, where there's likely to be the remnants of a small soaking pool. Bring a tarp, and be prepared to earn your soak; these pools don't see many visitors. Consider bringing a hammock, as there are no flat spots nearby for tents.

This is what we found at Bull Creek Hot Springs in fall 2013. Laying a tarp into the depression created a decent two-person soak. SALLY JACKSON

Note: On a cool morning we saw steam issuing from a rocky outcrop on the other side of the valley. It looked like a destination best suited to mountain goats. Please let us know if anyone figures out how to reach these springs (nzhotsprings@gmail.com).

92 Anderson Hot Spring

General description: A hot pool screened by trees in a creek canyon, near a dirt road. Keep swimwear handy.
Elevation: 3,200 feet
General location: 2 miles northeast of Garden Valley
GPS: N44.10295 / W115.92906

Map: Boise National Forest (spring not marked). See map on page 203.
Restrictions: This privately owned spring has a long history of public use, but this access could change. The parcel of land including the spring was for sale when this edition went to print.
Contact: Emmett Ranger District, Boise National Forest

Finding the hot spring: From SR 55 at Banks, take the Banks-Lowman Highway (CR 17) east to Garden Valley. Turn left just west of town onto Granite Basin Road (FR 668). Bear right at a junction in 2 miles onto Anderson Creek Road (FR 669). The road soon dips to bridge the creek. Park wherever you can find space, and follow a 0.1-mile path on the north bank downstream to the pool.

This secluded little pool at Anderson Hot Spring is just far enough off the beaten track.
Evie Litton

One lost and another found

While looking for a sandal that had disappeared in the night from under the truck (what critters eat shoes?), I stumbled across another spring located in a meadow on the opposite bank. It's best accessed from the road. Cross the bridge and veer left toward the creek to where there's a small 109°F pool that has potential (GPS: N44.10351 / W115.92899). (Sally)

The Hot Spring

Users have dug out a soaking pool lined with cinder blocks in the bank above Anderson Creek. Hot water bubbles up through the sandy bottom, but because there's not a strong flow, the water gets murky after heavy use. There's morning shade, but in the afternoon both the water and the air temperature tend to get a bit too toasty for comfortable soaking. The site is just outside the forest boundary on Boise Cascade property but is open to the public as long as it's treated with respect. Remember: No glass containers, no soap or shampoo, and please pack out what you pack in.

The small meadow pool at Anderson Hot Spring
Sally Jackson

93 Campground Hot Springs

General description: A popular soak between a highway campground and the South Fork Payette River. Swimwear is a must.
Elevation: 3,100 feet
General location: 6 miles southeast of Crouch

GPS: N44.05410 / W115.90811
Map: Boise National Forest (springs marked). See map on page 203.
Contact: Emmett Ranger District, Boise National Forest

Finding the hot springs: From SR 55 at Banks, take the Banks-Lowman Highway (CR 17) east, past Garden Valley, to Hot Springs Campground near milepost 14. There's a pullout on the bank, and a slippery 300-foot path leads down to the pool.

The Hot Springs

A comfortable soaker big enough for a family group has been dug out of the bank well above the river. The shallow pool offers a toasty soak year-round courtesy of a shower pipe that transports the flow from the 111°F springs. At the river's edge you may find one or more seasonal dips not far from a concrete slab that once supported a public bathhouse.

With its easy access, Campground Hot Springs is jumping during the summer months, but often deserted come fall. SALLY JACKSON

E. Out of Lowman

Hot Springs and Hikes

The Banks–Lowman Highway (CR 17) reaches hot pools at Pine Flats (94) on the South Fork Payette River. Then, SR 21 passes easy-access soaks at Kirkham (95) near Lowman en route to Tenmile (96) and Bonneville (97). Next, Sacajawea (98) leads hikers into the western Sawtooths. In the wilderness to the north is a hike to Bear Valley (99) and a backpack to Trail Flat (100) and Sheepeater (101) on the Middle Fork Salmon River, with a bonus dip at Dagger Creek (102) near the trailhead. New to this edition is Deadwood (103), northwest of Lowman, which is most commonly accessed from the Banks–Lowman Highway.

Season

Although early summer through fall is the prime time, the uppermost pools at Pine Flats, Kirkham, and Bonneville are usable all year. Spring runoff buries Tenmile and Sacajawea and prevents access to Bear Valley before late summer. The rest can be enjoyed whenever the roads are open, but the trek down the Middle Fork is best after July. The hiking season in the high Sawtooths generally runs from late July through mid-September. Summer weather tends to be hot with occasional thunderstorms and with cold nights at higher elevations.

Note: The only services near Lowman are the district ranger station and a few highway pit stops offering gas, meals, and very limited supplies.

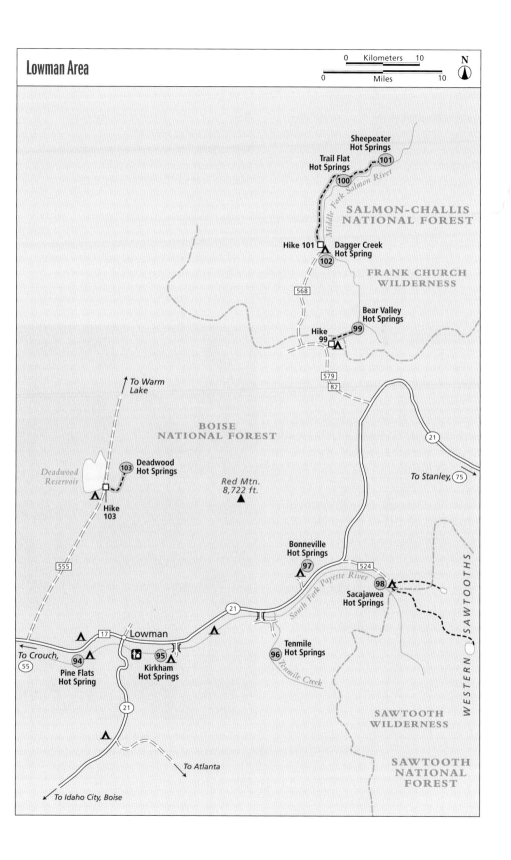

Lowman Area

Kilometers 10
Miles 10
N

Sheepeater
Hot Springs
101

Trail Flat
Hot Springs
100

Middle Fork Salmon River

SALMON-CHALLIS
NATIONAL FOREST

Hike 101
Dagger Creek
Hot Spring
102

FRANK CHURCH
WILDERNESS

568

Bear Valley
Hot Springs
99

Hike
99

To Warm
Lake

579

82

BOISE
NATIONAL FOREST

21

*Deadwood
Reservoir*

103
Deadwood
Hot Springs

Hike
103

To Stanley 75

Red Mtn.
8,722 ft.

555

Bonneville
Hot Springs
97

524

South Fork Payette River

98
Sacajawea
Hot Springs

WESTERN SAWTOOTHS

21

To Crouch,
55

17

Lowman

94

Pine Flats
Hot Spring

95

Kirkham
Hot Springs

Tenmile
96 Hot Springs

Tenmile Creek

SAWTOOTH
WILDERNESS

21

SAWTOOTH
NATIONAL
FOREST

To Atlanta

To Idaho City, Boise

94 Pine Flats Hot Spring

General description: Hot dips and cliffside showers near a family campground, on the South Fork Payette River. Bathing suits are required.
Elevation: 3,600 feet
General location: 5 miles west of Lowman
GPS: N44.06038 / W115.68886 (waterfall pool)

Map: Boise National Forest (campground named but spring not marked)
Restrictions: Day-use parking fee required. Signs state NO NUDITY, PETS OR GLASS.
Contact: Lowman Ranger District, Boise National Forest

Finding the hot spring: Pine Flats Campground is located below the Banks-Lowman Highway (CR 17), 5.7 miles west of Lowman and 28 miles east of Banks. Drive down and park at the west end by the fee station. Follow the signed path 0.4 mile downstream to a gravel bar. Look for the hottest pools on paths that wind up the back side of a cliff; cooler soaks at the bottom.

The Hot Spring

There's usually a pool 20 feet above the river on the downstream side of the geothermal outcrop and another up near the top. Both are big enough to pack a couple of human sardines side by side—and hot enough to cook them. Most of the springs are issuing out of the rocky hillside at 140°F, so take care with bare feet, and so on. Cooler pools at the bottom collect the runoff, and a large swimming hole at the river's edge adds the final touch. Those who prefer more privacy can wade along the base of the cliff in late summer to find yet another hot pool with a shower hidden in the rocks just around the bend.

This waterfall-fed pool at Pine Flats Hot Spring would be more popular except that it's often inaccessible until late summer, when the river level has fallen. SALLY JACKSON

95 Kirkham Hot Springs

General description: Hot waterfalls and pools below a highway campground on the South Fork Payette River. Swimwear is a must.
Elevation: 4,000 feet
General location: 4 miles east of Lowman
GPS: N44.07251 / W115.54545

Map: Boise National Forest (campground named but springs not marked). See map on page 221.
Restrictions: Day-use parking fee required. Signs state No Nudity, Pets or Glass.
Contact: Lowman Ranger District, Boise National Forest

Finding the hot springs: Drive 4.3 miles east of Lowman on SR 21. Cross the bridge to Kirkham Campground, and park at the west end. The forest service collects a day-use fee, but penny-pinchers can park outside and walk in. Follow a short path down to the river.

This edition's coauthor enjoys one of the many soaking options at Kirkham Hot Springs.
SALLY JACKSON

The Hot Springs

In plain view below the highway, these popular pools are frequently filled with boisterous teenagers and large family groups. All the pools are down by the river, with the exception of a couple of often-overlooked pools up near the parking area. The bedrock pools down by the river, interspersed with steaming showers from the 135°F springs, come in all sizes, shapes, and temperatures. Kids of all ages love to leap off the rocks into deep holes in the river, and older folks lie scattered about on boulders, dozing in the sun. For a bit more privacy, you might find a small pool or two under the bridge. The adjacent campground adds to the congestion here; it's usually Winnebago City on summer weekends. It's worth it to try early mornings or the off-season months.

Note: The once-wooded hills around Kirkham were devastated by a severe windstorm in addition to the 1989 Lowman Fire, but it's not clear what hit this area hardest—wind, fire, or the recent boom in tourism. The forest service now enforces strict rules on everything from swimwear and user fees at the hot springs to primitive camping, allowed only in designated sites, along the crowded river corridor between Pine Flats and Bonneville Hot Springs.

96 Tenmile Hot Springs

General description: Creekside soaks on an abandoned road near the South Fork Payette River. Swimwear is first come, first served.
Elevation: 4,700 feet
General location: 15 miles east of Lowman

GPS: N44.09772 / W115.37672
Map: Boise National Forest (springs not marked). See map on page 221.
Contact: Lowman Ranger District, Boise National Forest

Finding the hot springs: Take SR 21 about 13 miles east of Lowman or 8.5 miles past Kirkham to a turnoff between mileposts 85 and 86. Bridge the river and then immediately bear left onto Tenmile Road (FR 531). Stay on this dirt road, ignoring any turnoffs, including Tenmile Creek Road to the right. Follow Tenmile Road upstream to a bridge washout, 2.3 miles from SR 21; park where you can.

Cross the creek and continue on foot. You'll pass a spot where the creek takes a huge bite out of the old road, but this can be skirted with care. When you reach a grassy strip, you'll notice a thermal stream alongside the creek. Follow the flow upstream to its source. Tenmile is 0.5 mile from your car.

The Hot Springs

Users have built a toasty pool within the thermal stream. It's usable during the runoff, but it's shallow, usually lined with plastic, and runs a tad hot. Not far upstream there's a separate source right by the creek, and by midsummer a soaking pool or two will surface. Users dig a ditch from the creek to lower the temperature and must rebuild the pool(s) and the ditch each year after the runoff. Visitors bring a shovel or take potluck in this poor man's alternative to Bonneville.

There's often a good creekside pool by midsummer at Tenmile Hot Springs. SALLY JACKSON

97 Bonneville Hot Springs

General description: Private bathing and communal soaking in a scenic canyon, very near a popular family campground. Nude bathing permitted in bathhouse only.
Elevation: 4,700 feet
General location: 19 miles northeast of Lowman
GPS: N44.15668 / W115.31412 (bathhouse)

Map: Boise National Forest (springs named). See map on page 221.
Restrictions: Day-use parking fee required. Signs state: No Nudity, Pets or Glass.
Contact: Lowman Ranger District, Boise National Forest

Finding the hot springs: Follow SR 21 about 19 miles northeast of Lowman or 6 miles past Tenmile to Bonneville Campground. Park at the far end and follow a creekside path 0.3 mile north to the springs.

The Hot Springs

There is no time a hot soak is more welcome than right after a cold hike. The relief is immediate and the contrast between hike and soak unforgettable. Bonneville is a haven, especially if you are just off the trail. An aging bathhouse straddles the outflow, and hoses channel hot water into a bathtub that you can drain and refill after each use. Your clothes stay dry while your tired body gets wet.

The springs check in at temperatures up to 185°F. They flow past the bathhouse and tumble directly over a rocky cliff into a chain of pools that line one arm of Warm Spring Creek. There's also a secluded waterfall pool or two upstream. The bathhouse at Bonneville is usable year-round and accessible in winter by cross-country skiers. The off-season months are the only time for a quiet soak at this all too popular retreat.

The bathhouse perched high near the sources at Bonneville Hot Springs guarantees a soak when the creek is in flood. Sally Jackson

98 Sacajawea Hot Springs

General description: Roadside hot dips on the South Fork Payette River, near the Grandjean Trailhead into the Sawtooths. Swimwear is a smart idea.
Elevation: 5,000 feet
General location: 26 miles northeast of Lowman

GPS: N44.16011 / W115.17797
Map: Boise National Forest (springs not marked). See map on page 221.
Contact: Lowman Ranger District, Boise National Forest

Finding the hot springs: Drive 21 miles northeast of Lowman or 2 miles past Bonneville on SR 21 and turn right onto graded FR 524, signed to Grandjean. Drive 4.7 miles. Pass Waipiti Creek Bridge turnoff (on your right) and continue straight for 0.6 mile. Park wherever you can find space, and climb down the rocks to the pools.

The Hot Springs

A number of soaker-friendly pools line a beach along the scenic river. The outflow from several springs, at temperatures up to 153°F, cools as it fans out down the bank. Fine-tune the pool temperatures by adding river water. Another welcome refuge for weary hikers, Sacajawea is located just 1 mile from one of the principal gateways into the Sawtooths. You couldn't ask for a nicer finish to any hike.

There's a chain of hot pools to enjoy at Sacajawea Hot Springs. Sally Jackson

99 Bear Valley Hot Springs

Hike 99 To Bear Valley Hot Springs

General description: A day hike or overnighter to a chain of pearls locked up in the Frank Church Wilderness. Swimwear is a mixed bag.

Difficulty: Easy except for a major stream ford

Distance: About 7.0 miles round-trip

General location: 45 miles northeast of Lowman; 29 miles northwest of Stanley

Elevation gain: +160 feet, -320 feet

High point: 6,360 feet (trailhead)

GPS: N44.4449 / W115.2395 (upstream pools); N44.4452 / W115.2383 (downstream pools)

Hiking and road map: Frank Church Wilderness, South Half (springs marked)

Restrictions: The main trail can only be attempted when the creek is running low.

Contact: Lowman Ranger District, Boise National Forest

Finding the trailhead: On SR 21, drive 37 miles northeast of Lowman or 21 miles northwest of Stanley. Turn west between mileposts 109 and 110 onto FR 82/579, signed to Bruce Meadows and Boundary Creek. At 8 miles a sign marks the turnoff to Fir Creek Campground. Turn right here, proceed 0.2 mile, and then take the left fork that soon ends at the trailhead beside Fir Creek Pack Bridge.

The Hike

Bear Valley Creek has a claim to fame apart from its hot springs. It joins Marsh Creek downstream to become the headwaters of the Middle Fork Salmon River. Cross the bridge onto Marsh Creek Trail (12). Follow the creek east for the first 1.5 miles, then watch for a spot in the second large meadow where the trail seems to disappear. It will reappear across the creek. This ford would be suicidal during high water—the stream is fast, a good 20 yards wide, and the footing is treacherous. It's also over knee-deep through mid-August.

After the ford the path winds through a tangle of lodgepole pines strewn about on the ground like an oversized child's game of pickup sticks. Cross three streams, then watch for a tree on your left at about 3.5 miles that bears an old yellow forest service sign that reads PUBLIC SERVICE SITE. Take your choice of faint paths winding down the steep slope. If the trail brings you to another major creek crossing, you've gone 0.2 mile too far.

Don't be discouraged when you reach the bottom and find only one murky, ankle-deep pool filled with algae. Stroll a ways downstream to a larger flow, and track it past a forested campsite to a chain of pools dropping step by step to the creek's edge.

An alternate route saves fording the creek as well as 0.5 mile of walking. It's a primitive path that follows the south bank from Fir Creek Campground to the point where the forest service trail crosses over. The catch is that it's badly eroded as it

One of the more impressive pools at Bear Valley Hot Springs Sally Jackson

traverses a slippery stretch well up the steep bank. It's not a route for small children or anyone afraid of heights. The prudent choice would be to hold off until late August and take the official trail.

The Hot Springs

There are two distinct sets of springs located about 100 yards apart, both with high flows and source temperatures of around 145°F. A faint trail is likely to bring you first to a tiered set of pools on an open rock-strewn hillside. All but the lowest of these are usually too hot for soaking.

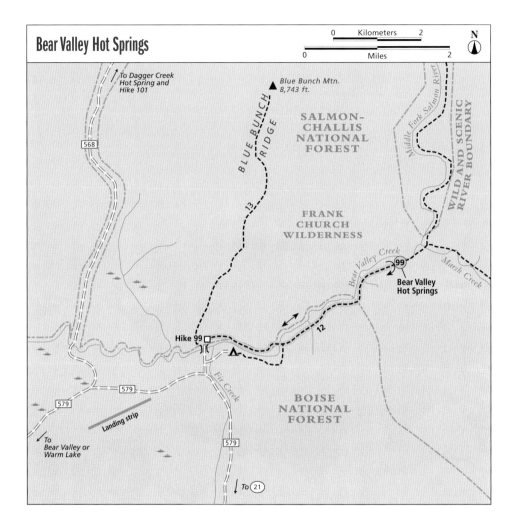

Downstream you'll find the best springs, with a hot stream and several large creekside pools. You can adjust the temperature in the lower pools by shifting the rocks around. But watch out for those nasty little red mites. They've been multiplying around here lately (see page 6 for information and advice on dealing with spider mites).

There are plenty of opportunities for primitive camping in the area. As this is a protected wilderness area, camping should be at least 200 feet from any water source.

100 Trail Flat Hot Springs

101 Sheepeater Hot Springs

Hike 101 To Both Hot Springs

General description: A backpack to a double bubble in the Middle Fork Salmon River Canyon. Public nudity is prohibited within the river corridor.
Difficulty: Strenuous
Distance: About 28 miles round-trip
General location: 60 miles northeast of Lowman; 44 miles northwest of Stanley
Elevation gain: +500 feet, -1,100 feet

High point: 5,800 feet (trailhead)
GPS: N44.60860 / W115.26926 (Trail Flat Hot Springs; 5,400 feet elevation); N44.62807 / W115.19823 (Sheepeater Hot Springs; 5,150 feet elevation)
Hiking and road map: Frank Church Wilderness, South Half (only Sheepeater is marked)
Contact: Middle Fork Ranger District, Salmon-Challis National Forest

Finding the trailhead: Follow the preceding road access but continue past the Fir Creek turnoff for another 1.6 miles. Turn right (north) on FR 568 and drive 10 miles to a junction near the end. The right fork goes to Dagger Creek Hot Spring (see following hike); and the left fork goes 0.6 mile to Boundary Creek Trailhead, 20 dusty miles from SR 21. Boundary Creek Campground is another 0.1 mile at the end of the road, where there is also day parking and access to the trailhead. The forest service has someone on duty there all summer. Directions given are from the large parking area 0.1 mile before reaching the campground.

The Hike

Two remote hot springs lie 6 miles apart near the upper end of the Middle Fork Salmon River. The streamside soaks at Trail Flat are submerged at high water but should be fine by midsummer, while Sheepeater's secluded dips lie on a rocky terrace well above the river's grasp. The 100-mile-long river, the only navigable stream of such length in the Northwest where powerboats are banned, lies within the National Wild and Scenic Rivers system of the Frank Church Wilderness.

The route to both springs follows the west side of the river downstream from Boundary Creek, a launch site where rafts splash down over a 100-foot-high ramp. By early to mid-August, the rafts are flown to a lower put-in at Indian Creek. From this time on, the hot pools and nearby campsites should be deserted and the trail high and dry above the river. The access road is open until mid-October.

For the first mile or so, the Middle Fork Trail (1) winds through burnt wooded hills, passing side trails at Sulphur and Prospect Creeks. It reaches the river at 4 miles then crosses Ramshorn Creek. The bridge was dismantled in 2011—check with the

Checking out the upstream pool at Trail Flat Hot Springs MATT ROSENTHAL

forest service on their plans to replace it and also another at Elkhorn Creek. The path briefly hugs the river, then climbs well up the bank. As it traverses this slope, it seems to drape loosely from the base of one anchoring tree to the next like a Christmas tree chain drooping from bough to bough. There are no views until you reach an open hill above Trail Flat. Drop down a rocky slope to reach the campsites at 8 miles (elevation 5,400 feet). The pools lie along the rocky beach just below.

The 12-mile round-trip from Trail Flat to Sheepeater is the most scenic stretch of the hike; you can complete it in one long day with ample time to enjoy the soaking pools at both ends. The route stays close to the river much of the way, and when it climbs, it keeps the river in sight. Hills wooded with tall ponderosa pines alternate with boulder-strewn slopes, and there are many pleasant views up and down the canyon.

About a mile below Trail Flat, the path drops to ford Elkhorn Creek. It climbs and then dips again to cross Deer Horn Creek. When you pass Joe Bump's log cabin, followed by a grave marked ELMER SET TRIGGER PURCELL, PROSPECTOR/TRAPPER, 1936, you'll be in the homestretch. Sheepeater's springs are in an open area off to your left at 14 miles. There's a large camp by the river and another in a clearing just above.

The Hot Springs

Trail Flat usually has one large, 110°F pool at the downstream end of the 300-foot-long rocky beach. The steamy outflow runs through several increasingly cooler

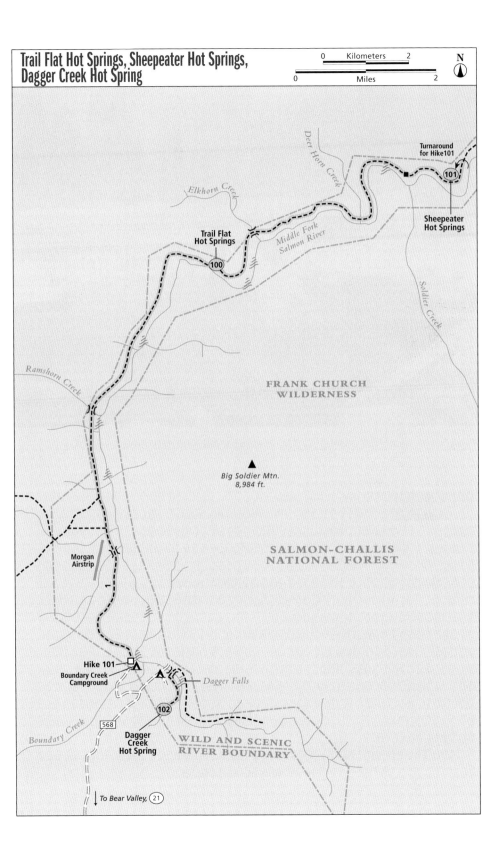

0   Kilometers   2

0   Miles   2

N

Deer Horn Creek

Turnaround
for Hike 101

101

Sheepeater
Hot Springs

Elkhorn Creek

Trail Flat
Hot Springs

100

*Middle Fork
Salmon River*

Soldier Creek

Ramshorn Creek

FRANK CHURCH
WILDERNESS

▲
Big Soldier Mtn.
8,984 ft.

SALMON-CHALLIS
NATIONAL FOREST

Morgan
Airstrip

1

Hike 101

Boundary Creek
Campground

Dagger Falls

102

Boundary Creek

568

Dagger
Creek
Hot Spring

WILD AND SCENIC
RIVER BOUNDARY

To Bear Valley, 21

One of several scenic pools awaiting the dedicated hiker at Sheepeater Hot Springs SALLY JACKSON

soaking pools fanning out to the river's edge. The sizes and shapes vary, as users have to scoop out new pools each year after the spring runoff. On a visit in 2012, this large pool had red spider mites, so we scooped out a bug-free soak at the smaller set of springs at the other end of the beach (see page 6 for information and advice on dealing with spider mites).

At Sheepeater you'll find a few soaking pools tucked up against the tree line on the far side of a damp, rock-strewn clearing that must be crossed to reach them. From the source pool, which runs 115°F, the outflow drops in steps and fans out into the marsh below. The soaking pools sit on rocky terraces beneath the source, each just a tad cooler than the one above. There's ample flow to keep them clean, but the flow also keeps them pretty toasty. In the center of the clearing, about 150 feet away from these pools, is a pool measuring 10 × 12 foot and 1 foot deep, with the source bubbling from its sandy center at 108°F. There's likely to be some dammed-up warm pools in the hot spring outflow about 0.1 mile away (just before it reaches the river).

Note: These hot springs receive high use during the early float season. Please treat them with TLC and use low-impact camping techniques.

102 Dagger Creek Hot Spring

General description: A peaceful soak near the trailhead for Trail Flat and Sheepeater. Swimwear is optional.
Elevation: 5,800 feet
General location: 60 miles northeast of Lowman; 44 miles northwest of Stanley

GPS: N44.52327 / W115.28389
Hiking and road map: Frank Church Wilderness, South Half (spring not marked). See map on page 233.
Contact: Middle Fork Ranger District, Salmon-Challis National Forest

Finding the hot spring: Follow the preceding road access to the junction near the end of FR 568. Take the right fork and proceed 0.7 mile to Dagger Falls Campground, where there's an information board and trailhead register. It's a hop, skip, and a jump down to the bridge. Don't cross it; instead veer right and follow an extremely faint trail upstream along the Middle Fork Salmon River (after 0.2 mile it sidles 30 feet above the river for a stretch). Hike a total 0.5 mile from the trailhead to the mouth of Dagger Creek, and then follow the creek 200 yards upstream to the pool.

The Hot Spring

This little dip has a double distinction. It's the only hot spring in the Frank Church Wilderness that doesn't require a rugged hike to reach. It's also the only one you can plop your tired body into right after a lengthy hike to other geothermal delights. It lies just within both the wilderness and the Wild and Scenic River boundaries and less than 1 mile from a quiet backwoods campground.

Dagger Creek Hot Spring perks up through the silty bottom of a rock-lined pool in the grass along the creek bank. The pool is shallow and barely big enough for a cozy couple to stretch out in, but the temperature, at a toasty 106°F, is hard to beat. It offers a handy remedy for stiff muscles after the trek to Trail Flat and Sheepeater.

103 Deadwood Hot Springs

Hike 103 To Deadwood Hot Springs

General description: Relatively unknown springs reached by a rugged and scenic drive followed by a pleasant day hike. You're unlikely to need a swimsuit.
Difficulty: Moderate
Distance: 7.0 miles round-trip
General location: 39 miles northwest of Lowman
Elevation gain: 400 feet, -100 feet
High point: 5,500 feet (at springs)

GPS: N44.30394 / W115.61303 (lower springs); N44.30451 / W115.61178 (upper springs)
Hiking quads: USGS Deadwood Reservoir and Whitehawk Mountain
Road map: Boise National Forest (springs not marked). See map on page 221.
Contact: Lowman Ranger District, Boise National Forest

Finding the trailhead: On SR 21, drive 10.6 miles west of Lowman (4.9 miles west of Pine Flats or 23 miles east of Banks) and turn north onto unpaved Scott Mountain Road (FR 555). After 9.8 miles of climbing, this road passes the turnoff to Scott Lookout. At 24 miles you'll pass Cozy Cove Campground and reach Deadwood Reservoir. Proceed 1 more mile; the signed Whitehawk Basin #199 Trailhead is immediately to the right after the bridge that crosses Deadwood River below the dam.

Note: There's also road access to the trailhead from the north (55 unpaved miles from Yellow Pine and 40 mostly unpaved miles from the Warm Lake area) via Deadwood Summit.

The Hike

Follow Deadwood River downstream for 1.25 miles, then turn left to follow Warm Springs Creek upstream in a northeasterly direction. At 2.25 miles, take the left fork (avoiding the trail that crosses the creek). After 3.3 miles you'll reach the first set of springs, which are positioned by the creek in an alcove at the downstream end of a giant granite mound.

The larger of the two rock-and-mortar pools tucked out of sight at Deadwood Hot Springs SALLY JACKSON

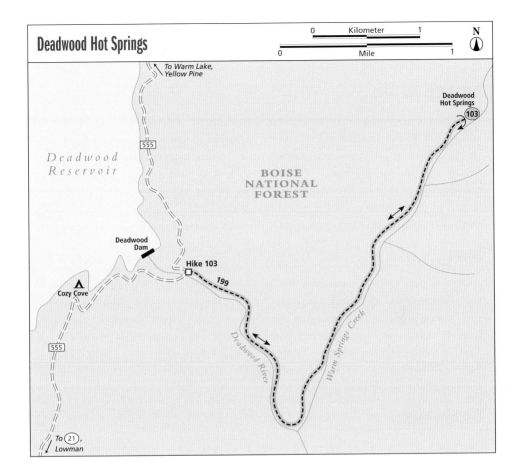

Deadwood Hot Springs

To Warm Lake, Yellow Pine

Deadwood Hot Springs

103

555

Deadwood Reservoir

BOISE NATIONAL FOREST

Deadwood Dam

Hike 103

199

Cozy Cove

555

Deadwood River

Warm Springs Creek

To 21, Lowman

The Hot Springs

The main soaking pools are located another 500 feet away near the upstream end of the granite mound. They can be reached by clambering up and around the mound or by crossing the creek a couple of times. Two rock-and-mortar pools have been ingeniously constructed side by side on a narrow ledge overlooking the creek. They are above the flood zone, and each is fed by a labyrinth of pipes connected to the many springs above, some reaching temperatures of close to 150°F. Both pools have outlet pipes for draining and cleaning. One pool is about 20 × 5 feet and 3 feet deep; the other is roughly circular and about a third this size.

F. Out of Atlanta

Hot Springs and Hikes

The Atlanta Trailhead into the western Sawtooths, 90 miles northeast of Boise, is accessed by 45 miles of dirt roads from SR 21. Trailhead soaks add much to the appeal of the area, as does the tiny backwoods town of Atlanta, established in 1864. From the hot springs just east of Atlanta (104–106), wilderness buffs can hike to Lynx (107), the uppermost soak on the Middle Fork. West of town, collectors can drive downstream to no fewer than eleven more soaks (108–118). Hikers will enjoy exploring the nearby Trinity Alps. Except for Lynx, this area is all in Boise National Forest.

Season

All the hot springs except Atlanta, Phifer, Loftus, and Sheep Creek Bridge are submerged during spring runoff. Many require a major river ford; the window is usually mid-August through early October. The hiking season in the high Sawtooths and Trinity Alps doesn't get under way until late July and usually runs through mid-September, while the foothills and the hot springs downstream enjoy a longer season. Summer weather can be hot, with cold nights at higher elevations. Hikers should be equipped for foul weather.

Getting to Atlanta

The best route from Boise leaves SR 21 about 19 miles above Idaho City or 15 miles south of Lowman. The next 30 miles of dirt are graded and signed, on FR 384 and FR 327, with a final 15-mile grind up the Middle Fork Road (FR 268). The slow route is the latter road all the way up, because the lower stretch is a tedious crawl past Arrowrock Reservoir. Thus the "eleven-soaks tour" along the middle stretch is recommended as a side trip from Atlanta.

You can also reach Atlanta from Featherville (Area G) via 23 miles of seasonal roads with a steep climb over James Creek Road (FR 126), a shortcut from FR 156. The latter connects Featherville with the Middle Fork Road 15 miles west of Atlanta. This is a longer but easier route that also accesses the Trinity Alps.

Note: Atlanta offers no services except a couple of rustic eateries, a post office, and a public phone. The nearest gas station is back in Idaho City. The historic Atlanta Cabin is available for a modest rental fee. (Contact the Idaho City Ranger District, or check online at recreation.gov.)

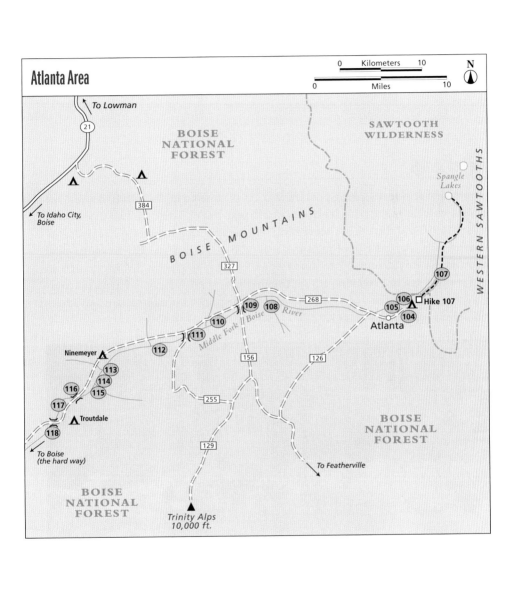

Atlanta Area

Kilometers 10

Miles 10

N

To Lowman

21

BOISE NATIONAL FOREST

SAWTOOTH WILDERNESS

WESTERN SAWTOOTHS

384

To Idaho City, Boise

Spangle Lakes

BOISE MOUNTAINS

327

107

268

Hike 107

106

105

104

Atlanta

Middle Fork Boise River

109

108

110

111

112

Ninemeyer

156

126

113

114

115

116

117

255

Troutdale

129

To Boise (the hard way)

To Featherville

BOISE NATIONAL FOREST

118

BOISE NATIONAL FOREST

Trinity Alps 10,000 ft.

104 Atlanta Hot Springs

General description: A roadside pool near the Atlanta Trailhead into the Sawtooths. Skinny-dippable after dark.
Elevation: 5,400 feet
General location: Just east of Atlanta

GPS: N43.81175 / W115.11026
Map: Boise National Forest (springs not marked). See maps on pages 239 and 243.
Contact: Mountain Home Ranger District, Boise National Forest

Finding the hot springs: Refer to "Getting to Atlanta" (see page 238). From the stop sign in town, continue nearly 1.2 miles northeast (bearing left at 0.3 mile) on the road to Power Plant Recreation Area, just past the turnoff to Chattanooga; then watch for a large pond on your right. A spur just beyond it has room for a couple of cars to park, and a short path leads to the pool.

The Hot Springs

A rock-and-masonry soaking pool sits in a grassy clearing in the woods. Because the pool is well above the river, it's usable nearly year-round. There are two pipes, one a toasty 113°F and the other a tepid 86°F, with a tap fitting to allow for temperature control. The user-built pool measures a good 6 × 12 feet and has an outlet pipe, allowing for easy draining. The runoff flows into the "frog pond," which doubles in hot weather as a fine swimming hole. You may have some hungry red mites for company, but for some the soak is worth the risk. (See page 6 for information and advice on dealing with spider mites.)

The pool at Atlanta Hot Springs is tastefully designed and solidly built. SALLY JACKSON

105 Chattanooga Hot Springs

General description: A five-star soak on the Middle Fork Boise River, near the Atlanta Trailhead into the Sawtooths. Swimwear is first come, first served.
Elevation: 5,360 feet
General location: Just east of Atlanta

GPS: N43.81287 / W115.11694
Map: Boise National Forest (spring not marked). See maps on pages 239 and 243.
Contact: Mountain Home Ranger District, Boise National Forest

Finding the hot springs: Refer to "Getting to Atlanta" (see page 238). From the stop sign in town, continue a bit over 1.1 miles northeast on the road to Power Plant Recreation Area (veering left at 0.3 mile). Just west of the pond by Atlanta Hot Springs, look for a side road to the left marked by a tree that bisects it. Follow it north 0.25 mile across a grassy flat. The flat is on private land; no camping is allowed. Park here; cross a ditch and for 200 feet follow an extremely steep and slippery path dropping down to the pool.

The Hot Springs

Bubbly springs at 120°F cascade over a cliff into a large, knee-deep pool lined with rocks and logs. It has a gravel bottom, and the temperature seems to stay around 100°F. There's also a little hot pot with a shower on a ledge 30 feet downstream from the main pool. This top-notch retreat is tucked between the base from the 100-foot cliff and the nearby river. The jagged Sawtooths across the canyon form a dramatic backdrop. It's a great place to pause and unwind between the rigors of a long, dusty trail and those of an even longer, bumpy road!

Water from the 120°F source cools as it cascades into the main pool at Chattanooga Hot Springs.
SALLY JACKSON

106 Greylock Hot Spring

General description: Another hot dip on the Middle Fork Boise River, at the Atlanta Trailhead into the Sawtooths. Swimwear is advised by day.
Elevation: 5,460 feet
General location: Just east of Atlanta

GPS: N43.81497 / W115.10822
Map: Boise National Forest (spring not marked). See maps on pages 239 and 243.
Contact: Mountain Home Ranger District, Boise National Forest

Finding the hot spring: Refer to "Getting to Atlanta" (see page 238). From the stop sign in town, continue nearly 1.4 miles northeast to Power Plant Recreation Area, just past Atlanta and Chattanooga Hot Springs. You'll see a large grassy clearing at the campground entrance. On the right is the Atlanta Trailhead; on the left is a loop to a group campsite on the bank. (There are many smaller campsites if you follow the road upstream.) Park at the clearing, and follow a track down to the riverside pools.

The Hot Spring

You can discover one more hot soak near Atlanta, and it couldn't be closer to either the trailhead to Lynx (see following hike) or fine campsites. The spring flows out across a gravel bar into one or more rocky soaking pools. The biggest pool wraps around a boulder and has a gravel bottom that four to six bodies can shoehorn into. The temperature runs at least 100°F and can be fine-tuned by adding river water.

Greylock is submerged during spring runoff, but because the following hike is best done in mid- to late summer, the timing should coincide. The site is visible only to people camping on the bank above, and the view across the rushing water to jagged Greylock Mountain, the spring's unofficial namesake, is nothing short of spectacular.

The late Skip Hill (past editor of the Hot Springs Gazette) *in his element at Greylock Hot Springs. He is missed far and wide by his fellow hot springing aficionados.* SALLY JACKSON

Atlanta Hot Springs, Chattanooga Hot Springs, Greylock Hot Spring, Lynx Hot Spring

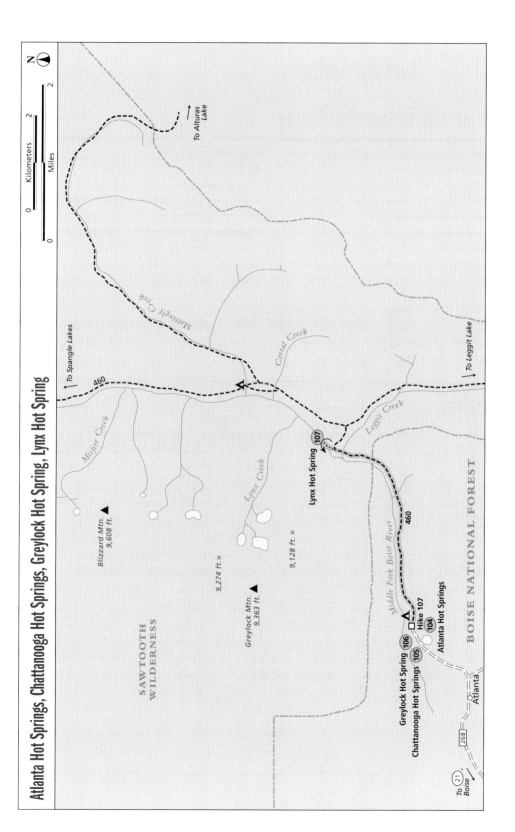

107 Lynx Hot Spring

Hike 107 To Lynx Hot Spring

General description: A day hike with a short bushwhack and two potentially serious river crossings to the uppermost hot spring on the Middle Fork and the only one in the wilderness. Swimwear is superfluous.
Difficulty: Moderate
Distance: About 7.4 miles round-trip
General location: Just east of Atlanta
Elevation gain: 200 feet

High point: 5,700 feet
GPS: N43.83326 / W115.05605
Hiking quad: USGS Atlanta East
Road map: Boise National Forest (springs not marked). See maps on pages 239 and 243.
Restrictions: Should only be attempted when river levels are low. A GPS unit is recommended, as some off-trail hiking is involved.
Contact: Sawtooth NRA

Finding the trailhead: Refer to "Getting to Atlanta" (see page 238). From the stop sign in town, continue nearly 1.4 miles northeast to the Power Plant Recreation Area and park at the large clearing near Greylock (see previous spring). Give the car a well-earned rest, and put your boots to work.

The Hike

Those not planning to backpack into the Spangle Lakes may be interested in this day trip to a mini-soak hidden at the river's edge at the base of a small gorge. The Atlanta Trailhead by the clearing near Greylock is not so obvious; neither is the trail initially. So we'll pick up the trail from near the end of the campground, where it becomes more defined. From the large clearing, wander through the campground to Campsite 15 where a faint trail behind the outhouse soon connects up with the main trail.

Stroll the Middle Fork Boise River Trail (460) east through a forest of Douglas fir and scattered meadows. After almost 3 miles, cross Leggit Creek (a difficult ford during spring runoff, as is the river). Continue up the trail another 0.25 mile and you'll see a small pond on your left. Depart the trail here and make your way to the river in a northeasterly direction (this will involve a short bushwhack).

Once you reach the river, head upstream and cross when the contours demand it then back again just before the spring. Less than 0.5 mile from departing the trail, you will come to a small rocky gorge containing a three-tiered waterfall (only partially visible). The spring is at the downstream end of this gorge on the southeastern side of the river.

The Hot Spring

Several small sources, some registering over 150°F, trickle down the bank into the river, where there may or may not be a usable pool—it's rebuilt by the few souls who frequent

A small tarp was put to good use yet again to build a temporary pool at the elusive Lynx Hot Spring. SALLY JACKSON

it each year after the river level drops. Bring a tarp if you want to guarantee a soak here. (As this is a wilderness area, the forest service asks that tarps not be left behind.)

Note: This spring is located almost 0.2 mile downstream from the river's confluence with Lynx Creek. There are some hot seeps up there, but nothing deemed soakable.

108 Weatherby (Hot Creek) Hot Springs

General description: Potluck dips up a creek on the opposite side of the Middle Fork Boise River. Naked bodies are welcome.
Elevation: 4,680 feet
General location: 13 miles west of Atlanta
GPS: N43.82324 / W115.31902

Map: Boise National Forest (springs not marked). See map on page 239.
Restrictions: Requires a major river ford
Contact: Mountain Home Ranger District, Boise National Forest

Finding the hot springs: Refer to "Getting to Atlanta" (see page 238) and take the dusty Middle Fork Road (FR 268) 13 miles downstream. Just east of an airstrip, take a spur road that drops down to the river. By mid-August you should be able to wade safely across to the mouth of the creek.

Hot Creek has a very narrow and brushy canyon. The creekbed is one way up but is not recommended unless you enjoy bushwhacking and rock climbing. The other way is to follow traces of a jeep track that climbs above and then along the west bank, watching for possible routes back down to the creek in about 0.5 mile.

Note: A quarter mile from the river, just above the jeep track, is a 119°F spring that is best described as a mud wallow heavily frequented by deer.

The Hot Springs

Weatherby, possibly the least-visited hot springs on the Middle Fork, has the advantage of invisibility from the road. Those who struggle up the creekbed will pass a couple of 85°F waterfalls and a waterslide whirlpool. Farther on they'll reach a chain of hot water faucets spurting under pressure from the rocky walls. What they won't find, without a shovel or plenty of luck, is a ready-made soaking pool. Bring a tarp if you're really serious about achieving full-body immersion at these springs.

109 Phifer (Weatherby Mill) Warm Spring

General description: A shower supplied by an artesian well on the Middle Fork Boise River. Keep swimwear handy.
Elevation: 4,400 feet
General location: 15 miles west of Atlanta

GPS: N43.81689 / W115.35537
Map: Boise National Forest (spring not marked). See map on page 239.
Contact: Mountain Home Ranger District, Boise National Forest

Finding the warm spring: Refer to "Getting to Atlanta" (see page 238) and take the Middle Fork Road (FR 268) 15 miles downstream on dirt to the intersection of FR 327 north and FR 156 south. Cross the river bridge and immediately turn left into a primitive camp. Park here and rock-hop across the creek, or drive across to the far end of a clearing (about 0.2 mile). The site, once part of the old Weatherby Mill, is currently a mining claim on public land.

The Warm Spring

Springwater gushing from an artesian well was once piped into a very funky bathhouse to provide the passerby with a torrent of 86°F bathwater. The old shack has finally collapsed, but the warm water still gushes from an overhead pipe. On Sally's last visit, some plywood scraps had been thrown together to form a three-sided shower cubicle. There's a circular tap on the well casing that supplies the flow to the shower.

Note to hikers: Not too far away are the Trinity Alps, a tiny wonderland of lakes and panoramic views along a 5.0-mile trail between Big Trinity Lake Campground and the lookout capping 10,000-foot Trinity Mountain. It's definitely worth the trip if you have a day to spare. Reach this area by either FR 156 or FR 255.

110 Granite Creek Hot Spring

General description: A roadside soak on the Middle Fork Boise River. Swimsuits are essential when standing up.
Elevation: 4,200 feet
General location: 18 miles west of Atlanta

GPS: N43.80288 / W115.40194
Map: Boise National Forest (spring not marked). See map on page 239.
Contact: Mountain Home Ranger District, Boise National Forest

Finding the hot spring: Refer to "Getting to Atlanta" (see page 238) and take the dusty Middle Fork Road (FR 268) 15 miles downstream to the junction of FR 327 north and FR 156 south. Continue 3.4 miles to a pullout 0.5 mile east of a sign for Granite Creek, and hop down the rocks to the pool.

The Hot Spring

Sun-warmed boulders line a large soaking pool at the river's edge just below the road. The outflow from the nearby spring (130°F) keeps the sandy-bottomed pool clean. From early to mid-season, users lower the pool temperature by removing a rock or two in the upstream dam. As the river level drops, dig deeper channels to keep cold water flowing in. The only drawback to this spring is the proximity of the dusty road.

Hats and drinking water are essential items for soaking on a sunny summer's day at Granite Creek Hot Spring. SALLY JACKSON

111 Dutch Frank (Roaring River) Hot Springs

General description: Steamy springs and tiny pools on the Middle Fork Boise River. Swimwear is a must.

Elevation: 4,100 feet

General location: 21 miles west of Atlanta

GPS: N43.78969 / W115.43571

Map: Boise National Forest (springs not marked). See map on page 239.

Contact: Mountain Home Ranger District, Boise National Forest

Finding the hot springs: Refer to "Getting to Atlanta" (see page 238) and take the Middle Fork Road (FR 268) about 21 miles downstream on dirt to the junction with FR 255, signed to Trinity Lakes, at the Roaring River bridge (6 miles west of the junction with FR 327 north and FR 156 south). Park across the river, and follow a short path upstream. Hikers: See note in Phifer (Weatherby Mill) Warm Spring (109).

The Hot Springs

A cluster of springs issues from the ground at temperatures up to 150°F, and steamy channels flow across a broad and highly visible flat on the south side of the river. A few small pools dug out of the rocks right at waterline allow a variable blend of temperatures. As the river level drops through the season, new dips must be dug lower down.

112 Brown's Creek Hot Spring

General description: Hot showerfalls on the wrong side of the Middle Fork Boise River. Swimwear and a life preserver are recommended.
Elevation: 3,900 feet
General location: 25 miles west of Atlanta

GPS: N43.77902 / W115.48588
Map: Boise National Forest (spring not marked). See map on page 239.
Restrictions: Requires a major river ford
Contact: Mountain Home Ranger District, Boise National Forest

Finding the hot spring: Refer to "Getting to Atlanta" (see page 238) and take the dusty Middle Fork Road (FR 268) about 25 miles downstream (3.5 miles past the bridge at FR 255 and 9.5 miles past the FR 327 north and FR 156 south junction). There's a pullout where you can look directly across at the plunge.

The Hot Spring

Hot water gushing from fissures in the rocks at 122°F cascades down a cliff in several graceful falls. One flows into a small alcove that is sometimes cemented in to form a single-soaker pool. It then flows down to a tiny beach into a shallow seasonal pool that's exposed at low water. This lovely site is a bit tricky to reach even when the river is at its lowest, which is usually late August through September. It's swift and deep at this bend, with rapids just downstream.

A hot shower awaits visitors at Brown's Creek Hot Spring after crossing the chilly Middle Fork Boise River. Sally Jackson

113 Ninemeyer Hot Springs

General description: Hot springs flowing down an open hillside, on the opposite side of the Middle Fork Boise River. Keep swimwear handy.
Elevation: 3,800 feet
General location: 30 miles southwest of Atlanta

GPS: N43.75562 / W115.57140
Map: Boise National Forest (springs not marked). See map on page 239.
Restrictions: Requires a major river ford
Contact: Idaho City Ranger District, Boise National Forest

Finding the hot springs: Refer to "Getting to Atlanta" (see page 238) and take the dusty Middle Fork Road (FR 268) nearly 30 miles downstream (5.4 miles past Brown's Creek) to Ninemeyer Forest Camp at milepost 38. The springs are on the opposite side of the river, just a short ways downstream of the camp. It's possible to ford the river here from around mid-August through early October.

The Hot Springs

Early-morning steam blankets the slopes above Ninemeyer as scalding 169°F water forms rivulets that flow downhill. The geothermal area forms a broad mound above the riverbank, and water pours over the lip. Scalding water also forces its way up from below and blasts out underwater into an alcove at the east end of the mound. Folks often try to dig out a dip or two right at waterline, but better pools can usually be built straight up the hillside. These are fed by separate, much cooler springs.

On an early October visit, the river was low enough to allow for a toasty 112°F soak in the large outflow channel about 150 feet downstream of the mound at Ninemeyer Hot Springs. Matt Rosenthal

114 Round the Bend Hot Spring

General description: A late-season soak around the bend from Ninemeyer, on the far side of the Middle Fork Boise River. Bathing suits are a must.
Elevation: 3,800 feet
General location: 30 miles southwest of Atlanta

GPS: N43.75620 / W115.57285
Map: Boise National Forest (spring not marked). See map on page 239.
Restrictions: Requires a major river ford
Contact: Mountain Home Ranger District, Boise National Forest

Finding the hot spring: Follow the preceding directions to Ninemeyer. Ford the river, and walk downstream 500 feet.

The Hot Spring

Many folks who manage to cross the river to Ninemeyer miss another geothermal display just around the downstream bend. Scalding water flows down a sheer cliff coated with streaks of orange algae and hits the river in a quiet eddy that can still be waist-deep by midsummer. The hot water fans out underwater, and within a 3-foot radius it might be possible to find a perfect temperature without any pool at all!

115 Pete Creek Hot Spring

General description: One last hot shower on the far side of the Middle Fork Boise River. Swimwear is essential.
Elevation: 3,700 feet
General location: 32 miles southwest of Atlanta
GPS: N43.73843 / W115.58372 ("Eagle's Nest" pool)

Map: Boise National Forest (spring not marked). See map on page 239.
Restrictions: Requires a major river ford
Contact: Mountain Home Ranger District, Boise National Forest

Finding the hot spring: Refer to "Getting to Atlanta" (see page 238) and take the dusty Middle Fork Road (FR 268) about 32 miles downstream (2.3 miles past Ninemeyer Camp) to a very narrow pullout across from the falls.

The Hot Spring

A 30-foot hot waterfall streams down the side of a cliff into the river on the far bank. By late August through early October, it should be possible to ford directly across and build a rocky pool beneath the spray. An easier ford may be located 300 feet downstream. There's also a small pool built near the top of the cliff. If you look closely from the road, you may spot what appears to be a white PVC drainpipe sticking out of a rock dam. It's worth investigating if you're prepared for a steep scramble. Known by some as the "Eagle's Nest," this two-person pool is fed by a small 138°F spring. The temperature can be adjusted by diverting the flow using rocks. Unplug the pool when you leave so that it stays free of algae.

The "Eagle's Nest" pool at Pete Creek Hot Spring will never be swept away by spring floods. SALLY JACKSON

116 Loftus Hot Spring

General description: Roadside grotto pools on a wooded bank above the Middle Fork Boise River. Swimwear is recommended if standing up.
Elevation: 3,600 feet
General location: 34 miles southwest of Atlanta

GPS: N43.72422 / W115.60455
Map: Boise National Forest (spring not marked). See map on page 239.
Contact: Mountain Home Ranger District, Boise National Forest

Finding the hot spring: Refer to "Getting to Atlanta" (see page 238) and take the Middle Fork Road (FR 268) nearly 34 miles downstream on dirt (1.7 miles past Pete Creek) to a pullout at milepost 34. Climb the short path up to the pools, but beware of poison ivy.

The Hot Spring

Users have dug out a pool beneath an overhanging rocky ledge, and the hot spring (129°F) trickles directly over the lip into the water below. The shallow pool, which runs a toasty 105°F to 108°F, is 8 feet in diameter with a sandy bottom. Once seated, if you can take the heat, you have a sense of total privacy. The outflow cools to 100°F en route to a second, smaller pool a few feet downhill. Loftus, a popular hideaway, can be enjoyed practically year-round.

The main pool at Loftus Hot Spring STEPHANIE ENSIGN

117 Smith Cabin Hot Springs

General description: Hot springs on both banks of the Middle Fork Boise River. Swimwear is a must.
Elevation: 3,550 feet
General location: 35 miles southwest of Atlanta

GPS: N43.71975 / W115.61816
Map: Boise National Forest (spring not marked). See map on page 239.
Contact: Mountain Home Ranger District, Boise National Forest

Finding the hot springs: Refer to "Getting to Atlanta" (see page 238) and take the Middle Fork Road (FR 268) about 34 miles downstream (0.2 mile past Loftus) on dirt to a bridge where the road crosses to the south bank. Continue 0.7 mile, and park wherever you can find room. Several tracks drop down to converge at the springs.

The Hot Springs

Springwater emerges from the riverbank at 140°F, and users seasonally dig a pool or two in the rocks right at waterline, where the temperatures can blend. By mid–August you should be able to safely ford the river upstream to more hot springs and a potential dip or two on the opposite bank.

Geothermal note: Locals report a number of springs and seeps in the stretch downstream to Sheep Creek Bridge. Not marked on any map, they can only be pinpointed by their early-morning steam.

118 Sheep Creek Bridge Hot Spring

General description: One last special, for the do-it-yourselfer, on the Middle Fork Boise River. Bare buns not recommended.

Elevation: 3,450 feet

General location: 38 miles southwest of Atlanta

GPS: N43.69632 / W115.65865

Map: Boise National Forest (spring not marked). See map on page 239.

Contact: Mountain Home Ranger District, Boise National Forest

Finding the hot spring: Refer to "Getting to Atlanta" (see page 238) and take the Middle Fork Road (FR 268) about 38 dusty miles downstream (2.7 miles past Troutdale Forest Camp) to a bridge at milepost 30 where the road recrosses the river. Driving in from the southwest via Arrowrock Reservoir, it's a windy and dusty 30 miles from SR 21. Park at the east end of the bridge by a trail sign, and follow a short path that forks to the right from the trail. The spring sits on a rocky bench above the river about 50 yards downstream of the bridge.

Riverside soaking at Sheep Creek Bridge Hot Spring is possible only when water levels are running low. The other option is to bring a tarp and build a pool higher up. SALLY JACKSON

The Hot Spring

Last on the Middle Fork list, this 142°F spring feeds into a scalding hot, algae-laden source pool 10 feet across. The outflow trickles down a boulder-strewn slope to the river. Dipping diehards sometimes dig a cooler pool out of the rocks lower down and use a tarp to keep it from draining dry, but you may need a bucket for adding river water. During a visit in early October, the river was running low enough to allow for some small rock-lined pools to be built on its edge where the springs were entering.

Note: If you happen to be heading farther down the road, check out the Twin Springs Resort 4 miles downstream. Hot springs on a cliff above the road are piped down to three riverside cabins, each with a hot tub on the deck—luxury soaks with a view for anyone tiring of the do-it-yourself routine.

G. Out of Featherville

Hot Springs and Hikes

The remote outpost of Featherville, faintly marked on the state map midway between Boise and Ketchum, is the gateway to hot springs along the South Fork Boise River and Smoky Creek. After a "bridge-stop" south of town (119), we take a back road into the Smoky Mountains. Heading east through Sawtooth National Forest, the scenic route accesses a variety of soaks as well as many fine campsites in exchange for 32 miles of washboard road. The first stop is Willow Creek (120), then popular Baumgartner (121). Next is the elusive Lightfoot (122), followed by a hike-in soak at Skillern (123) and a roadside dip at Preis (124). Last but not least comes a geothermal delight at Worswick (125).

Season

The limit on these soaks is the seasonal road, open from mid-May through October, and spring runoff at the streamside pools. The hiking season ranges from May through October in the lower elevations to late June through late September in the higher country farther east. Summer weather is generally hot, with scattered thunderstorms and cold nights at higher elevations.

Getting to Featherville

The most direct access from the outside world is via 74 miles of pavement leaving I-84 at Mountain Home: US 20 leads to the Pine-Featherville Road (FR 61) at milepost 127, which takes you north past Anderson Ranch Reservoir and Pine. Featherville can also be reached from Atlanta (Area F).

If you are traveling from the Twin Falls area, follow SR 46 north to Fairfield, home of the district ranger station, then continue north on FR 94 to hit FR 227 near Worswick Hot Springs, midway between Featherville and Ketchum. The 85-mile route is paved to the turnoff to Soldier Mountain, but the last 10 miles are slow. From Ketchum the route west on FR 227 is all on dirt, with a slow but scenic crawl over Dollarhide Summit.

Note: The only services you'll find in Featherville are a bar, a cafe, a tiny general store, and a public phone. The nearest gas station is 10 miles south in Pine.

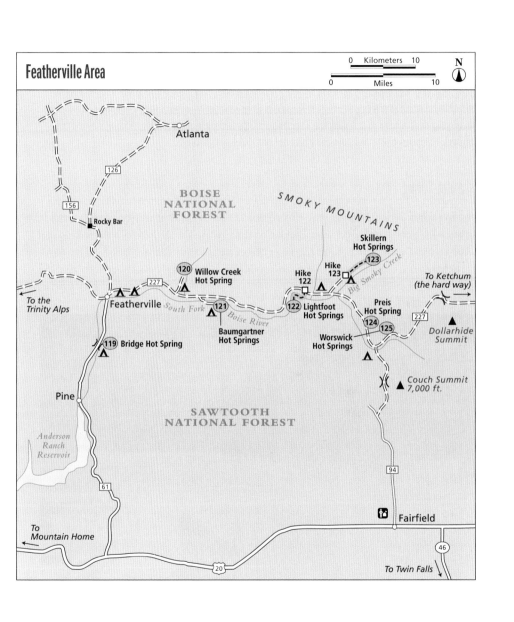

Featherville Area

0   Kilometers   10

0   Miles   10

N

Atlanta

126

BOISE
NATIONAL
FOREST

SMOKY MOUNTAINS

156

Rocky Bar

Skillern
Hot Springs

120 Willow Creek
Hot Spring

123

Hike
123

Big Smoky Creek

To Ketchum
(the hard way)

Hike
122

To the
Trinity Alps

227

Featherville   South Fork

121

122 Lightfoot
Hot Springs

Preis
Hot Spring

227

Boise River

Baumgartner
Hot Springs

124 125

Dollarhide
Summit

119 Bridge Hot Spring

Worswick
Hot Springs

Pine

Couch Summit
7,000 ft.

Anderson
Ranch
Reservoir

SAWTOOTH
NATIONAL FOREST

61

94

To
Mountain Home

Fairfield

20

46

To Twin Falls

119 Bridge (Elks Flat) Hot Spring

General description: Popular roadside soaks on the South Fork Boise River. Swimwear is essential.
Elevation: 4,340 feet
General location: 6 miles south of Featherville

GPS: N43.53982 / W115.28910
Map: Boise National Forest (spring not marked). See map on page 259.
Contact: Mountain Home Ranger District, Boise National Forest

Finding the hot spring: Refer to "Getting to Featherville" (see page 258) and take the paved South Fork Road (FR 61) a scant 6 miles south of the FR 227 junction (4.5 miles north of Pine) to the highway bridge that spans the river. The springs are by a pullout near the north end of the bridge, accessed by turning into the aptly named Hot Springs Drive.

The Hot Spring

Springwater emerges from the riverbank at 140°F, and steamy channels trickle across the gravel and sand into a series of shallow pools. Bathers dig these seasonal dips right at waterline, where the river water mixes into the hot pools. Sixty yards downstream of the bridge, a separate spring flows through a culvert into the last pool(s) downstream.

The source area at Bridge Hot Springs SALLY JACKSON

120 Willow Creek Hot Spring

General description: A toasty soak by a creek-side path, near the South Fork Boise River. Swimwear is optional.
Elevation: 5,200 feet
General location: 8.6 miles east of Featherville

GPS: N43.63719 / W115.13053
Map: Sawtooth National Forest (spring marked). See map on page 259.
Contact: Fairfield Ranger District, Sawtooth National Forest

Finding the hot spring: Refer to "Getting to Featherville" (see page 258) and take Baumgartner Road (FR 227) 6.8 miles east of town to FR 008. Turn left, pass Willow Creek Campground, and go 1.8 miles to a horse camp at road's end. A wooded path follows the creek 0.75 mile upstream to the pools.

The Hot Spring

Bubbles rise to the surface of a source pool at 131°F through a jungle of algae, and seasonal soaking pools can be dug out of the thermal stream as it winds its way across a grassy flat. The temperature drops to lukewarm as it flows into the creek, so you can pick a spot where the temperature suits your fancy.

The thermal stream at Willow Creek Hot Spring (usually) has several pools en route to the creek.
MATT ROSENTHAL

121 Baumgartner Hot Springs

General description: A campground swimming pool near the South Fork Boise River. Public nudity is prohibited.

Elevation: 4,900 feet

General location: 11 miles east of Featherville

GPS: N43.60245 / W115.07086

Map: Sawtooth National Forest (springs marked). See map on page 259.

Restrictions: Parking fee required; day use only

Contact: Fairfield Ranger District, Sawtooth National Forest

Finding the hot springs: Refer to "Getting to Featherville" (see page 258) and take Baumgartner Road (FR 227) 10 miles east on dirt (3.1 miles past Willow Creek) to the turnoff to Baumgartner Campground. This camp is a fully developed site, which is rare in these parts. You'll find the pool near road's end.

The Hot Springs

A 15 × 20-foot concrete pool houses the outflow from Baumgartner Hot Springs. The pool, furnished with decking and benches, is maintained by the forest service and kept at 102°F to 104°F. There's a fee for camping, but passersby can use the pool free of charge once they've paid the day-use parking fee. It's open daily, dawn to dusk, from around May 20 through late September. Alcohol or glass containers are prohibited.

John Baumgartner deeded the site to the forest service for public camping and bathing "in its natural state so far as that is practicable." It's about as far from its natural state as any you'll find in this guidebook, but it's equally far from the commercial resorts at the other end of the spectrum. All things are relative, and the forest service has done a tasteful job of developing it.

For a bit of civilized soaking, check out Baumgartner Hot Springs' popular swimming pool.
SALLY JACKSON

122 Lightfoot Hot Springs

Hike 122 To Lightfoot Hot Springs

General description: A day hike to thermal streams on the wrong side of the South Fork Boise River. Swimwear is optional.

Difficulty: Easy

Distance: About 3.0 miles round-trip

General location: 20 miles east of Featherville

Elevation gain: Minimal

Hot springs: 5,300 feet

GPS: N43.6050 / W114.9509 (estimate)

Map: Sawtooth National Forest (springs named)

Restrictions: Possible river ford

Contact: Fairfield Ranger District, Sawtooth National Forest

Finding the trailhead: Refer to "Getting to Featherville" (see page 258) and take FR 227 about 20 miles east (1.6 miles past the Lightfoot Hot Springs sign) on dirt to a footbridge across the river to Boardman Creek Trail.

Note: In 2012 this footbridge was closed; the forest service is hoping to replace it in the next year or two.

The Hike

There's a bit more to Lightfoot than the algae-laden swamp in the ditch beside the road. The rest lies hidden across the river. Reach it by fording near the sign (not recommended during high water) or by driving upstream to the footbridge (if it's been replaced) and following a user-built path back downstream on the opposite bank. Start hunting for clues after you pass a cabin in the woods and enter a clearing.

The Hot Springs

Three adjacent springs issue from the ground at 119°F and form shallow streams. One boasts a 110°F source pool with a layer of algae on top and bottom. Another, closer to the river, contains a tiny seasonal pool dug out of a rocky wash. Both are usable in a pinch, and chances are you'll have them all to yourself. The outflow and temperature vary greatly from one season to the next, so there's no guarantee of a soak. The fun is in the search. Check for red mites (see page 6 for information and advice on dealing with spider mites).

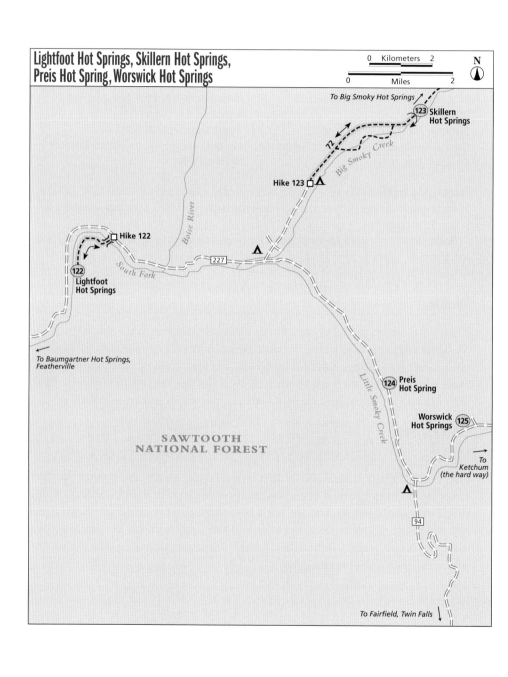

Lightfoot Hot Springs, Skillern Hot Springs, Preis Hot Spring, Worswick Hot Springs

0   Kilometers   2

0   Miles   2

N

To Big Smoky Hot Springs

123 Skillern Hot Springs

72

Big Smoky Creek

Hike 123

Boise River

Hike 122

122
Lightfoot Hot Springs

South Fork

227

To Baumgartner Hot Springs, Featherville

Little Smoky Creek

124 Preis Hot Spring

Worswick Hot Springs 125

To Ketchum (the hard way)

SAWTOOTH NATIONAL FOREST

94

To Fairfield, Twin Falls

123 Skillern Hot Springs

Hike 123 To Skillern Hot Springs

General description: A day hike to secluded hot pools in the Smoky Mountains. Swimwear is superfluous.
Difficulty: Moderate
Distance: About 5.0 miles round-trip
General location: 25 miles east of Featherville
Elevation gain: +300 feet, -100 feet

High point: 5,800 feet
GPS: N43.64780 / W114.81550
Hiking quad: USGS Paradise Peak
Road map: Sawtooth National Forest (springs named on both map and hiking quad)
Contact: Fairfield Ranger District, Sawtooth National Forest

Finding the trailhead: Refer to "Getting to Featherville" (see page 258) and take FR 227 about 24 miles east (4 miles past the footbridge to Lightfoot) on dirt to a turnoff signed to Big Smoky. It's also the same distance from Fairfield, and it's 5.5 miles from FR 94. The side road soon forks right, passes Big Smoky Guard Station, and ends in 1.5 miles at Canyon Campground. The trailhead is at the end of the loop. Motorcycles are allowed on the trail.

The Hike

After the first easy mile, Big Smoky Creek Trail (72) hugs the stream a bit too closely, requiring four crossings, so an alternate route has been built up the bank. The high trail not only keeps your feet dry but also offers views up and down the canyon. Grass and sagebrush speckle the southeast-facing hills. The cooler slopes across the canyon are wooded with ponderosa pine. At 2.0 miles the trails converge by the creek, and you'll reach the springs in another 0.5 mile. *Note:* You'll pass several trails branching left, including one signed to Skillern Creek. Don't be tempted—stay in the main canyon.

The Hot Springs

Water gushing from the rocks at 140°F cascades down a cliff, then flows across a grassy flat to the creek. Here you'll find one or more seasonal pools where you can blend the temperatures into a half-decent soak, but only if you keep stirring nonstop. Upstream, around the side of the cliff, there's a hidden pool partway up the side. This little gem, a depression in the rocky wall well above the high-water mark, features a steamy shower spraying the surface and a rock-and-log dam to contain it.

Geothermal note: A second hot spring 6 miles upstream at around 6,550 feet, marked on the national forest map and named Big Smoky on the state geothermal map, has a couple of small pools that are rarely visited by humans but are very popular with the elk and deer population (GPS estimate for Big Smoky Hot Springs: N43.701 / W114.738).

124 Preis Hot Spring

General description: A tiny roadside hot box in the Smoky Mountains. Swimwear is essential when standing up.
Elevation: 5,700 feet
General location: 27 miles east of Featherville

GPS: N43.57585 / W114.83091
Map: Sawtooth National Forest (spring named). See maps on pages 259 and 264.
Contact: Fairfield Ranger District, Sawtooth National Forest

Finding the hot spring: Refer to "Getting to Featherville" (see page 258) and take FR 227 about 27 miles east (3.5 miles past the Skillern turnoff at Big Smoky Creek) on dirt. It's 2.2 miles from FR 94. There's no landmark except for a small rock pile near the road.

The Hot Spring

Rocks form a screen around a 3 × 4-foot box recessed into the ground. Springwater bubbles up into the cozy container at around 105°F, and the temperature can be lowered by plugging the inflow. You can drain and refill the box after each soak, and a submerged bench makes a handy seat. The dubious function of the border, besides providing the only landmark, is to conceal the box itself. It's not high enough to screen any soaker over age 5 from full view by passing motorists.

125 Worswick Hot Springs

General description: A hot springer's fantasy spread out on both sides of the road, in the Smoky Mountains. Swimwear is advised in the daytime.
Elevation: 6,000 feet
General location: 32 miles east of Featherville

GPS: N43.56231 / W114.79497 (culvert); N43.56382 / W114.79611 (upper springs)
Map: Sawtooth National Forest (springs named). See maps on pages 259 and 264.
Contact: Fairfield Ranger District, Sawtooth National Forest

Finding the hot springs: Refer to "Getting to Featherville" (see page 258) and follow FR 227 for 2.1 miles east of the junction with FR 94—a total of nearly 32 long and dusty miles from Featherville. There's ample space south of the road to park or pitch a tent.

The "Culvert Pool" at Worswick Hot Springs usually runs a bit cooler than those up the hill.
MATT ROSENTHAL

The Hot Springs

A complex of fifty springs issues from a grassy hillside at temperatures up to 180°F and branches into a thermal stream flowing at a staggering rate of 250 gallons per minute. It runs through a series of pools, flows through pipes under the road, and then snakes across a flat into Little Smoky Creek. The temperature rises through the summer as the output of an incoming cold stream diminishes.

There's a toasty soaker dammed with a log partway up the hill on a side road, a rock-lined pool by the culvert, and one or more shallow pools near the creek. During an early June visit, the upper pool clocked in at 110°F, the "Culvert Pool" at 100°F, and the creekside one at 95°F. On a subsequent October visit, the upper pool was still 110°F, but the creekside pool was way too hot while the "Culvert Pool" measured 108°F. The area around Worswick is home to a number of unique plants, including a variety of tiny sunflower. Wildlife frequent the springs when human life has left. The number of visitors has increased over the years, and it's important to remember the basics: Tread lightly, and leave no trace. Red mites sometimes frequent these springs (see page 6 for information and advice on dealing with spider mites).

H. Out of Ketchum

Hot Springs and Hikes

From Ketchum, roadside hot springs fan out in four directions. To the south is a spring at Magic Reservoir (126). To the southeast we find an oasis at Milford (127) on the way to Craters of the Moon. Next come some scenic soakers west of town at Frenchman's Bend (128) and Warfield (129). Then SR 75 runs northwest through the Sawtooth NRA, where a dip at Russian John (130) on the way to Stanley combines well with alpine hikes into the Smoky Mountains.

Season

While the pools at Milford and Russian John are reachable year-round, they're not hot enough for winter use. The streamside dips west of Ketchum are limited by spring runoff. Magic works best in the fall or winter months. The hikes in the high country of the Smoky Mountains are best done in July through mid-September. The summer climate varies with changing elevations, so come prepared for the full gamut.

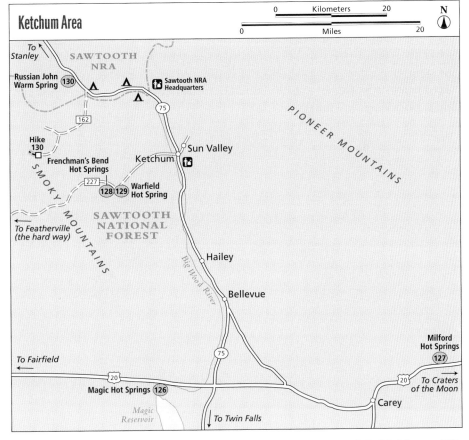

126 Magic Hot Springs

General description: Potluck soaks in a dry field above Magic Reservoir. Swimwear is essential.
Elevation: 4,800 feet
General location: 32 miles south of Ketchum

GPS: N43.32774 / W114.40030
Map: State highway map (springs not marked). See map on page 269.
Contact: None available

Finding the hot springs: From SR 75 in Ketchum, drive south 26 miles, then take US 20 west 5.7 miles to the Hot Springs Landing sign at Magic Reservoir, between mileposts 172 and 173. Turn south for 0.5 mile to the boat ramp parking lot, and walk 40 yards west to the springs.

The Hot Springs

The source (125°F) originates on private fenced land and flows down a very long channel into the north end of Magic Reservoir. A motley assortment of tubs and pools has appeared and disappeared below the fence over the years. The setting is a grassy/weedy field, and the reservoir is usually nowhere in sight. It might be worth checking out late in the year, when the air temperature doesn't match the temp in the pool(s). Coauthor Sally first visited these springs in 2007 and found a large tarp-lined pool full of clean 104°F water. On a fall 2012 visit, there was a small shallow pool of the same temperature that had been crudely dammed with logs. Due to the presence of red mites, she opted not to bathe on this occasion (see page 6 for information and advice on dealing with mites).

127 Milford (Wild Rose) Hot Springs

General description: A lava-rock hot pool on the road to Craters of the Moon. Swimwear is recommended when standing up.
Elevation: 5,000 feet
General location: 55 miles southeast of Ketchum

GPS: N43.36468 / W113.78906
Map: BLM Shoshone District (springs marked). See map on page 269.
Contact: Shoshone Field Office, BLM

Finding the hot springs: From SR 75 in Ketchum, drive south 26 miles, then take US 20 east 19 miles to Carey. Continue 9.7 miles to a pullout on the north side, midway between mileposts 214 and 215, or 15 miles west of Craters of the Moon Visitor Center. Follow a path 80 yards north to the pool.

The Hot Springs

A desert oasis bordered by sunflowers lies barely concealed from the busy highway behind a lava ridge. The pool, encased in chunky black lava rock with a gravel bottom, is roughly 15 × 20 feet and more than 4 feet deep at the near end. In late 2012 there was still a large floating deck made of plywood. The 101°F springs provide a comfortable soak in a unique setting.

The springs are on public land, but the pool itself is on a parcel owned by the Milford Sweat family. The owners don't mind people using the pool as long as they don't abuse the privilege. No soap or shampoo, no glass containers, and please pack out what you pack in.

Note to hikers: Craters of the Moon National Monument is well worth a visit. A variety of hiking trails access points of interest in the lava-strewn landscape, including several caves and tunnels. The visitor center has all the specs, and there's a campground at the start of the loop drive.

The lava-rock pool at Milford Hot Springs has year-round access. SALLY JACKSON

128 Frenchman's Bend Hot Springs

General description: Popular roadside soaks on a creek in the Smoky Mountains. Swimsuits are required.

Elevation: 6,300 feet

General location: 10.5 miles west of Ketchum

GPS: N43.64112 / W114.49070

Map: Sawtooth National Forest (springs not marked). See map on page 269.

Restrictions: Day use only. See also list below.

Contact: Ketchum Ranger District, Sawtooth National Forest

Finding the hot springs: From SR 75 in Ketchum, take the Warm Springs Road (FR 227) west on a surface that deteriorates from pavement to gravel in 4 miles. Park in the designated area just beyond a bridge at 10.3 miles, and walk 70 yards upstream to the pools.

The Hot Springs

Frenchman's Bend consists of a highly seasonal soaking pool or two nestled in the creekside boulders right below the road. The clear, sulfur-infused springwater bubbles in at 124°F, but the pool temperature is easy to lower by shifting rocks in the dam. There should also be a pool or two on the opposite bank a few yards upstream that emerge from the spring runoff a bit sooner—the sources for these springs are 138°F.

Note: The site has rules posted that are strictly enforced: no public nudity, no alcohol or glass containers, no parking except in designated areas, and no soaks between 10 p.m. and 4 a.m. The list may be objectionable to some, but it has alleviated the overuse/abuse problems encountered in the past. The access road is plowed up to the homes about half a mile back, and folks sometimes ski in for a quiet winter soak.

You have to be up early for a quiet soak at Frenchman's Bend Hot Springs. SALLY JACKSON

129 Warfield Hot Spring

General description: A "borderline soak" on the edge of Warm Springs Creek, just downstream from Frenchman's Bend. Swimwear is a smart idea.

Elevation: 6,300 feet

General location: 10.5 miles west of Ketchum

GPS: N43.64033 / W114.48720

Map: Sawtooth National Forest (spring named). See map on page 269.

Restriction: Can only be attempted when the water is low

Contact: None available

The lowdown: This spring is located on private property on which a large house has been built, and the once-popular soaking site is now posted with NO TRESPASSING signs. The law, however, states that private property extends only to the high-water mark. Because the hot water flows into the creek, this means that when the water is low in late summer or fall, pools can be legally dug and legally reached by following the low-water line instead of the private road.

Finding the hot spring: Follow the preceding directions to the parking area for Frenchman's Bend, then follow the creek 0.2 mile downstream. Unfortunately, this isn't as easy as it sounds. There's no route along either side, so you'd have to wade downstream from Frenchman's Bend. The creekbed is full of slippery rocks and deep holes, and the house is in plain sight.

The Hot Spring

Warfield Hot Spring sits out on what was once a quiet grassy flat that's now occupied by a house, bordering a bend in the creek downstream from Frenchman's Bend. Hot water seeps out of the ground at 119°F and flows down the bank into the creek. To reach it takes twofold courage: to tackle a stream wade that's difficult even in late summer and to risk a confrontation with irate homeowners, even though you're within your legal rights. Then a pool must be dug out from scratch in the creekside rocks with no guarantee of a decent soak. Would the soak be worth the hassle? Only you can decide.

130 Russian John Warm Spring

General description: A roadside retreat with a mountain view. It's semi-skinnydippable.
Elevation: 6,900 feet
General location: 18 miles northwest of Ketchum

GPS: N43.80678 / W114.58721
Map: Sawtooth National Forest (site named but spring not marked). See map on page 269.
Contact: Ketchum Ranger District, Sawtooth National Forest

Finding the warm spring: From Ketchum drive 18 miles northwest on SR 75, the Sawtooth Scenic Biway. The turnoff is located 2.5 miles past Baker Creek Road (see Hike 130). Turn west onto an unmarked dirt road just south of milepost 146, then continue south to the parking area. A short path leads to the pool.

Russian John Warm Spring is a pleasant retreat despite the nearby highway. Stephanie Ensign

The Warm Spring

A short stack of logs barely shelters an old sheepherder's soaking pool from sight of the busy highway 200 yards away. Springwater perks up through the sand into a user-friendly pool 6 feet across and 2 feet deep. The sides have been reinforced with mortar. The pool runs 85°F to 95°F; it's a pleasant soak in a semi-secluded spot.

Hike 130 Baker Lake

General description: A brisk stroll to a popular lake in the Smoky Mountains, near Russian John Warm Spring
Difficulty: Moderate
Distance: About 4.0 miles round-trip
General location: 25 miles northwest of Ketchum

Elevation gain: 880 feet
High point: 8,800 feet
Hiking quad: USGS Baker Peak
Road map: Sawtooth National Forest
Contact: Ketchum Ranger District, Sawtooth National Forest

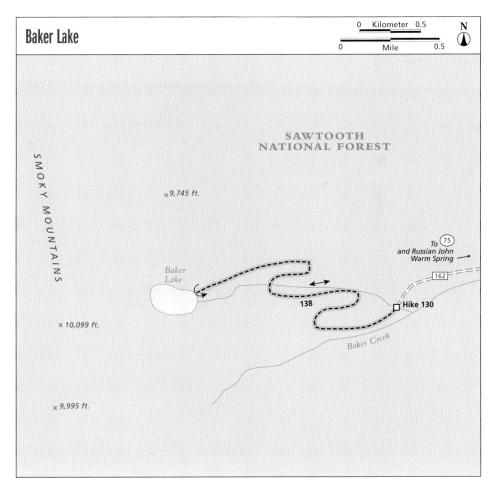

Finding the trailhead: From Ketchum drive 16 miles northwest on SR 75. Turn left onto Baker Creek Road (FR 162), 2.5 miles south of Russian John, and drive 9 dusty miles to the road-end parking area and trail sign.

The Hike

This pretty lake, a pleasant family outing, is well worth the short climb. Tall stands of fir rim the grassy shore, and pink granite cliffs cast their reflections in the clear water. Baker Lake Trail (138) starts off by crossing a branch or two of Baker Creek and then follows a track up a grassy hillside and through a forest. The route then follows a wooded ridge westward to the lake.

I. Out of Stanley

Hot Springs and Hikes

The Salmon River near Stanley is home to a family of roadside hot dips (131–137) as well as a variety of alpine hikes in the eastern Sawtooths. A remote trail north of Sunbeam leads to a chain of wilderness hot springs on Upper Loon Creek (138–141). Following SR 75 farther east, a back road leads to Lunchbreak (142) and another to a bath at Slate Creek (143). Still farther east, a longer back road accesses a hike in the White Clouds en route to soaks at West Pass (144) and Bowery (145). Everything in this area, except for Loon Creek, is within the Sawtooth NRA.

Season

Elkhorn's "boat box" is usable year-round, and the tubs at West Pass and Bowery would be except for the seasonal road. The riverside pools are underwater during runoff. Access to Upper Loon depends on road closures; the prime time for soaks is July through October. The high Sawtooths are often obscured by snow until late July and snowed in again by mid-September. Summer weather brings warm days and cold nights at higher elevations, and you should travel prepared for rain or even snow.

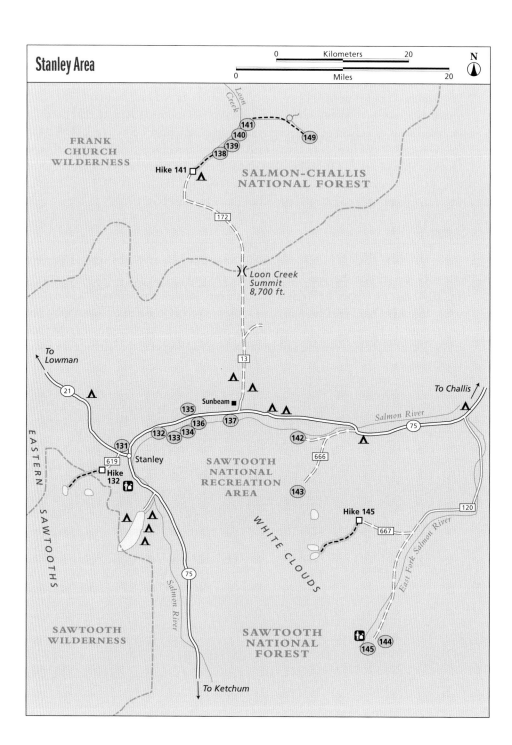

Stanley Area

0 Kilometers 20
0 Miles 20

N

FRANK
CHURCH
WILDERNESS

SALMON–CHALLIS
NATIONAL FOREST

Loon Creek

141
140
139
138

149

Hike 141

172

Loon Creek
Summit
8,700 ft.

13

To
Lowman

21

To Challis

Salmon River

Sunbeam

135
136
132 133 134
137

142

75

131

619 Stanley

SAWTOOTH
NATIONAL
RECREATION
AREA

666

143

Hike
132

Hike 145

667

120

WHITE
CLOUDS

East Fork Salmon River

EASTERN
SAWTOOTHS

75

Salmon River

SAWTOOTH
WILDERNESS

SAWTOOTH
NATIONAL
FOREST

145 144

To Ketchum

Hot Springs near Stanley

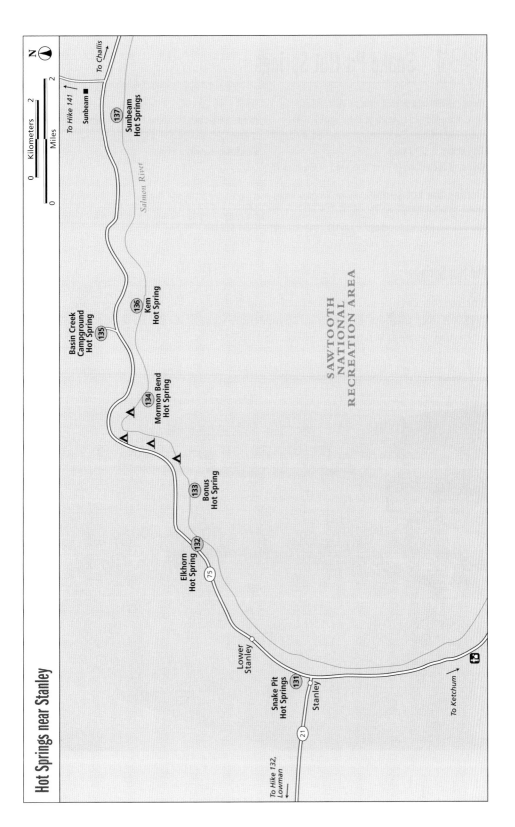

131 Snake Pit Hot Springs

General description: A perennial creekside pool with stunning views of the nearby Sawtooth Mountains. Swimwear is required by day.
Elevation: 6,200 feet
General location: On the outskirts of Stanley

GPS: N44.22190 / W114.93121
Map: Sawtooth National Forest (spring not marked). See map on page 279.
Contact: Sawtooth NRA

Finding the hot springs: From Stanley head north on SR 75 to mile marker 190 and turn left at the Stanley Museum. Continue 0.3 mile on this unpaved road to a large parking area on the left. From here, walk across a bridge; the springs are on the left.

The Hot Springs

The roughly circular pool is 18 feet across and 2 feet deep. It contains clear water that perks up from the bottom. The pool's temperature varies with the air temperature, but in warmer weather it tends to hover around 103°F.

The pool at Snake Pit Hot Springs is much nicer than its name would indicate! MATT ROSENTHAL

132 Elkhorn Hot Spring (the "Boat Box")

General description: A riverside hot tub and pools below the highway, near the eastern Sawtooth trailheads. Swimwear is essential.
Elevation: 6,100 feet
General location: 3.4 miles east of Stanley

GPS: N44.24481 / W114.88608
Map: Sawtooth National Forest (spring not marked). See map on page 279.
Contact: Sawtooth NRA

Finding the hot spring: Drive 3.3 miles east of the Stanley junction on SR 75. Watch for a small pullout by the river in the middle of a left curve. Park here and climb down the rocks.

The Hot Spring

This is the first of several hot dips along the Salmon River Scenic Biway, which begins east of Stanley. One or two seasonal pools and a year-round hot tub tucked between boulders mark the highly visible spot. Scalding-hot 136°F water is piped under the highway to the tub. If the previous visitors have left the hose in the tub, you either have a long wait for it to cool down or can scramble back and forth to the river with a bucket. If somebody has made off with the bucket, you're out of luck.

The latest tub at the "boat box" is round, but the name hasn't changed. STEPHANIE ENSIGN

Hike 132 Alpine, Sawtooth, and McGown Lakes

General description: A day hike or overnighter featuring alpine views and the largest lake in the Sawtooths, near Elkhorn Hot Spring

Difficulty: Moderate

Distance: About 12 miles round-trip

General location: 5.5 miles west of Stanley

Elevation gain: +2,090 feet, -280 feet

High point: 8,800 feet

Hiking quad: USGS Stanley Lake

Road map: Sawtooth National Forest

Contact: Sawtooth NRA

Finding the trailhead: Drive 2.5 miles west of Stanley on SR 21. Turn left onto gravel Iron Creek Road (FR 619) and drive 3 miles to a campground loop at the road end. The trailhead is located near the far end of the loop.

The Hike

The star attraction of this highly popular trip is the giant sapphire oval of Sawtooth Lake. Craggy Mount Regan dominates the skyline directly across the granite bowl, and trails around both sides offer a variety of unobstructed views. This may well be the most photographed scene in the Sawtooths. (**Note:** Campfires are prohibited within 200 yards of both Alpine and Sawtooth Lakes.) The Iron Creek Trail (640) meanders southwest for the first 1.25 miles to the wilderness line. Next it passes Alpine Way (528) branching east, signed to Marshall Lake. The route west curves gently to a second junction in a boggy flat, then angles up an open slope above Iron Creek Valley. Splash across Iron Creek and climb to an overlook of lovely Alpine Lake in 4.0 miles. A spur drops to the north shore, and Alpine Peak stands out to the south above the treetops.

The main trail snakes above Alpine Lake. The ridgetop has views of peaks to the north and south and overlooks the Iron Creek Valley stretching east toward Stanley. A little more scenic climbing brings you past a small tarn in an alpine valley to the outlet and northern end of the largest lake in the Sawtooths at 5.0 miles (8,430 feet).

Starkly beautiful Sawtooth Lake stretches a full mile from head to toe and 0.5 mile across. A deep basin of granite slabs outlines the oval shape, and a few twisted trees cling for survival to the steep walls. The jagged contours of Mount Regan shoot 1,760 feet skyward from the surface at the far end. There are very limited spots to camp at Sawtooth Lake.

There's a junction by the outlet. Before going on to McGown Lakes, take the left fork to a granite knoll with a full view across the lake. The scenic path hugs the shore for an easygoing mile to a flower-lined pond directly beneath Mount Regan before dropping through a glacier-cut gap to reach Baron Creek Trail in 6.0 lightly traveled miles.

The main trail branches west to climb 360 feet in a 0.5-mile traverse across the north wall. This spectacular stretch offers an eagle's perspective across the full length

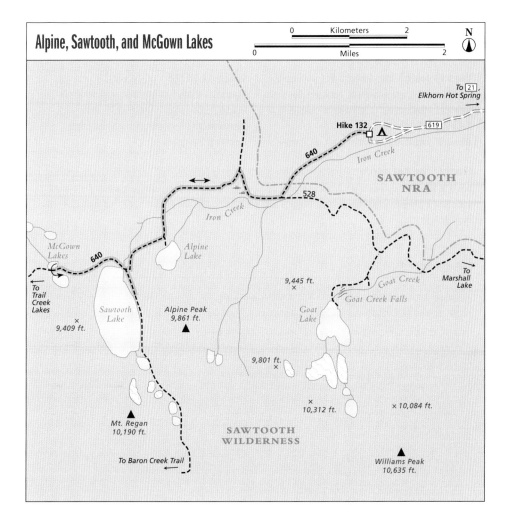

0   Kilometers   2

0   Miles   2

N

To 21,
Elkhorn Hot Spring

Hike 132

619

640

Iron Creek

SAWTOOTH
NRA

528

Iron Creek

McGown
Lakes

640

Alpine
Lake

To
Trail
Creek
Lakes

9,445 ft.
×

Goat Creek

To
Marshall
Lake

Goat Creek Falls

Sawtooth
Lake

×
9,409 ft.

Alpine Peak
9,861 ft.

Goat
Lake

9,801 ft.
×

×
10,312 ft.

× 10,084 ft.

▲
Mt. Regan
10,190 ft.

SAWTOOTH
WILDERNESS

To Baron Creek Trail

▲
Williams Peak
10,635 ft.

of the lake to Mount Regan and the gap carved in the far wall. The path crests at 8,800 feet, the high point on the hike, then quickly drops into a rocky valley to reach the largest McGown Lake just south of the trail at 6.0 miles.

The McGown Lakes lie in shallow rock basins below low peaks. They haven't much to offer other than a couple of campsites, a few stunted trees, and the magnificent route connecting them with Sawtooth Lake a mile away.

133 Bonus Hot Spring

General description: An extra hot pool on the far side of the Salmon River, near the eastern Sawtooth trailheads. Swimwear is essential.
Elevation: 6,100 feet
General location: 3.6 miles east of Stanley

GPS: N44.24776 / W114.88378
Map: Sawtooth National Forest (spring not marked). See map on page 279.
Restrictions: Requires a major river ford
Contact: Sawtooth NRA

Finding the hot spring: From the Stanley junction, go 3.5 miles east on SR 75 to the first big bend in the river downstream from Elkhorn Hot Spring (see preceding) and just west of milepost 193. You'll have to grab the nearest pullout and walk back. Aim for the far bank, but only when the river level is low.

The Hot Spring

Steamy water channels across a meadow, cooling to around 100°F as it reaches the river. It sits 0.2 mile downstream from the "boat box" at Elkhorn and is visible on the far bank. Like Mormon Bend, it can also be easily accessed by raft once the river is down. If you're serious about obtaining a soak at Bonus, bring a shovel and tarp to form your own pool.

134 Mormon Bend Hot Spring

General description: A hot dip on the far side of the Salmon River, near the eastern Sawtooth trailheads. Swimwear is advised when standing up.
Elevation: 6,100 feet
General location: 6.8 miles east of Stanley

GPS: N44.26012 / W114.83929
Map: Sawtooth National Forest (spring not marked). See map on page 279.
Restrictions: Requires a major river ford
Contact: Sawtooth NRA

Finding the hot spring: From the Stanley junction, go 6.6 miles east on SR 75 to Mormon Bend Campground. The spring is 0.2 mile east of milepost 196 on the far bank. The road into the camp branches. There's a free parking strip just to your right, and the road to your left soon reaches the camp's east end (Campsite 15) and a short path to the river. Take a bead across a gravel bar in the middle, angling downstream to the inside curve on the far side. The spring is invisible unless occupied.

The Hot Spring

A channel of steamy hot water flows into a rock-lined soaking pool or two that surface after the runoff. It requires a major river ford, which by midsummer shouldn't be too tricky, but offers a high chance of a quiet soak unobserved by passing cars.

Note: You could make a half-day outing by renting inflatable kayaks in Lower Stanley and paddling from there to both Bonus Hot Spring (see preceding spring description) and Mormon Bend for a double dip.

The graceful curve of the river at Mormon Bend Hot Spring SALLY JACKSON

135 Basin Creek Campground Hot Spring

General description: Creekside soaking pool(s) hiding a short way off the highway, near the eastern Sawtooth trailheads. Daytime skinnydipping isn't recommended.
Elevation: 6,100 feet
General location: 8 miles east of Stanley
GPS: N44.26426 / W114.82031

Map: Sawtooth National Forest (spring not marked). See map on page 279.
Contact: Sawtooth NRA
Note: The campground for which these springs were named has been permanently closed down; the nearest campground is now Mormon Bend Campground, 1.4 miles to the west.

Finding the hot spring: Drive 8 miles east of the Stanley junction on SR 75 to Basin Creek Bridge, and park in the small pullout beside it. Walk 150 feet up the unpaved road before dropping down to the creek on a narrow trail that covers the last 400 feet to the spring.

The Hot Spring

The spring issues out of the creek bank near the base of a large and distinctive rock outcropping. Small seasonal pools usually appear in the summer months—their temperature is controlled with a mix of creek water.

Keep an eye out for this prominent rock when tracking down Basin Creek Campground Hot Spring. SALLY JACKSON

136 Kem Hot Spring

General description: Hot dips sandwiched between the highway and the Salmon River, near the eastern Sawtooth trailheads. Swimwear is essential.
Elevation: 6,100 feet

General location: 8.3 miles east of Stanley
GPS: N44.26413 / W114.81170
Map: Sawtooth National Forest (spring not marked). See map on page 279.
Contact: Sawtooth NRA

Finding the hot spring: Drive 8.3 miles east of the Stanley junction on SR 75. Just beyond Basin Creek Bridge (see preceding spring description), there's a large pullout with a restroom on the right; a 400-foot path drops to the hot spring.

The Hot Spring

This site offers a bit more seclusion than the other roadside dips east of Stanley. It's at the base of a bank below the busy highway; motorists aren't likely to notice a few bathers unless they know just where to look.

One or more soaking pools border the river. You can move the rocks to either divert the 133°F inflow or admit river water. The pools swamp during high water, and the rocks wash away; they take on a new look every summer depending on the talents of the volunteers who rebuild them.

There are no telltale signs to give Kem Hot Spring's location away unless it's occupied.
SALLY JACKSON

137 Sunbeam Hot Springs

General description: Highly visible pools squeezed between the highway and the Salmon River. No nudes, just "prudes and prunes."
Elevation: 6,000 feet
General location: 12.2 miles east of Stanley

GPS: N44.26755 / W114.74984
Map: Sawtooth National Forest (springs named). See map on page 279.
Contact: Sawtooth NRA

Finding the hot springs: Drive 12.2 miles east of the Stanley junction on SR 75 (4 miles past Kem Hot Spring or 1 mile west of Sunbeam Village). Look for an old stone bathhouse and interpretive signs at a large turnout. A short path leads upstream to the pools; another goes downstream to a separate source.

The Hot Springs

One last cluster of highway hot soaks lines the Salmon River Scenic Byway from Stanley to Challis. Near-boiling water at 170°F is piped beneath the highway from the springs and flows across a gravel beach into several popular pools at the river's edge. Bathers can adjust the rocks to create a variety of soaking temperatures. Succeeding pools, each cooler than the one above, emerge as the river recedes through the summer. Some years the downstream source has a tiny tub perched in the rocky bank to collect the flow. It's worth checking out but requires a bucket for adding river water.

The historical bathhouse has been repaired and restored, and a stone outhouse in the same style has been built nearby. This work was done in conjunction with the Idaho Centennial Historical Site near Sunbeam Dam.

"No words needed!" SALLY JACKSON

138 None Too Soon Hot Springs

139 Upper Loon Hot Springs

140 Crescent Moon Hot Springs

141 Owen Cabin Hot Springs

Hike 141 To Four Hot Springs

General description: A day hike or overnighter to a chain of pearls lost in the Frank Church Wilderness. Keep swimwear handy.
Difficulty: Moderately easy
Distance: 11.5 miles round-trip
General location: 46 miles northeast of Stanley
Elevation gain: +240 feet, -640 feet

High point: 5,400 feet (trailhead)
GPS: N44.641830 / W114.741150 (Upper Loon; estimate)
Hiking and road map: Frank Church Wilderness, South Half (springs marked)
Contact: Middle Fork Ranger District, Salmon-Challis National Forest

Finding the trailhead: Drive 13.2 miles east of the Stanley junction on SR 75 (1 mile past Sunbeam Hot Springs) to Sunbeam Village. Turn left onto the Yankee Fork Road (FR 13) and drive 8 easy miles north to Bonanza, home of the historic Yankee Fork Dredge that sits marooned in a small pond walled in by the rocks it dredged out of the creek.

Bear left beyond the barge onto rocky Loon Creek Road (FR 172), which follows Jordan Creek north past other historic sites to Loon Creek summit. The seasonal road snakes over the 8,700-foot crest that forms the wilderness boundary and down the far side to eventually reach the road-end trailhead 35 miles from the highway. Tin Cup Campground, 0.5 mile from the end, provides a welcome rest.

The Hike

A series of wilderness hot springs lie at close intervals on Upper Loon Creek in the Salmon River Mountains north of Sunbeam. All are located on the east side, which is also the trail side, of the broad creek, and all branch into steamy channels that either trickle or tumble down the rocky banks.

Loon Creek Trail (101), a pleasant stroll, is far less tiring than the access road. The canyon walls are coated with grass and sagebrush on the south-facing slopes, while the hills facing north are lightly wooded with Douglas fir. The upper canyon consists of talus slopes and rock outcrops patched with lime yellow and orange lichen. Beyond

Enjoying a mid-September soak at Owen Cabin Hot Springs, where there's no cabin but still plenty of hot water. SALLY JACKSON

an 800-foot rock face, the path fords small streams fringed by grassy flats. The route closely follows the lively creek. In August and September you can sometimes see salmon struggling up the rapids to reach their spawning grounds. The trail bridges Loon Creek at 3.0 miles, passes a few campsites, and soon reaches a stretch of mid-summer berry picking interspersed with more easy stream hopping.

At 4.8 miles you'll pass the first hot spring, None Too Soon. It sneaks out 100 feet down the bank and spreads across a gravel bar that can be easily spotted from the trail above. At 5.2 miles you'll pass a shady campsite beside the remains of a log cabin in a tangle of greenery down by the creek. This is the landmark for Upper Loon, which begins near the trail and flows 30 feet down the rocks. Just around the next bend, at

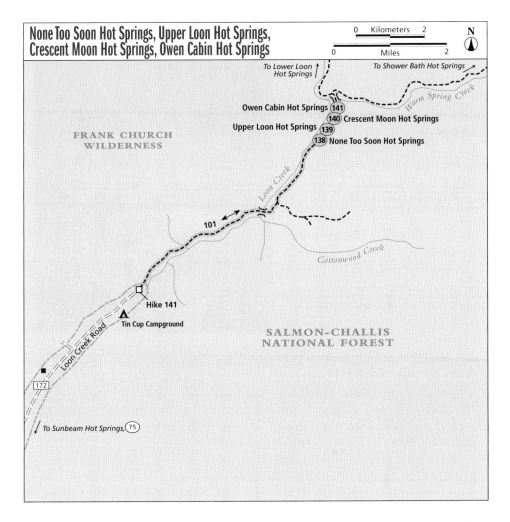

0   Kilometers   2

0   Miles   2

N

To Lower Loon
Hot Springs

To Shower Bath Hot Springs

Warm Spring Creek

Owen Cabin Hot Springs (141)

(140) Crescent Moon Hot Springs

Upper Loon Hot Springs (139)

(138) None Too Soon Hot Springs

FRANK CHURCH
WILDERNESS

Loon Creek

101

Cottonwood Creek

Hike 141

Tin Cup Campground

SALMON–CHALLIS
NATIONAL FOREST

Loon Creek Road

172

To Sunbeam Hot Springs (75)

5.4 miles, two hot waterfalls plunge over a 20-foot cliff into Crescent Moon. The pools below can only be seen from the edge of the cliff. At 5.7 miles, Owen Cabin flows gently through a meadow forming another 20-foot hot cascade as it enters the creek.

The Hot Springs

None Too Soon seeps from the creekside rocks at 140°F and fans out across the bar. Shallow pools can be scooped out in the more promising spots, and by late summer there may even be one or two established when you arrive. It doesn't offer much to entice the true hot spring gourmet but will serve as snacks in a pinch when the more popular soaks downstream are occupied. The access to the springs is via a steep, rocky slope.

Upper Loon gushes from several sources at 145°F but cools a bit in the 30-foot trip down to the river. Multiple streams give users much to work with, and by midsummer you'll find one or more well-built soaking pools, complete with cold water channels and premixing pools, nestled into the rocks. Upper Loon also provides the shadiest campsite around—the coveted spot by the cabin.

Crescent Moon, the star attraction, won't make her appearance before late summer, when the creek pulls back the curtain to let her shine forth. Many visitors miss the show altogether. If your timing is right, you'll discover the fabled crescent-shaped pool at the base of a steamy waterfall where green moss and ferns hug the bank beneath the misty spray. The pool wraps around a granite slab (hence the name) and juts out into the main current. The source is a staggering 160°F, so even allowing for some cooling en route,

The five-star pool at Crescent Moon Hot Springs has a narrow window of opportunity. EVIE LITTON

the cold mix is essential. Gaps in the rocky dam create a marbling of hot and cold currents within. Just upstream, a second hot waterfall splashes into a tiny pool with built-in shower, which also stays submerged until late summer.

At Owen Cabin, the springs emerge at 136°F in a meadow about 500 yards upstream of the few rusty remains of the long-gone Owen Cabin. The streams twist through the grass and down a 20-foot rock bank to fill a shallow, rock-lined pool by the creek. Few visitors stop here unless the upstream pools are occupied. The site offers solitude but requires more maintenance as the price for a soak.

With time to spare: From this point there's a choice of extensions to this trip. You could take Warm Spring Creek Trail 8.5 miles upstream as an alternate way to Shower Bath Hot Springs (see hike 149 and the Stanley Area Map). The primitive route involves fording the creek six times, but it passes another wild gem—a privately owned but rarely visited shower shack and hot tub at Foster Ranch. You could also continue down Loon Creek Trail all the way to Lower Loon, Whitey Cox, and Hospital Bar Hot Springs (see hike 152), which might be an easier access than the one described.

142 Lunchbreak Warm Spring

General description: A lukewarm pool on the wrong side of the Salmon River, not far from Slate Creek Hot Spring. Swimwear is advised when standing up.

Elevation: 5,700 feet

General location: 20 miles east of Stanley

GPS: N44.25452 / W114.61350

Map: Sawtooth National Forest (spring not marked). See map on page 278.

Contact: Sawtooth NRA

The choices: Lunchbreak sits on the far bank of the Salmon River between Snyder Springs and Torrey's Resort (between mileposts 209 and 210). There are three ways to get there. With a raft you could paddle across to it. Without a raft you could ford the river by late summer, aiming for a beach with benches and tables plus a pair of outhouses partway up the bank. (The tables and benches are provided by a local outfitter and disappear after the rafting season.) The third choice, described below, is via a high-clearance unpaved road.

Finding the warm spring: To get there with dry feet, drive 24.4 miles east of Stanley on SR 75. Turn right onto Slate Creek Road (FR 666) just past a highway bridge over the river between mileposts 213 and 214. Go 0.8 mile to a bridge spanning Slate Creek. The left fork goes to Slate Creek Hot Spring (see following hot spring description). Take the right fork, a very narrow and rocky road that follows the river upstream. Continue just over 3.3 miles and look for the outhouses on your right. Park beside them, and follow a short path down to the beach.

The Warm Spring

What this little retreat offers during the float season is fine seating accommodations for floaters, waders, and back-road drivers alike to enjoy their midday munchies. Lunchbreak also provides a modest soaking pool fed by a thermal spring that bubbles up through a silty bottom. The pool, bordered with rocks, is about 5 × 8 feet and just lukewarm (it registered 95°F on a warm September day).

Though the pool is unnoticeable to passing motorists when unoccupied, a soaker at Lunchbreak Warm Spring would be easy to spot. SALLY JACKSON

143 Slate Creek (Hoodoo) Hot Spring

General description: A soaking box on a dirt road in the White Clouds. Naked bodies are usually welcome.
Elevation: 7,040 feet
General location: 32 miles east of Stanley

GPS: N44.17204 / W114.62417
Map: Sawtooth National Forest (spring named). See map on page 278.
Contact: Sawtooth NRA

Finding the hot spring: Drive 24.4 miles east of Stanley on SR 75. Turn right on Slate Creek Road (FR 666) just past a highway bridge over the Salmon River between mileposts 213 and 214. Go 7.2 miles south on dirt to a road washout. You must currently walk the last 0.25 mile to the site on what little is left of the old road. One precarious stretch crosses a steep landslide.

The soaking box at Slate Creek Hot Spring was built where the old bathhouse stood.
STEPHANIE ENSIGN

The Way It Was

Slate Creek Hot Spring sure has a history of ups and downs. Some years you could drive right up to it; others you had to park behind a locked gate installed by the now-defunct Hoodoo Mine. In good years you'd find an old, funky but functional bathhouse that concealed a first-class soaking box. In bad years you'd arrive to discover—poof!—the bathhouse had collapsed. This landmark was standing in 1997, only to be swept downstream, along with a huge chunk of the access road and surrounding landscape, when Slate Creek flooded its banks in 1998.

The Hot Spring Today

Landslides and floods may continue to threaten this area, but the hot spring site is back in business. It currently has a user-built, 6-foot-square soaking box with recessed seating on three sides. Built over the foundation for the old bathhouse, the box is reinforced with rebar and braced by boulders. The plumbing consists of one pipe feeding steamy 125°F springwater into the box, a second (crucial) pipe admitting cooler water from a nearby source, and a drainpipe with a plug. There is also a seasonal creekside pool in the rocks below. The water has a faint smell of sulfur—or at least it seemed faint after visiting the potent West Pass Hot Springs earlier in the day (see the following spring)! With or without that great old bathhouse, Slate Creek remains a highly scenic spot to visit and, for the life of the cold-water pipe, an enjoyable soak.

144 West Pass Hot Spring

General description: A remote collection of bathtubs near a dirt road in the White Clouds. Wear what you normally bathe in.
Elevation: 6,800 feet
General location: 66 miles southeast of Stanley

GPS: N43.98103 / W114.48438
Map: Sawtooth National Forest. See map on page 278.
Contact: Sawtooth NRA

Finding the hot spring: From Stanley take SR 75 east about 38 miles (4 miles past Clayton) almost to milepost 227; turn south, across from a highway campground, onto the East Fork Salmon River Road (FR 120). Pavement turns to gravel in 16 miles, and Big Boulder Creek Road (see following hike) goes straight where the main road veers left at 17.5 miles. The seasonal road eventually passes a camping area at 26 miles. Next come two gates 1 mile apart. The road is likely to be muddy from the second gate onward. Between the gates the road bridges West Pass Creek by a cabin. Bear left just past the second gate on a track that climbs 0.2 mile above the creek to a flat area. Park here, and take the lower path for 200 feet past an abandoned mine down to the tubs. The spring is a total of 28 miles from the highway.

Note: The unpaved road to these high elevation springs is not plowed. Expect it to be closed from around mid-October though late-May.

The Hot Spring

Hoses from the old mine shaft supply 118°F water to three bathtubs perched side by side above West Pass Creek. Folks can lower the soaking temperature by diverting the hoses. The water has a strong mineral smell, and its lime-green cast makes you feel like you're afloat in a margarita. There's also a seasonal pool or two down down by the creek. An August 2012 visit found West Pass Hot Spring in good order, including the addition of a 150-gallon Rubbermaid tub that was ideal for two.

Enjoying the newest tub at West Pass Hot Spring
STEPHANIE ENSIGN

145 Bowery Hot Spring

General description: A high-tech spa on the East Fork Salmon River, in the White Clouds. Highly skinnydippable.
Elevation: 6,800 feet
General location: 67 miles southeast of Stanley

GPS: N43.97534 / W114.50006
Map: Sawtooth National Forest (site named but spring not marked). See map on page 278.
Contact: Sawtooth NRA

Finding the hot spring: Follow the preceding road access past the turnoff to West Pass Hot Spring, and continue 0.5 mile to a locked gate. Park here and walk the road toward Bowery Guard Station, turning left just before the bridge on a path to the tub, 0.3 mile altogether. The spring is 28.5 miles from the highway.

The Hot Spring

As of summer 2013, Bowery was still sporting a barn-red fiberglass spa with all the bells and whistles attached. It's been recessed, along with a matching tongue-and-groove skirting, into a custom-fit plywood deck. It features a railing at one end for clothes and towels.

Steamy water is gravity-fed from the 119°F spring. Lower the temperature by diverting the hose and adding a few dozen buckets of river water. The spa can be refilling while you sunbathe on the deck. Two buckets were on hand for our visit.

Note: There are often volunteer rangers based at the nearby Guard Station over the summer months.

Soaking up the sun, scenery, and good water at Bowery Hot Spring SALLY JACKSON

Hike 145 Island and Goat Lakes

General description: A long day hike or over-nighter to alpine lakes in the White Clouds, en route to West Pass and Bowery Hot Spring
Difficulty: Strenuous
Distance: About 13 miles round-trip
General location: 59 miles southeast of Stanley

Elevation gain: +2,220 feet, -240 feet
High point: 9,240 feet (Island Lake)
Hiking quads: USGS Boulder Chain Lakes and Livingston Creek
Road map: Sawtooth National Forest
Contact: Sawtooth NRA

Finding the trailhead: Follow the preceding road access to Big Boulder Creek Road (FR 667) and drive 4 miles to a trail sign near the dilapidated Livingston Mill. Turn left to the trailhead parking area (Livingston Mill–Castle Divide Trail 047).

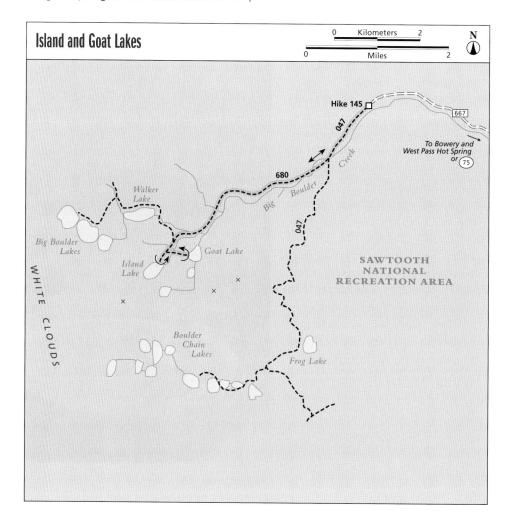

The Hike

This popular trail, which also accesses Walker Lake and the Big Boulder Lakes, is one of the shortest routes into the White Cloud Mountains. The Boulder Chain Lakes to the south see fewer visitors but also require twice the hiking distance to reach. Bordered by granite slabs and lofty peaks, these lakes offer stiff competition to the well-known Sawtooth Range farther west.

The Livingston Mill–Castle Divide Trail (047) crosses sagebrush flats backed by red rock towers. At 2.0 miles this trail branches south (left) to Frog Lake and the Boulder Chain Lakes. Stay on the right branch, which becomes Big Boulder Creek Trail (680). It works up through a forest of lodgepole pine and aspen, dips across Quicksand Meadows, crosses side creeks on logs, and then climbs past the rushing outlet of Goat Lake to the Walker Lake junction in just over 5.0 miles.

Climbing to Island Lake, the path weaves back and forth across the stream. In a marsh 0.4 mile up, a faint 0.5-mile trail forks left across a rocky saddle to Goat Lake. You'll reach a campsite at Island Lake less than 1.0 mile from the Walker Lake junction. Talus slopes and trees border Goat Lake beneath a wall of colorfully banded rock that striates Granite Peak beneath a skyline of pinnacles. Narrow Island Lake, dotted with two islands, is rimmed by granite benches, a cliff on one side, and a small meadow at the upper end.

With time to spare, this trip combines well with Walker Lake, just 1.0 mile above the junction. The 0.5-mile-long lake, misnamed Walter on the USGS quad, is backed by cliffs and a double-tipped peak. A cross-country route from here climbs 2.0 miles to the Big Boulder Lakes—Cove, Sapphire, and Cirque—nestled in the White Clouds at a high point of 10,000 feet. (**Note:** Campfires are not permitted at Big Boulder Lakes.)

J. Out of Challis

Hot Springs and Hikes

This Frisbee-shaped area on the Idaho A–K Area Map will send you flying all the way from Barney (146), on BLM land in the remote Pahsimeroi Valley 65 miles southeast of Challis, past Cronks Canyon (147), to a hair-raising but spectacular drive northwest of town that climbs a convoluted crest deep into the Frank Church Wilderness. At 29 miles, a path plunges to geothermal delights at Sitz Bath (148) and Shower Bath (149). At the road's end, a long descent to the Middle Fork Salmon River reaches hot soaks at Lower Loon, Whitey Cox, and Hospital Bar (150–152).

Season

Barney, a cool soak at a high elevation, is best on a hot summer day. Cronks is submerged until late summer. Prime time for the wilderness hot spring treks is midsummer through early fall. Off-season use is hampered by seasonal road closures, high-elevation trailheads, and spring runoff on all but Barney. You should prepare for nippy or foul weather at the start of the season that shifts to hot and dry toward the end.

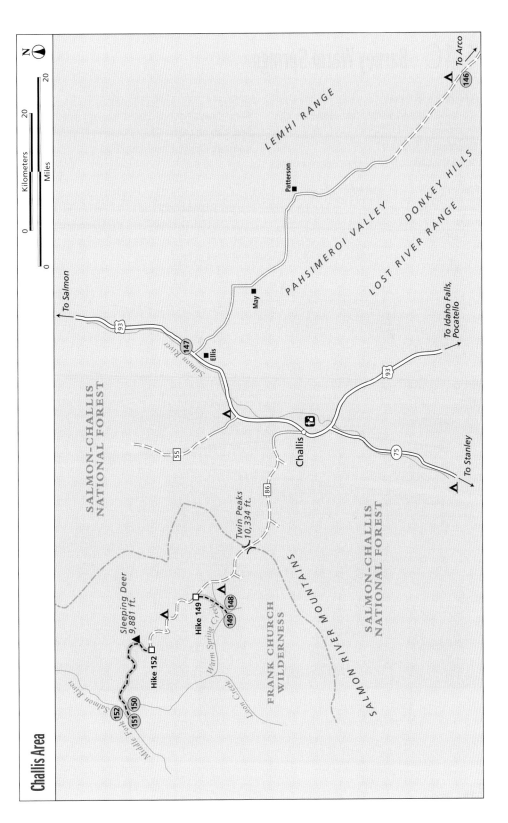

Challis Area

146 Barney Warm Springs

General description: A roadside warm pond in a remote desert valley. Skinnydippable with discretion.
Elevation: 6,400 feet
General location: 65 miles southeast of Challis

GPS: N44.26907 / W113.45053
Map: Challis National Forest (spring named). See map on page 301.
Contact: Challis Field Office, BLM

Finding the warm springs: Go north from Challis 18 miles on US 93 to Ellis (from Salmon head south for 41 miles on US 93 to reach Ellis). Take the Pahsimeroi (Farm to Market) Road 34 miles southeast on pavement plus another 13 miles on gravel to Summit Creek BLM Campground. At the south end of camp, a short spur goes west to the pond. The road continues 9 miles on gravel plus 33 on pavement to intersect SR 33 just northeast of Arco.

Barney Warm Springs supports a healthy population of tiny tropical fish that someone planted years back. They sometimes nibble—but it doesn't hurt! MATT ROSENTHAL

Barney flows to the surface of a waist-deep pond within an enclosure of logs. The temperature hovers around 83°F. One old-timer says the logs were once a corral, back before the pond was filled by damming the springs. Another story has it that the logs are the remains of an old house that once sat over the pond. The group that spins this tale can all remember swimming underneath the house as kids back in the 1940s.

In any case, the pond makes a refreshing stop on a hot summer day. On one side of the sagebrush valley are the Donkey Hills, backed by the Lost River Range. On the other side is the Lemhi Range, capped by 11,612-foot Bell Mountain.

Warning

Locals also whisper of one giant mutant fish that dwells in the depths of the pond. It's a purple monster that's been named for the spring, and it favors (and savors) very small swimmers. And any reader who swallows this tall tale fully deserves to be swallowed by Barney. (Evie)

147 Cronks (Royal Gorge) Hot Spring

General description: A late-season soak sandwiched between a busy highway and the Salmon River. Swimwear is advised when standing up.
Elevation: 4,700 feet

General location: 20 miles north of Challis
GPS: N44.71908 / W114.01842
Map: Challis National Forest (spring not marked). See map on page 301.
Contact: Challis Field Office, BLM

Finding the hot spring: Drive north from Challis 18 miles on US 93 to Ellis, a name on the map with just a post office on the ground. Continue 2.4 miles to Royal Gorge RV Park and Cabins and go almost 0.5 mile more. Cronks hides just below the busy highway at mile 266.7. The road cuts through a scenic narrow gorge here, but there's no landmark at the spot. There's no decent pullout either, so you'll have to continue until you find one. As you walk back along the riverbank toward Challis, go 200 feet past a road sign with an arrow, then scramble down the rocks to the pool.

The roadside soak at Cronks Hot Spring is thankfully not visible to the traffic above.
SALLY JACKSON

Where the grass is greener

The couple who introduced me to Cronks had just dragged me on a wild goose chase across the canyon on a road that became a jeep track, a hike straight downhill, plus a scramble along the riverbank on sharp rocks and through scratchy brush. All this on a day that was more than 100°F to check out a mystery hot spring 200 yards upstream from Cronks. And what did we find? A few seeps in the rocks and one stagnant pool. By the time we'd backtracked across the canyon, the sun had set and the temperature had dropped 15 degrees, the highway traffic was gone, and the modest little pool at Cronks felt like the finest five-star soak in the West. (Evie)

The Hot Spring

Squeezed between the road embankment and the river is a rock-lined, sandy-bottomed pool that will seat three in a pinch and enjoys a fine view of the canyon. It's a soak that few folks have heard of, much less sampled.

Sally's note: The pool temperature was a toasty 110°F the evening I was there. My weary muscles approved, as I'd just hiked up and out from Mormon Ranch Hot Springs.

148 Sitz Bath Hot Springs

149 Shower Bath Hot Springs

Hike 149 To Both Hot Springs

General description: A grueling day hike or overnighter to a geothermal fairyland in the Frank Church Wilderness. Swimwear is superfluous.

Difficulty: Strenuous

Distance: About 12 miles round-trip

General location: 29 miles northwest of Challis

Elevation gain: +100 feet, -2,340 feet

High point: 8,040 feet (trailhead)

Hiking and road map: Frank Church Wilderness, South Half (Shower Bath named)

Restriction: Shower Bath requires a major creek crossing.

Contact: Middle Fork Ranger District, Salmon-Challis National Forest

Finding the trailhead: The odyssey begins in Challis. Go west into town and turn right onto Challis Creek Road. Drive 9 paved miles into Salmon-Challis National Forest, where pavement ends and Sleeping Deer Road (FR 86) begins. Bear right at 10.5 miles and right again at a confusing junction at 15 miles. Climb a rocky surface to crest at 9,000 feet on Twin Peaks Saddle (the wilderness boundary). The seasonal road irons out somewhat beyond the top but becomes very narrow; sheer drop-offs are offset by wall-to-wall views. Watch for the Mahoney Creek Trail sign on your left at around 29 miles. It's a mile or so past Mahoney Springs Camp and opposite the Fly Creek Trailhead.

Note: See hike 152 for another adventure at the end of the road. Refer also to "With time to spare," at the end of hike 141 for an alternate way to Shower Bath from Upper Loon Hot Springs via Warm Springs Creek. This route is very rough and involves downed trees, several tricky fords, and possible landslides.

The vision and the challenge: Imagine camping at one modest little hot springs (Sitz Bath), then stumbling knee-deep in a torrent of icy water through a deep chasm that sees maybe an hour of sun a day, rounding the last bend numb and exhausted, and finding paradise spread out before you. Steamy water flows over the sides of a wide alcove and splashes into rocky bowls below. Clouds of spray billow out over a soft green carpet beyond the pools.

Like the legendary Shangri-la, Shower Bath lies at the end of an exhausting and difficult trek. Some 29 teeth-jarring miles on a knife-edge road are followed by a trail diving downhill into a stream that you must navigate through a narrow gorge. The last 300-yard stretch can be waist-deep through late July; when flooded, Warm Spring Creek can't be waded with any degree of safety.

Warning: Fires affected a large section of this forest in 2007. The access since then has been prone to erosion and charred trees falling across roads and trails. Rangers recommend having an ax or handsaw in your vehicle to clear the road. Be sure to check with the forest service in Challis before attempting the trip.

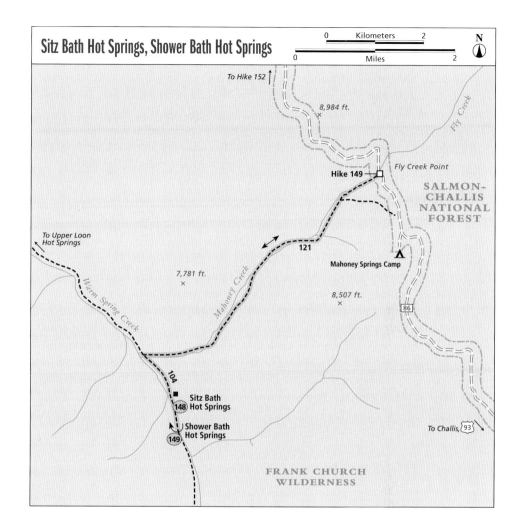

Sitz Bath Hot Springs, Shower Bath Hot Springs

0   Kilometers   2

0   Miles   2

N

To Hike 152

8,984 ft.

Fly Creek

Hike 149

Fly Creek Point

SALMON-
CHALLIS
NATIONAL
FOREST

To Upper Loon
Hot Springs

121

Mahoney Springs Camp

7,781 ft.

Mahoney Creek

Warm Spring Creek

8,507 ft.

86

104

Sitz Bath
148 Hot Springs

Shower Bath
149 Hot Springs

To Challis, 93

FRANK CHURCH
WILDERNESS

The Hike

Drop over the edge on a path that plunges 760 feet in the first mile to reach a spring, two log huts, and a junction where two trails join to follow Mahoney Creek downhill. The route dives another mile through heavy timber to a side stream, after which the grade becomes more moderate. The sinuous track weaves across Mahoney Creek wherever the canyon walls get too snug on one side. When you're not fording the creek, you'll be jumping the many side streams that feed it. Continue down through a blend of pine, fir, and aspen to finally bottom out on a sagebrush flat at Warm Spring Creek, with a total loss of 2,340 feet in 5 miles.

Take a breather and stroll upstream on Warm Spring Creek Trail (104) past the old Warm Spring Ranger Cabin, built in 1910. To find Sitz Bath, continue 0.25 mile and look for a side path dropping through the woods to a flat by the creek and a camping area. Follow the creek 50 yards upstream to reach the spring at the upper end of a gravel bar at 5.5 miles. It's best to camp in the meadow and do the wading to Shower Bath with minimum gear in a daypack.

To reach Shower Bath continue on the main trail to the mouth of the narrows. Prepare for a cold plunge as rock walls 200 feet high funnel the path into the swift-moving creek. Work your way upstream, taking care to avoid the deeper holes. The path emerges briefly along the west bank, then drops back into the stream. Tiny hot springs trickle down the sheer walls, but these aren't the ones you came this far to see. Round the final bend and haul out on dry land on the west bank at 6 miles (5,800 feet).

The Hot Springs

Sitz Bath doesn't surface before late summer. Once the creek is down, the remnants of a previous pool should reappear on the gravel bar. Rangers have reported that a recent landslide has reduced the size of the pool, and what's left may be pretty small. The 109°F source flows into the creek and cools just a tad before entering the pool. The heat may feel better after the return trip through the narrows.

At Shower Bath a broad wall of water trickles and tumbles in an 80-foot drop over the rim, and rainbows shimmer as sunlight pours through the mist. Gushing from the ground above at 120°F, the flow cools to a perfect soak in the tiny pools directly below. Lichen speckles the rock-ribbed walls; thick grasses carpet the floor. A warm stream meanders through the meadow to other pools spread out by the creek. Enjoy your stay, but please treat the fragile ecosystem around the springs with the respect it deserves.

Hikers will find one or more rocky soaking pools at Shower Bath Hot Springs hidden behind a curtain of steam and fine spray. EVIE LITTON ▶

150 Lower Loon Hot Springs

151 Whitey Cox Hot Springs

152 Hospital Bar Hot Springs

Hike 152 To Three Hot Springs

General description: A rugged backpack featuring wilderness hot dips in the depths of the Middle Fork Salmon River Canyon. Public nudity is prohibited within the river corridor.
Difficulty: Extremely strenuous
Distance: About 41 miles round-trip
General location: 43 miles northwest of Challis
Elevation gain: +120 feet, -5,420 feet

High point: 9,340 feet (trailhead)
Hiking and road map: Frank Church Wilderness, South Half (Whitey Cox and Hospital Bar named)
Restrictions: Hospital Bar requires a major river crossing.
Contact: Middle Fork Ranger District, Salmon-Challis National Forest

Finding the trailhead: See the access warning given for the previous hot springs, and follow the spine-tingling access road described there. Continue along the narrow crest to reach the road-end trail sign at 43 total miles. Perch your vehicle in the tiny pullout, and dig out your dusty boots.

Note: There's an alternate way to these hot springs via Loon Creek (see "With time to spare" at the end of hike 141). It's 40 miles round-trip but is said to have an easier grade and a better trail.

The Hike

A long and lonesome journey offers the more adventurous hiker a chance to sample a broad cross section of the Frank Church Wilderness as well as a triple dip at the rainbow's end. The primitive path begins in subalpine forest on a frosty mountaintop. Two life zones, 14 miles, and well over 5,000 feet below, the path comes to rest in the semiarid canyon carved by the Middle Fork Salmon River. Sagebrush lines the way to Whitey Cox, a twilight forest frames the stroll up Loon Creek to one of the finest hot pools in the wilderness, and a major river crossing highlights the route to Hospital Bar.

The soaking pool at Lower Loon Hot Springs, visited chiefly by river rafting groups, has all the key ingredients to keep a boater or backpacker happy for hours. Evie Litton ▶

High lakes below the trailhead draw keen anglers, and the distant hot springs attract seasonal boatloads of river rats, but the rugged backcountry sees far fewer visitors. Pristine scenery and solitude more than make up for the roundabout route.

The first mile of the Martin Mountain Trail (103) contours around a knoll studded with whitebark pine to a junction on a high saddle. The right fork takes you down a precipitous slope, where it traverses beneath the lookout to another saddle 200 feet below the first. This stretch is usually snow covered until mid-July. The path is hard to trace across the second saddle.

The route drops between granite slabs to a long meadow at the head of Cache Creek. Five glacially carved lakes fan out at 0.5-mile intervals. You'll pass the first lake in the marshy meadow and see a log cabin nearby. There are good campsites at the head of the lake and beside the cabin, elevation 8,685 feet. The trail contours an open ridge that overlooks Cache Creek Canyon and the second lake, bordered by meadows. As the trail swings around the headwall, there are views of other lakes and the rugged Salmon River Mountains below. You'll reach a signed junction at 4.0 miles.

Turn left and zigzag down a grassy slope on the Woodtick Cutoff Trail past a small lake to reach a branch of Cache Creek 400 feet below. Ford the creek to meet the rugged trail you'll be following down to the river. This 10-mile stretch offers few level campsites and difficult access to water.

This area burned intensely in 2007, and the Cache Creek Trail (100) is in rough shape, with numerous downed trees and rockfalls. This damaged trail dives down the headwall of the craggy canyon. The route passes burnt forests and lush meadows; at times you'll hear the roar of Cache Creek far below. As you continue the grueling plunge, grass and sagebrush begin to speckle the dry south-facing slopes, and the cooler hills facing north become wooded with stocky pines.

Near the bottom, ford the stream at two crossings where you can count on wet feet. Shortly beyond the last ford, the trail comes to rest at a junction. Bear left on the Middle Fork Trail to Loon Creek Pack Bridge, at 4,030 feet, 14 miles and 5,300 feet below the trailhead. Turn left across the bridge to find Lower Loon 0.25 mile upstream.

For the 7-mile round-trip from here to Whitey Cox, head 0.5 mile downstream to the river and swing west up the Middle Fork Trail. The gentle route passes sagebrush slopes dotted with age-old ponderosa pines. You'll spot some campsites down on a sandbar dominated by one tall pine 3 miles upstream. The springs are on the second bench above it, at 4,160 feet. The lower bench holds a tadpole-laden pond and the grave of Whitey Cox, a miner who died in a rockslide while prospecting the area.

Hospital Bar is a 6-mile round-trip downstream on the Middle Fork Trail from the Loon Creek Pack Bridge. You'll reach Cave Camp at a sharp bend in the river at 3 miles (4,000 feet). It's a good spot to pitch a tent. Across the river and just downstream are the hot springs and a large rafter's camp. It shouldn't be tough to thumb a ride over during the float season, and by late summer a strong swimmer could make it. The camps on both sides have protected beaches, and the river here is smooth. Contact

Lower Loon Hot Springs, Whitey Cox Hot Springs, Hospital Bar Hot Springs

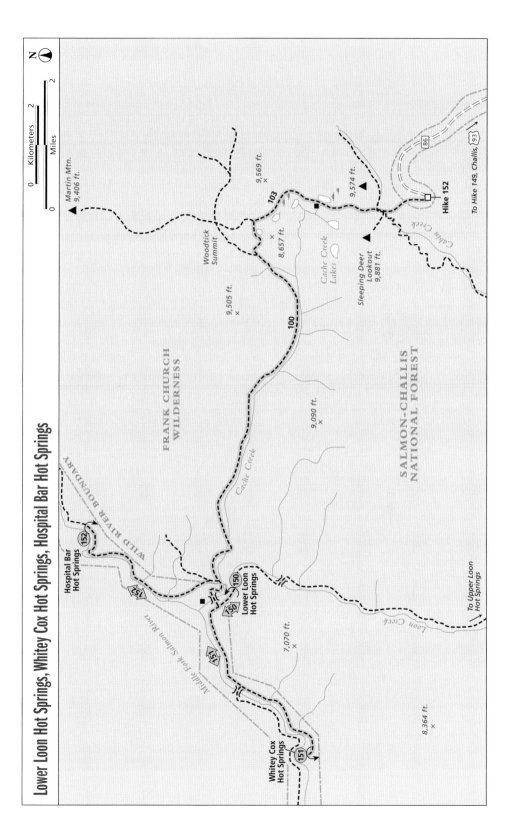

N

0   Kilometers   2
0   Miles   2

Martin Mtn.
9,406 ft.

9,569 ft.
×

103

Woodtick Summit

8,657 ft.
×

Cache Creek Lakes

Sleeping Deer Lookout
9,881 ft.

9,574 ft.

86

To Hike 149, Challis, 93

Hike 152

Cabin Creek

9,505 ft.
×

FRANK CHURCH WILDERNESS

100

SALMON-CHALLIS NATIONAL FOREST

9,090 ft.
×

Cache Creek

WILD RIVER BOUNDARY

Hospital Bar Hot Springs

152

151

Middle Fork Salmon River

150

150

Lower Loon Hot Springs

7,070 ft.
×

To Upper Loon Hot Springs

Loon Creek

8,364 ft.
×

151

Whitey Cox Hot Springs

the Middle Fork Ranger District, Salmon-Challis National Forest, for an update on river level and safety.

The Hot Springs

At Lower Loon you'll discover a rectangular pool lined with split logs that's at least 20 feet long, 10 feet across, and 3 feet deep. The pool is fed by several springs with temperatures around 104°F. The water flows through a long pipe into the crystal-clear pool. One side is shaded by a canopy of evergreen boughs, while a few planks on the creek side form a sundeck. The setting is a blend of seclusion and open views.

The few shallow soaking pools at Whitey Cox lie in a meadow strewn with wildflowers. By late summer the 105°F springs have slowed in their flow, and their silty bottoms stir up easily. There have also been reports of red mites at these springs (see page 6 for information and advice on dealing with the mites). The pools don't have much to offer the gourmet hot springer other than countless acres of solitude, a pleasant view across the canyon, and the highly scenic stroll along a wild and grand old river. The single riverside pool at Hospital Bar usually surfaces by mid-July. Rocks keep the river out, a healthy flow keeps it clean, and the nearby source (108°F) keeps it pretty toasty. Steamy water flows down a rock wall into the small pool, and while the river's still within reach, cold water can be added to taste. River runners rebuild the pool every year and tend to keep it occupied.

Note: All three of these hot springs receive high use during the float season. Please treat them with TLC and practice low-impact camping techniques.

K. Out of Salmon

Hot Springs and Hikes

Running south of Salmon, US 93 accesses a hike to Goldbug's thermal cascades (153). Far west of town, a remote trail in the Frank Church Wilderness plummets to Mormon Ranch Hot Springs (154). A trip southeast of town passes Sharkey (155), while a jump north and west hits a hike-in dip at Owl Creek (156) and a soak at popular Panther (157). Back roads farther northwest climb to a remote bathhouse at Horse Creek (158). This dispersed batch of bubblies resides in Salmon–Challis National Forest with the exception of Sharkey, which sits on BLM land.

Season

Goldbug is at its best from late runoff in early summer through the fall months. The wilderness treks are limited to midsummer through early fall due to high-elevation trailheads and seasonal roads. Sharkey and Panther can be accessed most of the year, but high elevation narrows access to Horse Creek to the few months between snowfalls. Owl Creek must be done after the runoff. Summer weather varies from hot and dry at lower elevations to cool and frequently rainy at higher elevations.

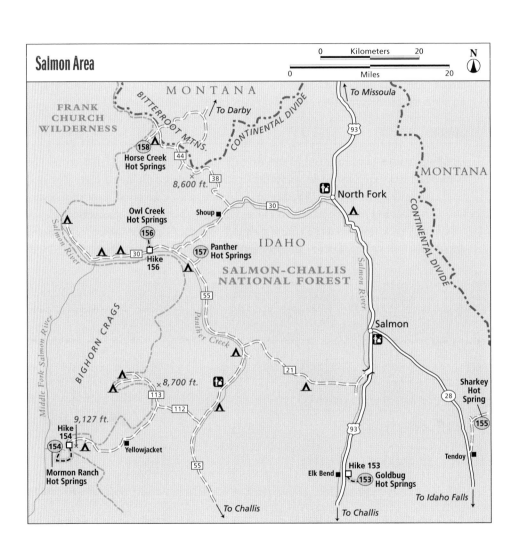

Salmon Area

0 Kilometers 20

0 Miles 20

N

MONTANA

To Missoula

FRANK
CHURCH
WILDERNESS

BITTERROOT MTNS.

To Darby

CONTINENTAL DIVIDE

93

MONTANA

158

Horse Creek
Hot Springs

44

×
8,600 ft.

38

North Fork

30

Shoup

CONTINENTAL DIVIDE

Owl Creek
Hot Springs

156

Hike
156

30

157

Panther
Hot Springs

IDAHO

SALMON-CHALLIS
NATIONAL FOREST

Salmon River

55

Salmon

Salmon River

BIGHORN CRAGS

Panther Creek

Middle Fork Salmon River

21

Sharkey
Hot
Spring

28

×8,700 ft.

113

112

155

9,127 ft.

Hike
154

154

×

Yellowjacket

Tendoy

Mormon Ranch
Hot Springs

55

Elk Bend

Hike 153

153

Goldbug
Hot Springs

To Challis

To Challis

To Idaho Falls

153 Goldbug (Elk Bend) Hot Springs

Hike 153 To Goldbug Hot Springs

General description: A day hike climbing to steamy soaks and hot waterfalls in a desert canyon. A bathing suit/birthday suit mix.
Difficulty: Strenuous
Distance: 4.0 miles round-trip
General location: 23 miles south of Salmon
Elevation gain: +920 feet, -120 feet
High point: 5,200 feet (Goldbug)
GPS: N44.9053 / W113.9296

Road map: Salmon National Forest (springs not marked)
Restrictions: Camping is not permitted within 500 feet of the springs. You'll pass a grassy campsite or two near the creek between the second and third bridge.
Contact: Salmon/Cobalt Ranger District, Salmon-Challis National Forest

Finding the trailhead: Drive 23 miles south of Salmon (0.8 mile past the Elk Bend store) on US 93. Near milepost 282, turn east on a short gravel road ending at the trailhead parking area.

A view down the canyon is one of the perks at one of Goldbug Hot Springs's many pools.
SALLY JACKSON

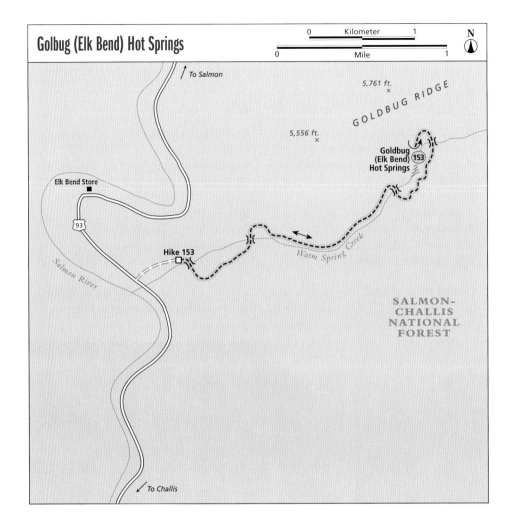

Golbug (Elk Bend) Hot Springs

0   Kilometer   1

0   Mile   1

N

To Salmon

5,761 ft.

GOLDBUG RIDGE

5,556 ft.

Goldbug
(Elk Bend) 153
Hot Springs

Elk Bend Store

93

Hike 153

Warm Spring Creek

Salmon River

SALMON-
CHALLIS
NATIONAL
FOREST

To Challis

The Hike

A trailhead bridge spans Warm Spring Creek, and switchbacks drag the path 200 feet uphill. The first 0.25 mile crosses private land, but as the route traverses an open slope, you'll pass a gate onto BLM land. The trail drops across a second bridge, where greedy cottonwoods and willows choke the creek in a green line winding up the valley between dry sagebrush slopes dotted with piñon and juniper. Ahead of you, Goldbug Ridge reveals a jagged slit. The path crosses a third bridge near the canyon's mouth and then zigzags up the wall. The last 0.5 mile is extremely steep and slippery and can be icy in winter.

Start peering through the foliage for pools interspersed in the cascade. First comes the late-season roller-coaster pool, which is very easy to miss. It features a bizarre waterslide that tumbles down from upper pools. Beyond are many other pools, most of them closer to the far bank. To reach these pools, climb to the fourth bridge and drop down the other side. Many pools disappear during spring runoff, and the creek temperature becomes somewhat cooler, so it may not be worth the trip at that time.

The Hot Springs

Hot and cold springs mix and emerge as geothermal cascades that flow over drop-offs. A chain of bubbly pools of varying size, shape, and temperature punctuates the spaces between falls. The hottest pools are found on the trail side of the canyon, cold in the center, and warm to hot pools on the far side. The current keeps them scoured clean.

154 Mormon Ranch Hot Springs

Hike 154 To Mormon Ranch Hot Springs

General description: A rugged overnighter to a remote wilderness soaking box near the Middle Fork Salmon River. Swimwear is superfluous.
Difficulty: Strenuous
Distance: 14 miles round-trip
General location: 80 miles southwest of Salmon
Elevation gain: +120 feet, -4,760 feet

High point: 8,940 feet (trailhead)
Elevation at springs: 4,300 feet
GPS: N44.95131 / W114.70598
Hiking and road map: Frank Church Wilderness, both halves (springs marked)
Contact: North Fork Ranger District, Salmon-Challis National Forest

Finding the trailhead: From Salmon drive 5 miles south on US 93. Bridge the river onto Williams Creek Road (FR 21) and climb 24 dusty miles west to Panther Creek Road (FR 55). Hang a left and go 13 miles to Porphyry Creek Road (FR 112). Turn right and follow signs to Middle Fork Peak. After a few more miles you'll pass the turnoff to the Bighorn Crags. Next you'll pass the rustic remains of Yellowjacket, a mining ghost town.

The seasonal road deteriorates in the final 14 miles, but those with high clearance should survive. Continue a few miles past the tiny campground to Middle Fork Peak Lookout (9,127 feet) at the end, a total of 75 long and dusty miles from the highway.

Note: There's a quicker way if you're coming in from the south. From Challis drive north 8 miles and turn left onto Morgan Creek Road (which is 9 miles south of Ellis). Proceed 33 miles through a small scenic gorge on Morgan Creek Road (turns into Panther Creek Road) and turn left onto Porphyry Creek Road (see preceding directions).

The Hike

Middle Fork Peak caps a sinuous ridge high in the Yellowjacket Mountains. The lonesome trail begins just south of the manned lookout and follows the ridge, dropping steadily in a giant half-circle around the Warm Spring Creek drainage. As it circles the head of the broad canyon, you'll enjoy panoramic views that are no longer obscured by tall trees after the fire that swept through the area in 2000. The trail is quite faint in places for the first couple of miles as you wind through the myriad blackened tree stumps and the granite outcrops that have now been exposed.

When you reach a point looking back to the lookout, the path begins plummeting in earnest, weaving in and out of gullies and across open slopes in a long descent to the canyon floor. The path crosses Warm Spring Creek and hugs the north bank en route to the river. Start watching about 0.5 mile downstream from the creek crossing for a side path through the grass and bushes on your left. Follow it across the creek to reach the springs (4,300 feet).

The time to visit Mormon Ranch Hot Springs is NOT when the air temperature matches that in the box. SALLY JACKSON

Mormon Ranch Hot Springs

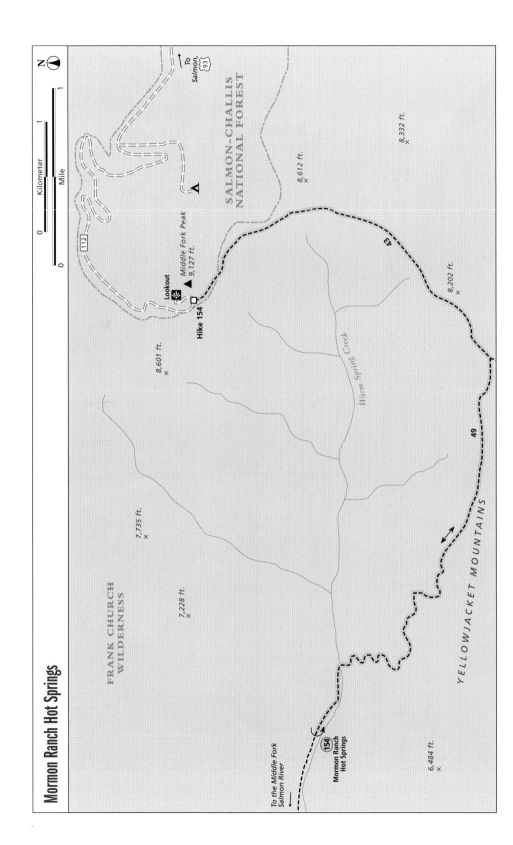

The Hot Springs

A length of pipe transports springwater at 116°F into a tongue-and-groove soaking box that measures 3 × 8 feet and 1.5 feet deep. The somewhat dilapidated box can hold a couple of cozy bodies. On a visit in September 2012, the pool's black plastic liner had seen better days, and the algae coating was difficult to clean out. Lining the pool with the trusty 6 × 8-foot tarp that we'd carried in allowed for a deeper and cleaner soak. The pool's temperature was a perfect 103°F. On a previous midsummer visit, the tub clocked in at 106°F, as did the air temperature, and there isn't any way to cool it short of diverting the pipe and waiting for the water to cool.

The setting is a sunny meadow screened by bushes from the creekside path, and you can pitch a tent nearby. The box gets far less use by passing river rats than the one at Lower Loon because it's located 1.5 miles up the trail from the river. When Sally was there, she got the distinct impression that these springs see very few visitors. The staff at the Middle Peak Lookout, who'd been stationed right above the trailhead for the past three summers and autumns, said that they knew of no other folks who'd hiked down to the springs from the lookout.

155 Sharkey (Tendoy) Hot Spring

General description: A hot spring with a colorful past and a bright future, on a dirt road above the Lemhi Valley. Swimwear is required.
Elevation: 5,300 feet
General location: 25 miles southeast of Salmon
GPS: N45.01061 / W113.61188

Map: Salmon National Forest (spring named)
Restrictions: There's a small day-use fee (an annual pass can be purchased from the BLM in Salmon). No overnight camping permitted. No dogs, soap, or glass containers. Closed Wednesday mornings for cleaning.
Contact: Salmon Field Office, BLM

Finding the hot spring: From Salmon take SR 28 about 20 miles southeast. Turn left at the Tendoy Store, then after 0.1 mile turn left again on gravel for 3 miles to Warm Springs Wood Road (FR 185). Turn right and go 2 miles uphill to the signed parking lot near the high voltage lines. The road is usable most of the year. Sharkey is on BLM land.

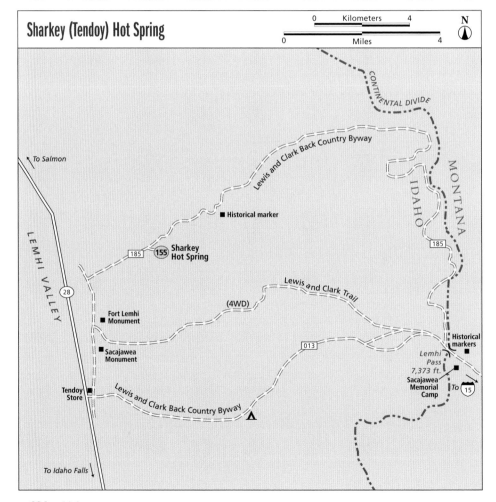

Sharkey Hot Spring got treated to a total facelift by the BLM in honor of Lewis and Clark. SALLY JACKSON

The Way It Was

Sharkey had its heyday in the mid-1920s. A local with a lease on the land and a claim to the water rights built a swimming pool with changing rooms and cabins. He piped cold water from 0.25 mile away and built the road up the hill. A swim cost two bits, and you could rent a swimsuit for the same price. All went well for many years, and Sharkey enjoyed great popularity as the community plunge. In the meantime, the BLM came into being, took a glance at the aging structures, and decided that Sharkey wasn't up to code. The whole works came down in the 1970s, and the site returned to its natural state.

Since that time there have been a series of user-built tubs at the site, but the problem has been temperature control. When Evie was there some years back, hot water was piped into a wooden box at a staggering 112°F, with no visible means of cooling it.

The Hot Spring Today

The BLM came to the rescue in 2001 and constructed not one but two concrete pools that can hold half a dozen soakers apiece. Cooler water from a cold bore is piped in along with the hot, and it stays around 103°F. The site is now complete with concrete decks and walkways, fencing around the pool area, spiffy changing rooms/ toilets, and picnic tables with fire pits. The setting is a sagebrush slope with no shade in sight, so wait for a cool day to fully enjoy it.

Historical notes: Several signs have been erected by the BLM giving information about the history surrounding the springs. *Pahyu-yuah* (hot springs) of *puha pah* (medicine water) were a sacred place for Lemhi Shoshone people.

The BLM marks the access road as a Lewis and Clark Backcountry Byway. Sharkey is the first unofficial stop on this 39-mile scenic drive that loops over Lemhi Pass. The narrow dirt roads can be impassable when wet.

156 Owl Creek Hot Springs

Hike 156 To Owl Creek Hot Springs

General description: A day hike to seasonal creekside hot pools in a wooded valley. Swimwear is first come, first served.
Difficulty: Easy
Distance: About 5.0 miles round-trip
General location: 50 miles northwest of Salmon
Elevation gain: 500 feet

High point: 3,800 feet
GPS: N45.34435 / W114.46398
Hiking and road maps: Frank Church Wilderness, North Half, or Salmon National Forest
Contact: North Fork Ranger District, Salmon-Challis National Forest

Finding the trailhead: From Salmon drive north on US 93 about 21 miles to North Fork. Take the Salmon River Road (FR 30) about 29 miles west, or 3 miles past the turnoff to Panther (see following hot springs description). Watch for the trail sign off to the right, and park wherever you spot a pullout along the river.

The Hike

The Owl Creek Trail (152) is a gentle grade up the east side of the creek. At 2.0 miles bear left and ford the East Fork of Owl Creek at a junction. Soon you'll pass the landmark to the springs, an old log cabin. Beware of poison ivy along the overgrown path, and take care crossing the creek. The springs are on the far bank, 100 yards or so beyond the cabin.

The Hot Springs

Owl Creek has one or two little soaking pools that surface after the runoff, and they take a bit of rebuilding each year. Hot water trickles down the rocky bank from several sources, which range from 95°F to 125°F; the pools can be cooled by adding creek water. The pools are sandwiched between the creek and a very steep bank, so when the water is high, there's not a soak to be had. The cabin is located on a small plot of privately owned land, so please pack out what you pack in and respect the landowner's rights.

Owl Creek Hot Springs, Panther (Big Creek) Hot Springs

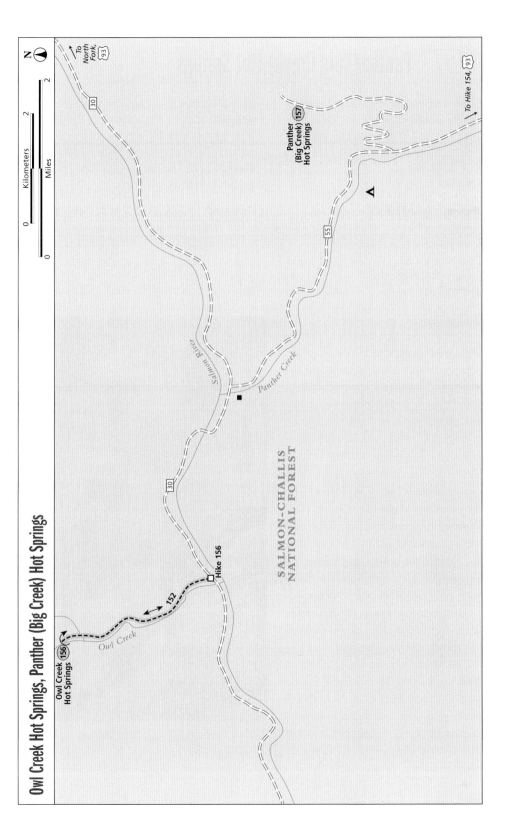

157 Panther (Big Creek) Hot Springs

General description: Problematic soaks with an abundance of scalding water and a seasonal lack of cold water on a grassy hillside near a dirt road. It's skinnydippable with discretion.
Elevation: 4,300 feet

General location: 55 miles northwest of Salmon
GPS: N45.30714 / W114.33895
Map: Salmon National Forest (springs marked). See maps on pages 316 and 327.
Contact: Salmon/Cobalt Ranger District, Salmon-Challis National Forest

Finding the hot springs: From Salmon take US 93 about 21 miles north to North Fork. Here the Salmon River Road (FR 30) heads west, past the turnoff to Horse Creek (see following hot springs description) and Shoup, where the pavement ends. Turn left 26 miles from North Fork on Panther Creek Road (FR 55). In 4 miles FR 60 climbs 4 miles uphill to a pullout where a 0.25-mile path drops to the springs.

The Hot Springs

On a hillside edged by ponderosa pines, users carve out soaking pools and dig trenches to regulate the temperature of a hot stream. Scalding water channels toward the pools but can be diverted by adjusting rocks. A small cold-water source also funnels in, and the balance is critical. The system works fine unless someone there before you messes up the plumbing. A visit in summer 2012 found all the pools too hot, as the cold water supply had all but dried up. Hiking downstream through poison ivy for another quarter of a mile revealed more pools, but they were still too hot for bathing. Panther is at its best in cooler weather and shines on through the winter months. The final road gets icy about halfway up, but locals often walk the last half for a steamy winter soak. For those into steam heat, there's even a dilapidated sauna hut built from rocks (take care not to get burned). The nearest campground is down on Panther Creek.

Just one of the dammed-up sections of the hot stream at Panther Hot Springs SALLY JACKSON

158 Horse Creek Hot Springs

General description: A roadside bathhouse sans roof near a remote campground in the Bitterroots. A haven for skinnydippers or chunkydunkers (ditto for swimsuiters).

Elevation: 6,000 feet

General location: 65 miles northwest of Salmon

GPS: N45.5031 / W114.4639

Map: Salmon National Forest (springs named). See map on page 316.

Contact: North Fork Ranger District, Salmon-Challis National Forest

Finding the hot springs: From Salmon zip 21 miles north on US 93 to North Fork and take the Salmon River Road (FR 30) west. At 17 miles, where the pavement peters out, turn right onto FR 38. Continue 13 miles, climbing switchbacks to the Bitterroot Divide on the Idaho-Montana border before taking a right fork. The sinuous road follows the crest and state line over a high point of 8,600 feet and after 4 more miles becomes FR 44, eventually passing a turnoff to Darby, Montana, at Horse Creek Pass. Another 4 miles brings you to FR 65 on the left and the shortest route to Darby on the right. The final lap plummets 3.6 miles to the bathhouse.

Note: Forest fires affected a large area surrounding Horse Creek Hot Springs in 2012. The access will now be more prone to erosion and charred trees falling across the roads.

Some quiet reflection inside the roofless bathhouse at Horse Creek Hot Springs Chris Andrews

The name game

While contentedly afloat, I began to notice the many names inscribed on the walls around the pool. Out of the chaos, a pattern began to emerge: "Abe 'n Deb," "Bear 'n Deb," "Jo & Jack & Deb," "Deb + Jim," "Pete 'n Deb," "Zeek 'n Deb." In the far corner was the exception: "Rob '90, w/o Deb." (Evie)

The Hot Springs

Bubbles stream up through the slab rock-and-sand bottom of a soaking pool big enough to float a small family. Over the 100°F pool sits a crude 8 × 10-foot bathhouse, roofless except for a covered area on the side for hanging clothes. A window looks out across a tree-lined meadow. A footbridge from the picnic area to the shack spans the outflow, which flows through an outdoor pool or two into Horse Creek. Horse Creek Campground is conveniently located less than a quarter of a mile to the east.

L. All by Themselves

Last but not least, we end up with a few leftovers: four rogue springs located surprisingly far afield from all of the other primitive soaks in Idaho. There's no way they would fit within the boundaries of the Idaho A–K Area Map, but you can spot Bear Creek and Alpine Hot Springs off to the southeast and Indian and Lower Indian Hot Springs to the south on the Idaho Map (page 147).

159 Bear Creek Hot Springs

Hike 159 To Bear Creek Hot Springs

General description: An overnighter for experienced trekkers only to a soaking pool in a mountain meadow near Palisades Reservoir. Naked bodies are welcome.

Difficulty: Strenuous

Distance: About 15 miles round-trip

General location: 62 miles southeast of Idaho Falls

Elevation gain: 1,200 feet

High point: 6,900 feet (at hot springs)

GPS: N43.269 / W111.304

Hiking quad: USGS Red Ridge

Road map: Caribou/Targhee National Forest (springs not marked on either map)

Restrictions: Should be done when the creek is low

Contact: Palisades Ranger District, Caribou-Targhee National Forest

Finding the trailhead: From Idaho Falls take US 26 east and follow signs to Palisades Reservoir. You'll reach Palisades Dam in about 55 miles. Turn right and cross the dam, then pass Calamity Guard Station and Campground. Turn south onto FR 058 and drive 5.6 miles on gravel to Bear Creek Campground and Trailhead.

Warning: This expedition is a challenge physically, with several major stream fords followed by a grueling climb; it's a navigational challenge as well. Not only aren't the hot springs marked on either map, but the final (crucial) path isn't shown. The USGS quad shows only Bear Creek Trail. The national forest map marks the trail going from Bear Creek up the ridge. But to home in on your goal, a GPS device would come in handy. If none of the above has slackened your enthusiasm, go for it. But don't go when the water level is high.

The Hike

Bear Creek Trail (273) begins at 5,700 feet and follows the creek upstream in a gentle grade. The tough part here is having to either ford several side streams on the way or take alternate routes up the steep bank to keep your feet dry. Either way you'll have to ford the North Fork of Bear Creek in 4 miles and then stay on South Fork Bear Creek Trail (274) as it crosses and recrosses the South Fork. Finally, about 6 miles upstream, the route crosses to the south bank. In about 200 yards it intersects the Warm Springs Trail (148) just before recrossing the creek. Watch closely for this junction—the trail sign is sometimes missing.

Here you'll leave Bear Creek behind and follow Trail 148, heading southeast up a very steep ridge and gaining nearly 900 feet in just under 1 mile. When you reach a crest, watch for a trail that bears left. This little path (not marked on any map) winds down and up, down and up, then down—landing you at the springs in just over 0.5 mile, a total of 1.5 miles from Bear Creek. There's a broad, level meadow for camping,

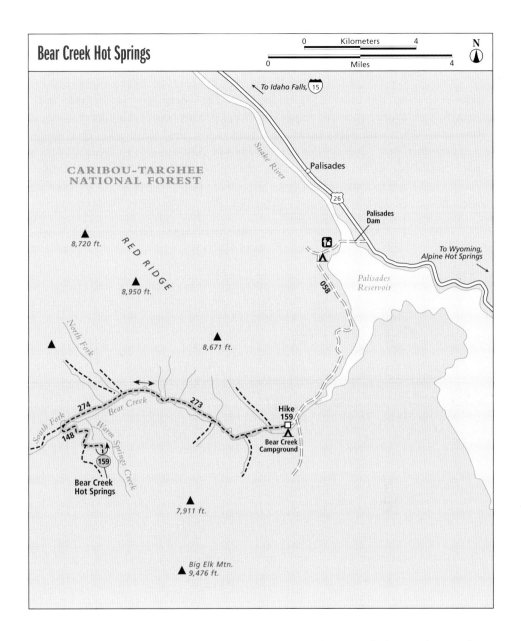

and a cold spring runs nearby. Route details are compliments of Chris Andrews, who worked hard to find and help fit the missing pieces (elevations, mileages, and final approach) in the puzzle.

Note: The trail number system has been upgraded in this area. If you have an old map, it will list different trail numbers for Bear Creek Trail (was 047) and South Fork Bear Creek Trail (was 048).

The Hot Springs

What awaits you after all this effort? Well, within the meadow there's a comfortable pool that's about 10 feet wide, 20 feet long, and 2 feet deep, bordered by rocks and grass. A log platform spans the deeper end. Springwater perks up through the sandy bottom at 98°F, releasing long streamers of bubbles that cling to your skin, then burst and fizz when they reach the surface. The outflow runs through a few small rocky pools nearby and forms a stream winding through the lush grass. This secluded site doesn't see much foot traffic. The few visitors that venture this far afield are chiefly a few hunters in the fall riding up in either Bear Creek or over Big Elk Mountain.

Hike 160 To Alpine Hot Springs

General description: A day hike to a late-season dig-your-own hot mud bath on the southwestern edge of Palisades Reservoir. Swimwear is advised if others are present.
Difficulty: Easy
Distance: 3.0 miles round-trip
General location: 84 miles southeast of Idaho Falls
Elevation gain: -50 feet
High point: 5,570 feet (at hot springs)

GPS: N43.20180 / W111.10749
Hiking quad: USGS Alpine
Road map: Caribou/Targhee National Forest (springs not marked on either map)
Restrictions: Springs are underwater when the reservoir is nearly full. Late summer and fall are your best bets for lower water levels.
Contact: Palisades Ranger District, Caribou-Targhee National Forest

Finding the trailhead: From Idaho Falls take US 26 east for 72 miles—just barely across the stateline to Alpine,Wyoming. At the junction turn south on US 89 and proceed 3.8 miles before turning right onto McCoy Forest Road (FR 087). Head back into Idaho down this unpaved road for 7.2 miles, past several informal campsites and McCoy Creek Campground before crossing a bridge spanning McCoy Creek. Park on the far side in a small pullout.

The hike to Alpine Hot Springs should look something like this, as the reservoir covers the springs when it's full. SALLY JACKSON

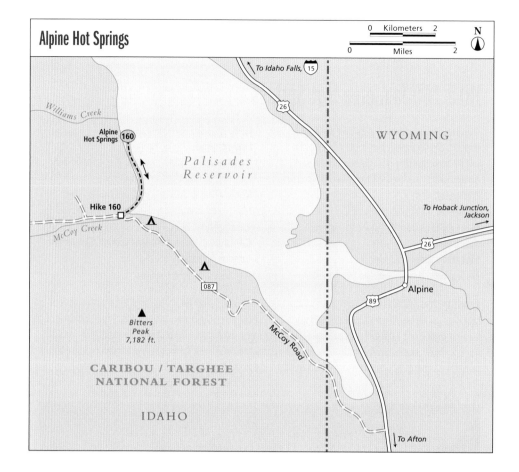

Alpine Hot Springs

The Hike

Follow ATV trails down the northwestern side of McCoy Creek toward the reservoir. In 0.5 mile bear left along the western edge of the (hopefully) dried-up shoreline. Make your way along the shoreline for almost a mile, keeping high enough to avoid muddy patches left by receding waters. Several warm and hot springs issue out of the mudflats below a small but distinct outcropping of brown, porous-looking rock.

The Hot Springs

The warmest springs are around 100°F. Bring a shovel; you may have to dig out a pool. There are panoramic views across the reservoir to the peaks of both Wyoming and Idaho. Be prepared for a warm wallow in the black oozing mud!

161　Lower Indian Hot Springs

General description: Modest pool(s) by the edge of the Bruneau River, best reserved for the cooler months. Swimwear is advised if others are present.
Elevation: 2,600 feet

General location: 40 miles south of Mountain Home; 11 miles southeast of Bruneau
GPS: N42.76731 / W115.72705
Map: *Benchmark: Idaho Road & Recreation Atlas* (springs marked as Bruneau River Hot Springs)
Contact: Bruneau Field Office, BLM

Finding the hot springs: From Mountain Home, take SR 51 south to the town of Bruneau, turning left (east) onto Hot Springs Road. Proceed 7.6 miles before turning right and crossing a bridge over the Bruneau River where the pavement ends. Continue 0.7 mile and turn left onto Blackstone Grasmere Road, which isn't signed. Drive 1.3 more miles, turn left down a narrow dirt road, and then bear right after 0.3 mile into a small, narrow canyon that requires high clearance. Proceed 0.5 mile; take a left fork and drive a final 0.2 mile before bearing right to park on the edge of the basalt cliff overlooking the lower Bruneau River canyon. Take the steep 100-yard path to the river; then turn left and head downstream for 50 yards to reach the riverside soaks (watch out for poison ivy).

　Note: This destination is best left for the cooler months, as there is minimal shade and searing summer temperatures.

The Hot Springs

Users have cemented in a 4 × 12-foot lava-rock pool by the spring sources that fills to about 104°F. It's just over 1 foot deep and has a smooth rock-slab bottom. There's usually a larger and cooler seasonal pool a couple feet below at river level. There used to be a large pool at the base of the cliff near the cave-like alcove, but there's no longer any sign of hot water at this spot. It's thought that the hot spring activity in the area has been diminishing due to pumping of groundwater for irrigation.

There might be more . . .

A quarter mile upriver of these springs is the confluence with Hot Creek. Maps show Falls Creek Hot Springs and Indian Bathtub Springs located 0.25 mile up this creek. They might be worth checking out, despite claims that they have dried up. Foot travel isn't recommended because of poison ivy. To drive there, continue south on Blackstone Grasmere Road another 1.6 miles before turning left and heading 0.9 mile down to Hot Creek (no guarantees on the road condition for this last stretch).

162 Indian Hot Springs

Hike 162 To Indian Hot Springs

General description: A short hike to a far-flung but high-flow delight in a remote desert canyon. Best left for the cooler months. Swimwear is optional.

Difficulty: Easy or moderate, depending on which trailhead you use

Distance: About 3.0 miles round-trip (may be shorter via the eastern access)

General location: 60 miles south of Bruneau

Low point: 3,700 feet (at hot springs)

GPS: N42.33655 / W115.64770 (source); N42.33768 / W115.64674 (soaking area)

Hiking quad: USGS Indian Hot Springs

Road map: *Benchmark: Idaho Road & Recreation Atlas* (springs marked)

Contact: Bruneau Field Office, BLM

Finding the trailheads: These springs can be accessed from the east or west. The eastern access is used more often, especially by boaters, to reach the launch site near the hot springs (high-clearance with four-wheel drive is highly recommended). Read on to make your decision. **Note:** Contact the BLM Bruneau Field Office to check on current road conditions.

Directions from the east (considered the easier way): From Mountain Home take SR 51 south to the town of Bruneau, turning left (east) onto Hot Springs Road. Reset your trip odometer to 0. Drive 36 miles west before turning west onto Three Creeks Road, where the pavement ends. At 40 miles turn right onto unmarked Bruneau Put-in Road. Begin to follow Bruneau River signs. At 45.8 miles take a left (west), and at 48.4 miles again turn left (west). At 48.5 miles turn right (west), and at 51.9 miles go left (southwest). At 52.7 miles turn right (west), and at 55.4 miles right again (southwest). At 55.7 miles the road becomes extremely difficult, and you may have to hike the remaining 1.8 miles or so to the hot springs. If your vehicle can continue, at 57.2 miles turn left at a T junction, where you should see a register box. Proceed 0.25 mile to the bridge, and park on the east (near) side. Alternatively, taking a right at the register box leads to river access and a wooded campsite. The bridge can't be driven on. **Note:** These directions are from the BLM website, as Sally only visited these springs from the western side.

Directions from the west (the hard way!): From Bruneau drive 40 miles south on SR 51 to the abandoned town of Grasmere (blink and you'll miss it). Turn left 0.4 mile south of Grasmere onto unpaved Roland Road and proceed 11.6 miles before turning left onto an unmarked road. Continue 1.5 miles, turning right just before reaching a ranch house. From here the road deteriorates dramatically as it becomes a rock-strewn affair. A four-wheel-drive, high-clearance vehicle and really good tires (preferably 10-ply) are essential. From the ranch turnoff, continue a slow and bumpy 6.7 miles, and then take a right fork in the middle of nowhere. Ignore a minor spur to the right 0.1 mile later, and proceed 3.7 miles to the ruins of a stone house perched on the canyon rim. Park your tired vehicle, and get ready to stretch your legs.

The Hike (from the west)

Beside the ruins, a narrow trail initially plunges into the canyon before softening out on a ridge leading down to the river and hot springs—a total of 1.6 miles and just over a 1,000-foot drop.

Bathing in the geothermally heated Bruneau River downstream from Indian Hot Springs
Stephanie Ensign

The Hot Springs

The magnificent hot spring source area is located on the western bank of the Bruneau River, 500 feet upstream from the crooked bridge. Thousands of gallons of 157°F water issue out of the hillside, forming a large deep stream of scalding water—take extra care with children and dogs in this area. The soaking zone is located downstream of the confluence of the river and this hot stream, usually just up from the bridge (this varies according to the river flow). No pool building is necessary. Just plop yourself into the river and hang onto a rock to maintain your position while the warm current washes over you—a five-star soaking experience!

The springs are located on private land. Please show respect for this area; practice low-impact techniques, and take your rubbish with you. There is a sheltered BLM camping area on the eastern side of the river just over a quarter mile from the springs.

Historical note: In spite of the remote location, these springs have a long history of visitation. According to archeologists, rich hunting and fishing grounds, along with the hot springs, attracted Native Americans to set up camps nearby. Early pioneers also used this route across the canyon, and you will see several remnants of stone houses from this era.

APPENDIX A: CONTACTS

Useful Websites

Most of the following agencies have websites that provide useful information, especially regarding road and trail closures. (You just need to know where to click!)

BC Park Service: env.gov.bc.ca/bcparks/

BC Forests (Ministry of Forests, Lands and Natural Resource Operations): gov.bc.ca/for/. Not a user-friendly site. Has information on road and trail conditions, but you have to go to the regions page and each region has a slightly different format. Look for road and/or engineering link; within them will be a link to a road conditions table. It sounds complicated, but it might be easier than tracking down someone to speak with you. BC Forests was the agency Sally had the most difficulty trying to contact.

Bureau of Land Management: blm.gov. Has a good search engine, so just type in the hot spring's name.

US Department of Agriculture Forest Service (USDAFS): www.fs.fed.us. A very user-friendly site. The "Alerts and Notices" links provide up-to-date information on road and trail closures, bridge washouts, etc.

Incident Information System: inciweb.nwcg.gov. Gives excellent updates on road and trail closures due to fires.

Government Agencies

If you need more detailed information or don't have access to the Internet, contact the following agencies for updates on weather and road conditions, hiking trails and stream crossings, hot springs, and other miscellaneous information. If the receptionist can't answer your questions, ask for someone in recreation. Maps may be purchased from these agencies, and many districts offer free trail printouts.

OREGON
Bureau of Land Management
Burns District
Hwy. 20 West
Hines, OR 97738
(541) 573-4400

Vale District
100 Oregon St.
Vale, OR 97918
(541) 473-3144
or Rome Launch Site Ranger Station
(541) 586-2612

Columbia River Gorge National Scenic Area
902 Wasco Ave., #200
Hood River, OR 97031
(541) 308-1700

Deschutes National Forest
Bend/Fort Rock Ranger District
63095 Deschutes Market Rd.
Bend, OR 97701
(541) 383-4000

Mount Hood National Forest
Clackamas River Ranger District
595 NW Industrial Way
Estacada, OR 97023
(503) 630-6861

Willamette National Forest
McKenzie River Ranger District
57600 McKenzie Hwy.
McKenzie Bridge, OR 97413
(541) 822-3381

Middle Fork Ranger District
46375 Hwy. 58
Westfir, OR 97492
(541) 782-2283

Umpqua National Forest
Diamond Lake Ranger District
2020 Toketee Ranger Station Rd.
Idleyld Park, OR 97447
(541) 498-2531

US Fish and Wildlife
Hart Mountain National Antelope Refuge
18 South G St.
PO Box 111
Lakeview, OR 97630
(541) 947-3315

Malheur National Wildlife Refuge
36391 Sodhouse Lane
Princeton, OR 97721
(541) 493-2612

Sheldon National Wildlife Refuge
PO Box 111
Lakeview, Oregon 97620
(541) 947-3315

WASHINGTON
Gifford Pinchot National Forest
Mount Adams Ranger Station
2455 Hwy. 141
Trout Lake, WA 98650
(509) 395-3402

Mount Baker–Snoqualmie National Forest
Darrington Ranger District
1405 Emmens Ave.
Darrington, WA 98241
(360) 436-1155

Mount Baker Ranger District
2105 Hwy. 20
Sedro Woolley, WA 98284
(360) 856-5700

Olympic National Park
Wilderness Information Center
3002 Mount Angeles Rd.
Port Angeles, WA 98362
(360) 565-3100; (360) 565-3130

BRITISH COLUMBIA

Note: Both the BC Forest Service and BC Park Service have undergone major restructures in recent years, with more changes likely in the future. This may result in further changes to the names and locations of some the following offices.

BC Forest Service
Chilliwack Forest District
46360 Airport Rd.
Chilliwack, BC V2P1 A5
(604) 702-5700

Kootenay Boundary Region
1902 Theatre Rd.
Cranbrook, BC V1C 4H4
(250) 426-1700

Selkirk Forest District
1907 Ridgewood Rd.
Nelson, BC V1 6K1
(250) 825-1100

Squamish Forest District
42000 Loggers Lane
Squamish, BC V0N 3G0
(604) 898-2100

BC Parks
Kootenay Park Services
6188 Wasa Lake Park
Wasa, BC V0B 2K0
(250) 422-3003

Kootenay Region
205 Industrial Rd.
Cranbrook, BC V1C 7G5
(250) 489-8540

Squamish Office (Lower Mainland Region)
Alice Lake Provincial Park
Hwy. 99
Squamish, BC V0N 1H0
(604) 898 3678, ext. 2224

West Coast Region
1240 Rathtrevor Rd.
Parksville, BC V9P 2H4
(250) 954 4618

IDAHO
Bureau of Land Management
Boise District
3948 Development Ave.
Boise, ID 83705
(208) 384-3300

Bruneau Field Office
3948 Development Ave.
Boise, ID 83705
(208) 384-3300

Challis Field Office
1151 Blue Mountain Rd.
Challis, ID 83226
(208) 879-6200

Salmon Field Office
50 Hwy. 93 South
1206 South Challis St.
Salmon, ID 83467
(208) 756-5400

Shoshone Field Office
400 West F St.
Shoshone, ID 83352
(208) 732-7200

Boise National Forest
Cascade Ranger District
540 N Main St.
PO Box 696
Cascade, ID 83611
(208) 382-7400

Emmett Ranger District
1805 Hwy. 16, #5
Emmett, ID 83617
(208) 365-7000
or
Garden Valley Ranger Station
(208) 462-3241

Lowman Ranger District
7359 Hwy. 21
Lowman, ID 83637
(208) 259-3361

Mountain Home Ranger District
2180 American Legion Blvd.
Mountain Home, ID 83647
(208) 587-7961

Idaho City Ranger District
Hwy. 21, Milepost 38.5
Idaho City, ID 83631
(208) 392-6681

Caribou–Targhee National Forest
Palisades Ranger District
3659 E Ririe Hwy.
Idaho Falls, ID 83401
(208) 523-1412

Clearwater National Forest
Lochsa Ranger District
502 Lowry St.
Kooskia, ID 83539
(208) 926-4274

Powell Ranger District
192 Powell Rd.
Lolo, MT 59847
(208) 942-3113

Nez Perce National Forest
Salmon River Ranger District
304 Slate Creek Rd.
Slate Creek Station
Whitebird, ID 83554
(208) 839-2211

Payette National Forest
Council Ranger District
2092 Hwy. 95
PO Box 567
Council, ID 83612
(208) 253-0100

Krassel Ranger District
500 North Mission St.
McCall, ID 83638
(208) 634-0600

McCall Ranger District
102 West Lake St.
McCall, ID 83638
(208) 634-0400

Salmon–Challis National Forest
Middle Fork Ranger District
311 N US 93
Challis, ID 83226
(208) 879-4101

North Fork Ranger District
11 Casey Rd.
PO Box 180
North Fork, ID 83466
(208) 865-2700

Salmon/Cobalt Ranger District
311 McPherson St.
Salmon, ID 83467
(208) 756-5200

Sawtooth National Forest
Fairfield Ranger District
102 First St. East
PO Box 189
Fairfield, ID 83327
(208) 764-3202

Ketchum Ranger District
206 Sun Valley Rd.
PO Box 2356
Ketchum, ID 83340
(208) 622-5371

Sawtooth National Recreation Area
Headquarters Office
5 North Fork Canyon Rd.
Ketchum, ID 83340
(208) 727-5000; (800) 260-5970
or
Stanley Ranger Station
HC 64, Box 9900
Stanley, ID 83278
(208) 774-3000

APPENDIX B: FURTHER READING AND INFORMATION

Marjorie Gersh-Young and Chris Andrews. *Hot Springs and Hot Pools of the Northwest* and *Hot Springs and Hot Pools of the Southwest* (Aqua Thermal Access).

These two books have long been standard references among serious hot springers. They feature all the commercial resorts, spas, and naturalist accommodations as well as many primitive springs. The Northwest book covers Alaska, Canada, Washington, Oregon, Idaho, Montana, and Wyoming. The website is hotpools.com. You can find one or both books in many bookstores or online.

Soakersforum.com is a hot springs community forum where serious soakers exchange information. There are some very knowledgeable folk out there who are willing to give you updates and clues on many an elusive hot spring if you ask the right questions!

HOT SPRINGS INDEX

★ new to this edition

ABOUT THE AUTHORS

Evie Litton broke loose from a career as a technical illustrator for the University of California in Berkeley to hit the road in 1983. She traded her civilized life for a van she called home and started exploring backcountry hot springs. This pursuit evolved in turn into the precursor of the book you see today. Since its debut in 1990, Evie spent the next fifteen years obsessed with keeping the text up to date, expanding it, and making improvements—an increasingly challenging job. After completing the fourth edition in 2005, she settled down in Arizona where she spends her winters in Tucson and summers in Flagstaff.

Evie leading a hike with friends in the Southern Arizona Hiking Club in Tucson BOB CARDELL

Sally Jackson first visited Idaho in 1996 armed with just a state map and a copy of *Hiking Hot Springs in the Pacific Northwest*. Thanks to this book, she was able to visit thirty-three free hot springs in twelve magical days! She was now firmly hooked on all things geothermal and very grateful that someone had written such a great guide for this region. Her good luck continued when she got to meet and befriend the author, Evie Litton, a couple of years later through mutual friends.

During more settled periods, Sally has been an economic statistician and also a park ranger (at a set of mountain hot springs!). A lot of her travels have been in the pursuit of hot water in North America, Italy, Japan, Turkey, New Zealand, and Fiji. She's lost count of the grand total but has visited over 280 hot springs in North America alone (including 126 of the 162 listed in this book). Her next major project will be working on the fourth edition of her guidebook *Hot Springs of New Zealand*, which will contain details on more than one hundred geothermal soaks.

Sally enjoying a five-star soak at Hot Springs Cove JOHN HERCHENRIDER